A Traveller's Guide to Historic British Columbia

Also by Rosemary Neering

The Canadian Housewife: An Affectionate History
Wild West Women: Travellers, Adventurers and Rebels
Down the Road: Journeys Through Small-Town British Columbia

A Traveller's Guide to Historic British Columbia

ROSEMARY NEERING

whitecap

Edited by Elaine Jones, third edition by Grace Yaginuma
Proofread by Ann-Marie Metten
Design by Michelle Mayne
Archival photographs, except as noted, from the British Columbia Archives (BCA).
Present-day photographs by Rosemary Neering, except as noted. Thanks to Gary Green,
Vivien Bowers and Alena Vackova for the photographic contributions, and to Joe Thompson
for his research contributions.
Maps by Stuart Daniel/Starshell Maps

Cover photo credits: main front cover photo (in Sandon) by David Gluns; front cover archival
photos, from top to bottom: image no. BCA A1028, BCA C4270 and BCA A2592 courtesy of the
Royal BC Museum, BC Archives; fourth image from top courtesy of the Revelstoke Museum and
Archives; image no. BCA H5813 and BCA A6403 from the Royal BC Museum, BC Archives;
archival photos on spine: BCA A1028, BCA B7602 and BCA G255 courtesy of the Royal BC Museum, BC Archives; back cover photos by Rosemary Neering (clockwise from left: near Trout Lake;
grist mill at Keremeos; and Quilchena Hotel near Merritt)

Printed in Canada

Library and Archives Canada Cataloguing in Publication

Neering, Rosemary, 1945–
        A traveller's guide to historic British Columbia / Rosemary
Neering. — 3rd ed.

Includes index.
ISBN 978-1-55285-987-2

        1. Historic sites—British Columbia—Guidebooks. 2. British
Columbia—History, Local. 3. British Columbia—Guidebooks.
I. Title.

FC3812.N43 2009   917.1104'5   C2008-905588-8

09 10 11 12 13   5 4 3 2 1

THIS BOOK is dedicated to those enthusiasts
who have worked to preserve evidence
of British Columbia's past, to those people
who have responded patiently and at length to my
many requests for information or who have sent me down
fascinating roads both literal and figurative,
and to those travellers of backroads and lonely paths
who have provided information and encouragement
in this documentation of the evidence of the province's history.
Your support has been invaluable.

CONTENTS

Chapter 6: The Interior Plateau 215

Chapter 7: The Coast 259

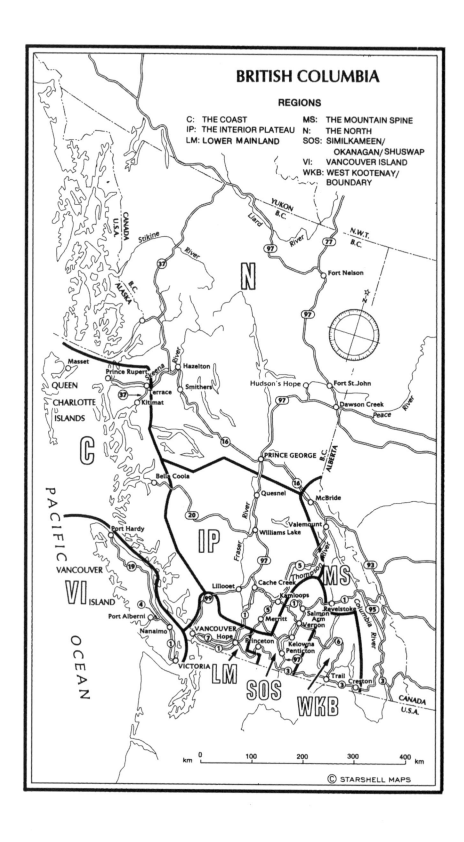

INTO THE COUNTRY OF THE PAST

From my vantage point high on the hill, the few remaining two-storey brick houses the Doukhobors built more than a century ago seem like tiny toys set amid the golden sweep of grass. Far to my left, piles of black slag that hearken back to the glory days of mining and smelting glisten in the sunshine. And spread out below on the floor of the valley is the present-day city of Grand Forks, its solid brick courthouse and courtly manors contrasting with the more modern motels and strip malls.

The panorama below me presents the physical evidence of history that is the essence of *A Traveller's Guide to Historic British Columbia*. From middens and totem poles to orchards, mining shafts and steel rails, this book chronicles the history visible to the traveller along the province's highways, streets and pathways. And with these markers of time and change come stories that bring the past alive.

Much has changed since this guide was first published some 15 years ago. Seated in a small theatre at Whistler, I watch and listen as the images on the screen take us soaring over the territory of the Squamish and the Lil'wat nations and into an ancient culture, then marvel at the craftsmanship behind the weavings and canoes displayed in the centre that opened in 2008. More places like this are starting to open across the province, providing a window to native cultures that in the past have been all but inaccessible to travellers.

Some evidence of the past slides into oblivion or is destroyed. Even as I finish the revisions to this guide, yet another pioneer hotel in yet another tiny town is destroyed by fire. But as more and more people value the evidence of the past, they find ways to restore and rebuild. Looking at a Doukhobor house in Grand Forks, I can still hear the soft shuffle of the owner's slippers as he led me up the worn wooden stairs some 25 years ago, his love for Doukhobor heritage clear in each touch of his hand on woven rug and carved wooden implement. But Peter Gritchen, the man who created a museum in this house, has died, and for a time it looked as though the house would be abandoned. Now it has been rescued and will live again as testimony to the vital spirit of its builders. In every region, those with a love for the past and the way it underlies our present have salvaged decrepit buildings, replanted heritage gardens and restored railway trails, trestles and tunnels.

The landscape itself is ever changing. I drive the back roads around Kelowna, in the Okanagan, and envision the grassy hills as they originally were, ranches where incomers pastured their horses and cattle. Fifteen years ago, orchards still dominated this region, though it was starting to change. Now, golf courses, sub-divisions and vineyards neighbour the remaining apple trees—and those trees, too, have changed, to modern varieties that bear their fruit tightly clustered on low branches easily reached without the giant ladders so common even several decades ago.

The search for historical detail has become much easier. Many books now detail the history of every part of British Columbia, and websites dedicated to that history are ever more numerous and of ever better quality.

Yet with all the changes, there is one constant. The thrill of discovery never palls as I approach each reminder of the past, each re-created native village, each tombstone shadowed in the undergrowth, each abandoned mine. When I walk a dusty track where little but flowers gone wild or hewn timbers in the brush remain of some homesteader's dream, I am transported to the country of the past and the stories that sustain it. I invite you to join me on that journey.

———•———

This book documents some of the evidence of the province's past and the changes in the province's landscape, from restored 19th-century streetscapes to dyked farm fields to re-created First Nations villages. It is not an exhaustive guide: if I had tried to record all the evidence, the book would be three or four volumes long and still incomplete. The choice of what went in and what did not had to be, to some extent, personal.

I have included evidence of First Nations history from 10,000 years ago to the present: pictographs, village sites and middens; buildings from 1850 to 1945; native museums and cultural centres that interpret native history and traditions from the beginning to the present; other museums that display native heritage; native nations that offer tours and trips that give the traveller a glimpse of First Nations past and present. Yet no guide to this rich heritage can do more than touch the surface of a long tradition and developing culture. Those who seek a deeper understanding of native history and culture will find many books and websites that delve into that history and culture.

When it comes to sites that stand witness to modern history, I have definite preferences. Sites of undoubted historic importance are included. But I would rather follow unpaved back roads to abandoned ruins than consider the architectural significance of big-city buildings. Pioneer cemeteries tell me better stories than restored Victorian courthouses. I prefer relatively undisturbed ghost towns that allow me to re-create an earlier world for myself to restorations where costumed actors do my imagining for me. I like to know why a landscape looks the way it does and how it used to look. I love a good or quirky story even though its historical significance may be slight. And I thrill at that moment of discovering some hidden evidence of history where I can suspend logic just long enough to imagine that no one has come this way for decades.

The guide is divided into sections, one for each region of the province. These regions, dictated by history and geography, are different from the tourist regions marked on many maps, which reflect current political realities and modern highway routes. History and geography tend to unify, for example, the coast of British Columbia from the Sechelt Peninsula to the Alaska Panhandle, rather than attaching pieces of it to the neighbouring inland regions.

In general, the material in each section moves from west to east, south to north. Where possible, directions use landmarks rather than distances. I get too frustrated every time I forget to note a starting point or reset the odometer to want to inflict that frustration on the reader.

A good map or set of maps is an essential companion to the guide. An up-to-date provincial map will provide general locations and show most routes discussed in the guide. The *British Columbia Road and Recreational Atlas*, published by Informap, maps most back roads. Many areas provide local brochures and maps that are an invaluable supplement. But in the backcountry, no map can supersede local information. If in doubt, ask at an infocentre, a museum, the local café, the police station, the logging-company office. However, the closure of Ministry of Forests offices in many smaller towns removes what was often the best source of information on area back roads. And a decision to end government maintenance of many forest service roads may make it difficult or impossible to reach remote sites.

Any survey like this relies heavily on those who have written before, and I acknowledge my debt particularly to those historians and authors who have meticulously documented the details of local history. Local histories, many unfortunately out of print, provide intimate details of a region's past. To find these books, ask at local museums, bookstores and libraries—or at the drugstore, general store or town newspaper office.

Museums and archives are treasure houses, improving all the time as small towns and bigger cities alike increasingly value the evidence of their histories. I sincerely thank everyone at every museum and every archives and historical society who responded to questions about changes and updates in their area; your help makes this a much better book. And thank you to those individuals in hamlets without infocentres or museums who gladly supplied information on what has changed and what remains in their part of the province.

A word of warning to the traveller: many museums, infocentres and historic sites, especially in smaller towns and rural areas, are closed from mid-September to June.

A new and invaluable resource since this book was first published is the Internet. Every large historic site and many smaller ones, plus almost every city, town or village in the province, has a website that provides much information.

Back-roading enthusiasts post background information and the current status of ghost towns, cyclists discuss how to gain access to historic trails, and hikers and horseback riders write about their various experiences. I have not listed web addresses throughout the book, since they change often. I'm willing to spend hours following a narrowing track into the bush in search of old buildings folding into the forest, but five minutes spent chasing a non-existent web address is so much wasted time: there's no delight in that investigation. But if you use a good search engine and seek entries under the name of the attraction or area you want to visit, you will be amply rewarded. Sometimes, these websites provide maps of the area or the attraction, so a visit to the virtual site before heading to the real one can be helpful.

Of course, it can also detract from the sense of discovery that comes from entering history less prepared.

---------•◆•---------

A brief summary of regional history begins each chapter of the book. Yet each time I set out to write an overview of the history of the entire province, that overview threatened to fill the whole book. The following provides the barest of bones, a context for the regional histories.

For several thousand (in some areas more than 10,000) years, the land was the domain of native peoples, who developed their cultures and traditions and used the resources of their regions in innovative and sustaining ways. Groups such as the Haida and the Kwakwaka'wakw on the Coast, the Okanagan and Ktunaxa people in the southern interior, and the Dakelh and Gitxsan in the north led vastly different lives. Yet all these nations built societies rich in material goods and spiritual expression. These cultures and traditions can be traced today in middens, artifacts and re-created historic villages. Though subsequent years saw the destruction of much native culture and the decimation of native populations, new museums, new reconstructions and the creation of new art attest to the revitalization of those cultures.

In the late 18th century, explorers and fur traders arrived by sea and land, mapping and charting, building posts, trading with the native peoples and getting their help as guides.

The 1858 gold rush in the Cariboo resulted in a radical change, including the creation of mainland British Columbia as a separate British colony. Later discoveries of precious metals did for other regions in B.C. what that early rush did for the Cariboo. In each case, prospectors, miners, merchants, hotel keepers, loggers, sawmill operators, clerks, families, camp followers and crooks avalanched into British Columbia, drawn by the inevitable exclamation marks of "Gold!" and "Silver!"

The mining camps rarely outlasted the minerals. But the discovery of rich ores was accompanied almost everywhere by the founding of more permanent towns on the new roads and railways opened to serve the mines. The building of the Canadian Pacific Railway across B.C. in the early 1880s, though, was spurred mainly by political, not economic motives, a promise made to entice B.C. into Canadian Confederation. Vancouver, Kamloops, Revelstoke and several dozen other cities and towns owe their existence to the CPR.

With better transportation came immigration booms, the sturdiest of these between 1890 and 1912. In 1891, some 98,000 people, 28 percent of them First Nations, lived in British Columbia. By 1911, 390,000 people lived here, just 5 percent of them First Nations. The Grand Trunk Pacific Railway was completed to tidewater in 1914; a third transcontinental railway, the Canadian Northern, was conceived, though not completed, in the same period. The two later merged with other lines into Canadian National Railways. Though the GTP resulted in the founding of Prince Rupert and the growth of Prince George, by 1914 the bulk of B.C.'s population still lived on Vancouver Island and in the Lower Mainland, Okanagan and Kootenay.

The boom died before World War I began. Some promising moments broke through the gloom in the 1920s, but British Columbia did not return to general prosperity until during and after World War II. This time, the north and the central plateau shared in the good times, with new roads and rail lines spearing into the Peace River country from the Cariboo and Prince George.

With each era, of course, came changes to the landscape, and new buildings in city, town and countryside. A certain logic underlies what has survived these changes and what has disappeared. Towns and camps that existed because mines, canneries or mills operated in the area rarely outlived the resources they were based upon. They are today's ghost towns. But some of the more solidly built towns still exist today; a languishing economy meant that developers saw little point in ripping down old buildings to erect new ones, and this helped preserve the evidence of history. In the same way, older areas of larger cities have often been best served by a degree of neglect, as poor and shabby neighbourhoods in older downtowns offered little to mall and subdivision developers. Where farmland surrounding the cities was overtaken by development though, only the rare farmhouse or pioneer church survived.

Landscape changes were often permanent. Dams built to provide hydroelectric power flooded huge areas of land and were particularly damaging to the native peoples whose best interests were regularly ignored. Ranches took the place of open country; some were in turn supplanted by orchard plots, then by housing developments or hectares of grapevines. The greatest landscape change of all, so pervasive that it would be simpler to list those places untouched than those places changed, came with logging. All across the province, forests were replaced by farm fields, towns and cities, blank hillsides and regimented rows of new plantings.

So much remains to remind us of our journey from past to present. I hope this guide begins to document the evidence of the past and that it lures into new and rewarding explorations those who love, as I do, wandering the back roads of history.

———•—•———

Change is one of the themes of this book and changes in some of the sites listed are inevitable. Buildings burn down, landscapes are converted to new uses and historic sites are rescued and restored. I welcome information about these changes. Please write to me c/o Whitecap Books, 351 Lynn Avenue, North Vancouver, B.C. V7J 2C4.

VANCOUVER ISLAND

PORT
HARDY

Port
McNeill

V A N C O U V E R

CAMPBELL RIVER

COURTENAY Comox

PARKSVILLE

NANAIMO

Tofino PORT
ALBERNI

Ucluelet

DUNCAN SALTSPRING
ISLAND

I S L A N D

VICTORIA

N

km. | 0 | 50 | 100 | 150 | 200 | km.

© STARSHELL MAPS

VANCOUVER ISLAND

"Vancouver Island has been not unaptly designated the England of the great Western ocean," wrote Matthew Macfie in the 1860s, "and it is no exaggeration to assert that it only requires a vigorous application of British capital, enterprise and labour in the development of its resources, to secure for it supremacy as a commercial and manufacturing centre in the Western Hemisphere."

Allowing for the hyperbole of a man who often let his words outrun his judgment, this assessment from the Victoria clergyman and writer seemed rational enough. In the 1860s, the island, and Victoria in particular, seemed poised to dominate the politics and economy of the continent's northwest coast. Indeed, to a great extent, it *was* the politics and economy of the northwest coast.

The trend began early in the history of the region. The many native nations that lived on the island, among them the Nuu-chah-nulth, the Kwakwaka'wakw and the Lekwammen, were among the most prosperous in North America. The ocean provided salmon (and other fish), shellfish and sea mammals such as whales. Cedar trees, suited for a multitude of purposes from building materials to basket making, clothed the coasts. What their own region did not produce, island First Nations could obtain from other areas, which they reached by canoe and along trade trails. The nations of the coast developed complex trade and diplomatic relations among themselves.

With plentiful and easily gathered resources, secure in permanent communities and seasonal sites along the island's coasts, the native groups developed highly evolved economic, social, religious and educational systems. Their art reached its height with the Kwakwaka'wakw, fine carvers of masks, totems and more utilitarian objects.

Explorers and traders who visited the northwest coast in the late 18th and early 19th centuries were equally well rewarded. So assiduously did they trade for sea otter pelts that they wiped out these animals along the coast. Though neither saw great commercial potential here, Spain and Britain fought, verbally though not physically, over the northwest coast. Britain won, and from 1794, the British flag flew over Nootka Island.

By the 1840s, another nation hungrily eyed the coast. The United States had to settle for half of what it wanted; in 1846, the Oregon Treaty declared Vancouver Island and the mainland north of the 49th parallel British while awarding Oregon and Washington territories to the Americans. Anticipating the decision, James Douglas and the Hudson's Bay Company in 1843 chose a location at the southern tip of Vancouver Island as their new northwest headquarters. Fort Victoria was built beside the present harbour, surrounded by "a range of plains nearly six miles square, containing a great extent of valuable tillage and pasture land." In 1849, the island was made a British crown colony.

Yet by 1850 only a few dozen Hudson's Bay Company employees and a handful of independent settlers had joined the native peoples as residents. James Douglas had much to do with this: he had no desire to see independent settlers on the island. He set the price of land so high and offered so little encouragement that few settlers arrived from Britain or from the United States.

His motives were relatively simple. He saw the commercial potential of the island and its value to the HBC, whose grip would surely be challenged by new immigrants. He was quick to exploit those resources that could profit the company. When coal was discovered at Fort Rupert, at the northern end of the island, Douglas sent for miners to work the deposits. The coal was of such poor quality that the mines were soon closed—but the miners established a Vancouver Island tradition by staging the island's first strike, a precursor of the often tumultuous relationship that would develop between those who harvested resources and those who profited from that harvest.

In 1850, new coal deposits were discovered at Nanaimo. Noting that both the

HBC and the new gold-rush settlements in California needed coal, Douglas sent a small group of miners north, then brought in 24 Staffordshire miners and their families. Nanaimo became the second permanent white settlement on the island.

By early 1858, a few hundred Europeans and about 15,000 native people lived on the island. One word changed all that. "Gold!" was the cry from the mainland, a cry heeded by thousands who flocked north from the declining gold fields of California. As word spread, thousands more took ship from Europe and from the American and Canadian east coast, bound for the tiny post on the southern tip of Vancouver Island.

Victoria was not prepared. In six months, it was transformed from a slow-moving outpost of empire to a raucous town of tents, log and clapboard houses, stores and hotels, churned and muddy streets and vast excitement. Though white Americans predominated, Black Americans, Canadians, Chinese, East Indians, South Americans, Mexicans, English, Scots, Welsh, Irish, Hawaiians and people of a dozen other nationalities hurried north to prospect for gold or to provide services for those who prospected.

Many were just passing through Victoria on their way to the fabled gold fields. But others came to stay for as long as the economy would support them. By late 1859, hastily built hotels replaced tents; independent outfitters and grocery stores competed with the HBC store; restaurants, saloons, barbershops, hairdressing salons and dry-goods stores stood beside the new wooden sidewalks, and gamblers, speculators and prostitutes engaged in activities that shocked the staid. Native people were exiled from their traditional locations, pushed aside for development of the town.

Many of those who made money from or in the gold rush retired to Victoria for the winters—or year-round—attracted by the mild climate and gentle contours of the area, greatly preferable to the deep winter snow, summer heat, mosquitoes and hard slogging of the Cariboo. Bankers, merchants, professionals of all kinds built their stately homes—some of which remain—along Victoria streets. Though Victoria's population, which had risen from 500 in 1857 to 5,000 in 1858, fell to 1,500 in 1859 as mining excitement abated, the Hudson's Bay outpost had become a permanent town.

The influx of new settlers changed forever the relations between the incomers and the original inhabitants of the land. Early explorers and traders were greeted as equals by the native nations, who engaged in trade—and the occasional battle—with the Europeans as they had among themselves. But the arrival of thousands of newcomers, many of whom despised the native peoples, was cataclysmic: the smallpox epidemic of 1862, for example, began with a few infected men arriving in Victoria by ship, and resulted in the deaths of up to two-thirds of the coastal native people.

It was a few years later, in 1865, that Matthew Macfie made his prophecy. He cast an eye upon the mineral deposits of the island and proclaimed them its economic future. He then declared that "it is now universally admitted that Vancouver Island and British Columbia produce the best qualities of timber to be found in the world," discoursed upon the fisheries and exhorted would-be immigrants to take advantage of what agricultural land existed. After making reference to Alexander the Great, Antiochus, Tamerlane, Nadir Shah, Mahomet and Caliph Omar, among others, Macfie cried out for a railway that would link Vancouver Island and British Columbia to the markets of the world. His proposed railway made "transcendent the prospects of Victoria."

The choice of Victoria in 1868 as the capital of the combined colonies of the island and mainland presaged a trend that would continue into the 20th century. Victoria would be the political capital of British Columbia and a slower-paced city where people came to relax or retire. As such, it grew; many of the impressive brick and stone buildings that still enhance downtown Victoria were built before 1900. But much of Victoria would be built on money that came from elsewhere. The Dunsmuir family, famous or notorious as late-19th-century entrepreneurs, made their money up-island, from the Nanaimo coal mines, from the building of the Esquimalt and Nanaimo Railway and from other ventures. In Victoria, they built Craigdarroch and Hatley castles, both enduring monuments to turn-of-the-century grandeur.

Life in Victoria contrasted with that up-island. The area around the capital was rapidly logged, so logging and milling operations moved on into forest farther north. Settlers and would-be farmers broke land in the Cowichan and

Comox valleys. Miners blasted and dug their way into the rock at Cumberland; at Nanaimo, they ran tunnels out under the water.

Relations between the men who ran the mines and those who worked them were often bitter. Mine owners played off white workers against Chinese labourers, who, jobless when they finished their work on the CPR, were powerless to fight low wages and unsafe conditions. Between 1884 and 1912, 373 men were killed in mine explosions. In 1912, Cumberland miners led by Albert "Ginger" Goodwin went on strike; in 1913, Nanaimo miners followed suit. The government sent in the army; the company sent in strikebreakers. The battles between management and labour have left an imprint: traditionally, much of Vancouver Island has voted for a left-wing political party.

George Vancouver, scanning the west coast mountain slopes, noted the size of the trees. Later incomers realized their economic potential. The HBC built the island's first sawmill in 1849; it was followed by more mills and bigger mills that processed more and more trees as the 20th century wore on. Hand logging gave way to horse logging; horses gave way to railways; railways gave way to roads and logging trucks, hauling timber from deeper and deeper in the forest. The crosscut saw was supplanted by the power saw, and the faller by the grapple yarder. Each change in technology made it possible for loggers to reach farther into the forest, to cut down a greater number of trees more quickly. In 1944, when H. R. MacMillan donated Cathedral Grove, a group of 800-year-old trees near Port Alberni, to the province for preservation, he anticipated, though perhaps not knowingly, the course of island logging. (See page 40.) Those who wish today to see virgin rainforest and centuries-old growth find few places to do so.

Major landscape change on the island came also from settlement: better transportation and roads, coupled with the pleasant climate and scenery, attracted many to towns and cities on the island's east coast from Victoria to Campbell River, and these communities still attract growth today—the 21st century has seen an unprecedented increase in housing prices and development.

Matthew Macfie was not wholly prescient. There was no way he could foresee the future of Vancouver Island in the 21st century, or, for that matter, the commercial future of the England he compared it to. Vancouver Island has

5

evolved rather differently than he predicted it would. Yet perhaps he may be allowed the last word.

He quotes from the journals of explorer George Vancouver: " 'To describe the beauties of this region will on some future occasion be a very grateful task to the pen of the skilful panegyrist. The serenity of the climate, the innumerable pleasing landscapes, and the abundant fertility that unassisted nature puts forth, require only to be enriched by the industry of man with villages, mansions, cottages, and other buildings to render it the most lovely country that can be imagined.'

"I am disposed," wrote Macfie, "to regard the language of Captain Vancouver . . . as sober and just."

————◆————

VICTORIA AND AREA

Long the domain of the Lekwammen, T'Souke, Beecher Bay and Wsanec (Saanich) peoples, the southern tip of Vancouver Island was the first part of the island permanently settled by non-natives. Today, this small area is home to more than half of the island's 750,000 people. This section of the guide covers the area from Port Renfrew, at the western end of the Strait of Juan de Fuca, through the western communities of Metchosin, Langford and Colwood; Victoria and its sister communities of Esquimalt and Oak Bay; and the Saanich Peninsula to Sidney and Swartz Bay. It begins in downtown Victoria.

Victoria

Downtown Victoria is a dream for those who are fascinated by the province's colonial history. Since many of its 19th-century buildings were solidly built of brick or stone, they escaped destruction by fire or neglect. Nor was the city plagued by massive downtown redevelopment. By the time economics might have allowed such redevelopment, citizens had realized the value of historic buildings in the central core, and the downtown area has, by and large, remained on a turn-of-the-century scale. Although a growing forest of condominium and commercial towers has slightly dimmed the pleasure of walking downtown with its Edwardian or Victorian buildings, much of the central core of historic Victoria still retains its low-rise charm.

Maps of the downtown area, useful for orientation, are available from the tourist infocentre at the corner of Government and Wharf streets. Also available here and at City Hall are guides to the historic buildings of James Bay, North Park and Fernwood, with a guide to Fairfield forthcoming.

This guide begins at the James Bay waterfront; the foot of Government or Douglas street makes an interesting starting place for a walk through James Bay and downtown.

Yellow-flowered broom bushes are so omnipresent along the seafront that visitors could be excused for thinking them native to the area. They are not. Broom seeds were brought here, probably by early settler Walter Colquhoun Grant. Grant didn't have much luck on Vancouver Island. His many enterprises, which included farming and sawmilling, were less than successful, and, at one point, he repaired to Hawaii to consider his future. He returned to Victoria, however, bringing with him broom seeds from plants grown in Hawaii by a Hudson's Bay Company employee who presumably started broom plants from Scottish seed.

The Victoria tradition of a drive along the waterfront is an old one, as is the practice of holding conventions in the capital city. Delegates to a 1907 conference take a carriage trip along McNeil Bay. (BCA A9194)

Along the seafront, too, the deep-blue, star-shaped flowers of camas bulbs that *are* native create a carpet in late spring. Camas bulbs were once an important food source for the native peoples who lived along the southern edge of the island.

A number of historic sites exist along the waterfront walkway. One of the most poignant is a simple gravestone in the ground beside Dallas Road just north of the entrance to the Ogden Point docks. It is dedicated to Hiwet, a young man of the Camel Point Indian village who was buried 300 to 1,000 years ago, unearthed in 1995 and reburied by his Lekwammen people that same year. North from the water, west of the park, is James Bay, one of the first residential areas settled in the 1860s. Two houses on lower Government Street date from the 1860s. A redwood house at 138/140 Government, the oldest remaining in the area, was built in 1861 in Italianate style for a Hudson's Bay Company official. A block away, at 207 Government, is the 1860s Carr family house where painter Emily Carr grew up. Restored and open to the public, it also features period gardens.

Huntington Place and Avalon Road in James Bay feature seven houses built between 1890 and 1907, in Queen Anne, late Victorian and Edwardian styles. In the 100-block of South Turner Street stand nine turn-of-the-century houses.

The area north of James Bay, around the Inner Harbour, was the site of HBC activities from 1843 on and of commercial and government activities after the gold rush transformed Victoria. Before the HBC arrived, the Lekwammen lived farther south and east at Cadboro Bay. Many moved to live around the fort but were banished by James Douglas to the Songhees land across the Inner Harbour. Native history from pre-contact days to the present is well presented at the Royal British Columbia Museum at Government and Belleville streets. The museum has garnered an international reputation for its innovative displays, among them a magnificent presentation of First Peoples culture and history, with the Kwakwaka'wakw house of the late Chief Kwakwabalasami (built in his honour by his descendants, the Hunt Family) and a moving presentation on the 1862 smallpox epidemic. Also at the museum are an Old Town streetscape, displays of the history of logging and mining and a replica of Captain Vancouver's ship the *Discovery*, featuring the captain's quarters. The B.C. Archives building next to the museum has changing photographic displays on the walls of its entrance lobby. Inside is the repository of records, writings, photographs and art on the history of the province.

Thunderbird Park, to the east of the museum, contains well-carved replicas of totem poles from coastal villages. Just below the poles is a traditional native Big House known as Wawadit'la, also called the Mungo Martin House.

Just east of the museum is the province's oldest standing house, Helmcken House, which was built in 1852 for B.C.'s first resident doctor, John Sebastian Helmcken.

Beside Helmcken House is a plank-sheathed, squared-log cabin built in the 1840s and used after 1858 as a schoolhouse by the Sisters of St. Ann. The order was founded in Quebec in 1850 to provide teachers for the public schools of the countryside. Eight years later, four sisters arrived here from Vaudreuil and set about establishing this school for young ladies of all religions. Members of the Sisters of St. Ann still live and work in British Columbia, teaching and doing pastoral and social justice work.

Another short block east, in grounds that front on Humboldt Street, St. Ann's Academy, its cornerstone laid in 1871, is well worth a look. Increasingly dilapidated and under threat in the 1980s and 1990s, the building was beautifully restored in 1998 and is a favourite location for weddings.

West of the museum and archives building are the Legislative Buildings; to the north is the Empress Hotel. Both are the creations of storied architect Francis Mawson Rattenbury, whose rather flamboyant life here was overshadowed by his murder in England some years later. Both buildings include a number of later additions. The Legislative Buildings, opened in 1897, replaced earlier, smaller government buildings. The building exterior features various architectural details, including statues immortalizing in stone a number of B.C. heroes and mythological figures. Tours and information on the history of the buildings are available.

Until the turn of the century, the tide flowed in over mud flats that separated the James Bay area from the rest of Victoria. Pedestrians and vehicles crossed on a bridge across the flats. Then the land was drained and dyked; the causeway

The bookstore Munro's is housed in the beautifully restored 1909 neoclassical Royal Bank of Canada building on Government Street in Victoria.

in front of the Empress Hotel runs on top of a dyke. The Empress, opened in 1908 as part of the Canadian Pacific hotel chain, rests on pilings driven deep into the drying mud.

Across the causeway, Government Street leads through Old Town, where history from gold rush through to 1914 is highly visible. Many of the buildings along these streets, designated heritage buildings, sport plaques that outline their past. The 1000-block of Government Street contains a half-dozen 1890s buildings, including the Bank of British Columbia building at Government and Fort, later occupied by the Canadian Imperial Bank of Commerce and now—how the temples of commerce have changed—a pub. Rogers' Chocolates at 913 Government is a Victoria institution. Charles Rogers, an immigrant American fruit dealer, began making chocolates in Victoria in 1885; his recipes are still in use. At 1116 Government, the Morris building houses a traditional tobacconist, as it has since 1892, still hanging on despite Victoria's vigorous anti-smoking policies.

A series of grey blocks inlaid into the brick sidewalks of Old Town traces the perimeter of Fort Victoria. On Government Street opposite the end of View Street, where a plaque describes the location of the fort, is the entrance to Bastion Square. The square, really a rectangle that runs through to Wharf Street, contains the former courthouse, board of trade building, law chambers and other historic buildings. The Maritime Museum of British Columbia, in the 1899 courthouse, presents displays on B.C.'s maritime history.

From the lower part of Bastion Square, an alleyway leads to Yates Street and a second alleyway continues between Yates and Johnson. This second alley (Waddington Alley) is paved with wooden blocks, replicas of those that originally muffled the noise of horses' hooves. At night, this alley can be as unsavoury now as it probably was 150 years ago.

The 500-block of Johnson Street, including the Paper Box Arcade and Market Square across the street, features some well-restored buildings from about 1900. Market Square bridges what used to be a ravine that divided Chinatown from the rest of Victoria. In early years, the ravine creek supplied water to some city dwellers. Later, it became a garbage dump. The brick buildings that now form the north row of Market Square date from the late 1890s, when Victoria's Chinatown, the first and at that time the largest in Canada, numbered more than 3,000 people.

The first Chinese in Victoria came from California, lured by the gold rush in 1858; most continued on to the Cariboo, but some stayed to found businesses or to work for other Victorians. The building of the CPR, completed in 1886, attracted thousands more Chinese to the city. Chinatown expanded and by 1910

Victoria in the 1860s had exploded from a sedate fur post to a town built in brick and wood. Here, natives sit in Bastion Square, near the centre of the old HBC post. (BCA H3766)

The Chinese Public School at 636 Fisgard Street opened in 1909. It is the home of the Chinese Consolidated Benevolent Association.

it covered some eight city blocks. It has since shrunk to the blocks between Pandora and Herald, Store and Government and east a further half-block.

Through Market Square and across Pandora is Fan Tan Alley, a narrow walkway that dates from the 1880s. It leads between brick buildings that used to house fan tan gambling clubs and cafés (the wooden buildings where opium was legally manufactured are long gone). Closed off by locked gates and guarded by watchmen who surveyed visitors through a peephole, Fan Tan Alley earned a reputation among white Victorians as a dark and mysterious, indeed sinister, place. In the 1940s, when war and conditions in China prevented the single

Many buildings on Fisgard Street in Victoria's Chinatown have recessed balconies, traditional feature of Chinese architecture.

13

Chinese men who made up a large percentage of Chinatown's population from sending money home, they gathered here to gamble in the clubs. As the Chinese population moved out into other areas of Victoria, Fan Tan Alley, like most of Chinatown, became increasingly rundown. Alley buildings were condemned in the 1970s but restored a decade later. Now the small shops are used by artisans and others. Signs in Chinese characters indicating the old fan tan clubs are still visible atop doorways and on the brick walls.

The alley leads to Fisgard Street and the heart of present-day Chinatown. Most of the older buildings date from Chinatown's heyday between 1890 and 1914. Some features to look for: recessed balconies on the second storeys, Chinese tile roofs, upturned corners, Chinese society (tong) signs. On the north side of Fisgard Street, Dragon Alley leads through what were once tenements and now are upmarket offices, studios and condominiums.

The Chinese Public School building on Fisgard east of Government opened in 1909 after the Victoria School Board ruled that Chinese children born outside Canada could not attend public schools. The Chinese Consolidated Benevolent Society sued to reverse the ruling but was unsuccessful and built its own school, the Zonghua Xuetang, where children of Chinese heritage learned both Chinese and English. The school still operates after regular school hours. The building combines a pagoda-style structure with Western decorative elements.

Back in the centre of downtown, the Rithet Building at 1117 Wharf was once a dockside warehouse. The building features a brick fountain that was originally a well in the lobby. South and on the other side of Wharf is the 1876 Dominion Customs House, now known as the Malahat Building.

As Victoria grew, new neighbourhoods developed, fell out of favour, then often returned to favour once more. To see some of the city's older and opulent houses, drive Rockland Avenue and St. Charles Street.

Christ Church Cathedral, at Quadra and Courtney streets, was built in 1929. Check out the bell tower (bells ring on Sundays) and the stained glass windows.

The list of historic buildings outside downtown is topped by Craigdarroch Castle, built by coal baron Robert Dunsmuir, who died in 1889 before the massive monument in marble, stone and wood could be completed. The castle, at 1050 Joan Crescent, is marked on tourist maps of Victoria. Restored and refurbished after a life as dwelling place, hospital, college, school board offices and music conservatory, it is open to the public.

Three houses outside downtown date well back. The second-oldest structure in the region—still a residence—is the Tod House at 2564 Heron Street in Oak Bay. John Tod was unknowingly a trendsetter: reputedly, he was the first person to retire in Oak Bay. An HBC chief trader at Fort Kamloops, he came to Victoria in the late 1840s and built this six-room squared-log dwelling, a variant on the one-storey Quebec farmhouses familiar to him from his childhood. It is said he married seven times and had ten children. The Tod House received much publicity in the 1950s and 1960s as a haunted house; skeletons and ghosts walked and chains rattled—or so the stories went—and people sought out the tunnels believed to have been used to bring in illegal Chinese immigrants from the beach some distance away. The house's reputation was reinforced in 1993 when a woman who lived in the house and suffered from anorexia hid for five days in an attic almost no one knew existed.

Point Ellice House, built in 1861 for gold commissioner and judge Peter O'Reilly and his family, has been restored and is open to the public. Afternoon tea is served in the gardens in the summertime. It stands alongside a shady lane in the industrial area north of downtown, at 2616 Pleasant Street, north of Bay Street.

The manor house at Craigflower Farm and the schoolhouse that served the children of farm labourers, at the corner of Craigflower and Admirals roads, are open to the public. Craigflower was one of four farms established by the HBC subsidiary, the Puget Sound Agricultural Company. The farm, started in the 1850s, survived until 1866, when it was sold off piece by piece. The buildings date from 1855 and 1856.

Four cemeteries tell the story of Victoria's early days. Pioneer Square, on Quadra Street between Rockland and Meares, was the first cemetery. A number of headstones dating from the 1860s are preserved there, including a monument erected by Ellen Carroll in memory of her three children, who died in 1860, 1861 and 1862, all on the first day of their lives—a sad reminder of the uncertainty of life in those pioneer days.

Off Fairfield Road east of Cook Street, Ross Bay Cemetery, dating from 1873, is perhaps the province's most interesting burial place. It was designed as a place for people to contemplate life and death. Among the celebrated British Columbians buried here are Matthew Baillie Begbie, British Columbia's first judge; William Fraser Tolmie, physician, botanist and politician; Roderick Finlayson, Fort Victoria factor (chief trader) from 1844; capitalist Robert Dunsmuir; Sir James and Lady Amelia Douglas (Douglas dominated British Columbia and Vancouver Island history and politics from 1843 to 1865); artist Emily Carr; and prospector and adventurer Nellie Cashman. Also buried is Billy Barker, gold prospector, whose discoveries on Williams Creek were the catalyst for the Cariboo gold rush. His grave has recently been marked with a 900-kilogram boulder that was originally close to the shaft of his miracle mine. Check the cemetery's website for maps that locate the graves of prominent occupants. You can also get a map and brochure at the travel infocentre.

But the social history revealed by the cemetery is at least as interesting as the graves of famous people. William Gladstone Kemp died in 1877, in an accident on board an HBC ship. Farmer George Deans was killed by the kick of a horse. Fanny Palmer, age 17, died when the steamer *Pacific* capsized near Cape Flattery in 1875. Mary McLeese died in 1876, two days after her infant daughter. Three of the 59 people killed when the Point Ellice bridge collapsed in 1896 are buried here.

The headstones challenge the idea of Victoria as a little bit of England. The francophone Sisters of St. Ann are buried here, as are Heinrich Bohrer, a music teacher who dropped dead during a lesson; Carlo Bossi, pioneer stonemason and merchant; George Katayama; Demetrius Changranes; Marie Larbonne; Joseph Bahash; James Siomax; and Nicholas Khanishten, a "chief of the Songish" who died at the age of 100.

The cemetery is divided into 24 sections, many of which correspond to religious—or in some cases racial—divisions. One corner of section K was set aside for Chinese and Japanese graves; section N was used after 1904 for those who came here from China, Japan and India. But section N was closest to the sea, and a heavy storm washed away part of it, setting coffins afloat and exposing graves. (The Ross Bay seawall was built in 1911, partly to prevent a recurrence of the flooding.)

The flooding convinced the Chinese community that they must find a new burial site. The one they chose is at Harling Point, at the end of Gonzales Bay (follow Crescent Road to its end at the seafront). Chinese who died in Victoria were buried in the Chinese Cemetery for six years; in the seventh year, the bones were dug up, prepared and stored in the bone house in the cemetery until there were enough for shipment back to China and a final resting place. That practice ended when China's doors closed in the 1930s. The cemetery was closed in 1950, but was restored in 2000 and is now a National Historic Site.

The Jewish cemetery, still in use as a cemetery today, is on Cedar Hill Road south of Hillside. The Jewish community was established early in Victoria. Temple Emmanuel, at 1461 Blanshard Street, was built in 1862, the first synagogue in British North America west of Toronto. Its restoration in the 1970s merited a heritage award. A gravestone at the cemetery commemorates the man who is thought to have been the first person buried there: Morris Price was killed at Cayoosh, en route to the goldfields in 1861. Also here is the grave of Sarah, wife of David Oppenheimer, one of five Oppenheimer brothers prominent in the early commercial and political life of British Columbia. David Oppenheimer was Vancouver mayor from 1888 to 1891. The brothers operated stores in the Cariboo and Victoria; they ran the first wholesale grocery business on the mainland and built the first brick building in Vancouver after fire destroyed their original store. The graveyard reminds us that Victoria in the 1860s was still a pioneer community. A number of gravestones are for children who died before they reached their third birthdays. Also in the cemetery is a Holocaust memorial.

Across Fairfield Road from the Ross Bay cemetery is Ross Bay Villa, an 1865 colonial cottage under restoration; the villa's garden contains many heritage plants.

ESQUIMALT, across the Johnson Street bridge from downtown Victoria, was the Royal Navy's choice as a harbour. As early as 1846, six Royal Navy ships anchored here. The Canadian Forces base still occupies a large section of land at the city's west end. Security precautions inaugurated at the base in 2001 require that visitors present photo identification at the gate if they wish to visit the CFB Esquimalt Naval and Military Museum.

Victoria's Chinese Cemetery looks out across the water; the bones of Chinese immigrants who died in Canada rested here for many years, then were transported to their final resting place in China.

In 1873, the federal government passed an order-in-council, fixing Esquimalt as the western terminus for the Canadian Pacific Railway. The rail line was to run from Esquimalt harbour to Seymour Narrows, north of present-day Campbell River, where, it was presumed, steamships or bridges would carry traffic to and from the mainland. Esquimalt harbour was later passed over in favour of the mainland harbour at to-be-built Vancouver, but a railway was still built: the Esquimalt and Nanaimo Railway was completed between those two communities in 1886. The E&N tracks still follow their old course along Victoria's Store Street through Esquimalt and north. The frequently threatened passenger service from Victoria to Courtenay still hangs on, though no one can say for how long.

Because the Hudson's Bay Company prevented, or imposed harsh conditions on, settlement near the fort, early would-be farmers followed the coasts west and north from Victoria. Though development in the western communities of Colwood, Langford and Metchosin has been rapid in the past few decades, some evidence of earlier times remains between the two-car garages of landscaped housing developments.

Fort Victoria residents seeking diversion rode their horses or came by wagon or buggy to such establishments as Four Mile or Six Mile House. Both, with renovations and additions, operate as pubs beside the Old Island Highway. The central part of Four Mile House was built in about 1856. Though a pub has existed on the Six Mile site for more than a century, present buildings date from the 1920s and later.

On the oceanfront in Langford (take Highway 1A/Sooke Road) west, then turn left at Ocean Boulevard, keeping left) is Fort Rodd National Historic Site. Beginning in 1864, artillery batteries were located at Rodd Point as a line of first defence for Royal Navy installations at Esquimalt. Fort Rodd ended its military duties in 1956. Fisgard Light here was the first permanent lighthouse on the coast, illuminated on November 16, 1860, just six weeks before the light at Race Rocks. Now automated, it still flashes its warning to ships. You can visit the lighthouse and the keeper's quarters. Look for historical exhibits in various buildings.

The Dunsmuir family were busy builders. A second stone monument to their opulent lifestyle is now part of Royal Roads University, which was for many years a military college. The main building of Royal Roads was originally Hatley Castle, built for James Dunsmuir. It contains 50 rooms. The beautifully landscaped grounds, including Japanese and Italian gardens, are open to the public (an admission fee is charged). The castle itself can be seen via guided tours.

St. Mary's Church, on Metchosin Road near the corner with Happy Valley Road, is known as the Easter Lily Church for the purple and white fawn lilies that throng the churchyard in mid-April. Consecrated in 1876, it is one of the older churches in continuous use on the island.

Just around the corner on Happy Valley Road is the Metchosin Schoolhouse, restored as a museum. Built in 1872, it was used until 1914, then off and on until 1949. Here also is a pioneer implement museum.

Check out nearby Lombard Drive to see a double row of poplars planted by a pioneer settler along the approach to his farm.

Sooke to Port Renfrew

Just before Sooke on Highway 14 along the west coast is a roadhouse that has served as a stopping place for travellers since the late 19th century. The 17 Mile House was built in 1900. Redoubtable innkeepers Mary Jackson and Edith Wilson served food and drink for decades. They are both long gone, and the pub no longer rents out rooms or finds itself busiest in hunting season, but it is a quirky place with uneven floors that still reflect its turn-of-the-century origins.

Some who arrived in the 1840s and 1850s tried first to settle in Metchosin, the area west of HBC lands, but the ground was stony and a harbour non-existent. So early settlers moved farther west, to Sooke. Walter Colquhoun Grant, whom many regard as the first independent white settler on Vancouver Island, built a homestead and a mill here in the 1850s, but to no avail. Grant's skills were not up to the task; all but bankrupt, he fled the area for more promising climes. A plaque at the corner of Sooke Road and Maple Avenue commemorates his efforts.

Among the heritage buildings still standing near Sooke are a trio built by people connected to Sooke's first permanent white settlers: John and Ann Muir, their daughter, Marion, and their sons, Andrew, John, Robert and Michael.

The Muirs arrived at Victoria from Scotland in 1849 to oversee the coal workings at Fort Rupert. When that operation failed, they moved to Fort Victoria, then pre-empted crown land at Sooke. They operated the first successful steam sawmill in B.C., built ships (among them the *Ann Taylor*) and ran some of the first logging operations along their section of the west coast.

Moss Cottage, transplanted from its original location to stand beside Sooke Region Museum just off Sooke Road (Highway 14) east of Sooke, was built sometime in the late 1860s. Mary Ellen Flynn came from Liverpool in 1869 to marry James Welsh, who worked for the Muirs, and the couple lived at Moss Cottage. Mary Ellen had five children in 11 years, then died in 1880. The cottage stayed in the Welsh family until 1977. It has been restored in turn-of-the-century style and is open to the public, with displays on logging, fishing and First Nations. Outside is a cast iron and glass dome, incorporating an unusual Fresnel lens from the storied Triangle Island lighthouse.

Woodside, at 7117 West Coast Road, is a two-storey, Georgian-style farmhouse, square and uncompromising, probably built in about 1869. It was the home of John and Ann Muir, and then of their son John and his wife, Annie. Woodside is still a private residence, looking much as it did a century ago.

Burnside, at 1890 Maple Avenue, home to Michael and Matilda Muir from its construction in 1870, is similar to Woodside and equally well preserved.

Some evidence remains of Sooke's changing economics. A brief gold rush in 1864 drew prospectors to the Leech River. But there's little left of Leechtown now. A hard-to-find cairn placed in 1928 marks the site of the government assay office, and weather-beaten boards in the forest testify to the old mining camp and subsequent explorations. Finding them may give you some idea of the travails of prospectors who travelled without maps or roads—as, indeed, may reaching Leechtown itself. You can hike or bike in along the Galloping Goose Trail, but road access west from Shawnigan Lake has been closed permanently and the logging roads that lead from Otter Point Road in Sooke to Leechtown may from time to time be closed to the public as well.

Farther along the coast, at the town of Jordan River, the dilapidated shell of the 1911 Jordan River powerhouse still stands near the Jordan River bridge. The powerhouse generated power for southern Vancouver Island until 1971, when the system was replaced by a new dam and powerhouse. The original hydro-producing system included two dams, a flume, a reservoir and penstocks that conveyed water to the powerhouse. Some Jordan River buildings—including the old school and the café—date from an army camp built in 1939 to protect the power source against enemy action. West of the town, For Sale signs indicate promoters' hopes of a new land rush to more than rival old gold rush times.

Still farther along the coast, at the end of the West Coast Road, stands Port Renfrew, born as a logging camp and for years the end point of logging railways that took timber from the hills to the coast. Had the owners of the ancient Port Renfrew Hotel been a little more stubborn, the hotel might have ended up at the bottom of the channel: a tale is told that a tugboat captain, who was refused service for himself and his men, encircled the hotel with his towline and threatened to pull it into the water. The men got their beer.

The West Coast Trail, the reincarnation of the old life-saving trail that ran from Port Renfrew to Bamfield farther north, now attracts thousands of hikers from around the world every year. Intended as a trail to safety for shipwrecked sailors who came to grief in the angry Pacific waters, it was paralleled by a rough telegraph line that allowed lighthouse keepers along the coast to summon help.

The guide now returns to the northern border of Victoria proper and the beginning of the Saanich Peninsula.

Saanich Peninsula

The Saanich Peninsula was and is the location of many Wsanec villages—"Saanich" comes from the native word *Wsanec*. As white settlers moved into the Victoria area from the 1850s on, they took up land on the fertile peninsula to the north of the fort and established farms. By the 1890s, two steam railways and one electric interurban system carried passengers between Victoria, Sidney and other peninsula communities. Railway buffs will note that the name of Veyaness Avenue is a corruption of the V&S, the Victoria and Sidney Railway, and that Lochside Road, with its many interruptions, follows the railbed of the Canadian National right-of-way, as does much of the Lochside Trail.

A pleasant driving route provides an introduction to much of the area's history. West Saanich Road was one of the original meandering routes through the peninsula; it also passes through a number of First Nations reserves. You can reach the road in a variety of ways. The simplest is to drive north on Highway 17 out of Victoria and take the Royal Oak exit. At the lights, turn left, then turn right onto West Saanich Road.

St. Michael and All Angels Church, on West Saanich about a kilometre from the corner of Wilkinson Road, was built in 1883 for a congregation of a hundred. Though the building was greatly expanded in 1953, it still retains its original Gothic revival style.

Benvenuto Avenue leads west to the Butchart Gardens. Jenny Butchart began creation of these 10-hectare, world-famous gardens in the pit of an exhausted limestone quarry that operated until the turn of the century; Robert Butchart used the limestone to make cement. Soil for the gardens was brought from nearby farmland by horse-cart. The original quarry pit is now the Sunken Garden. The chimney from a cement plant kiln still overlooks the old quarry.

At the entrance to Brentwood Bay is the simple white frame Sluggett Memorial Baptist Church, built in 1911.

Throughout the peninsula, elegant gingerbreaded farmhouses remain from the turn of the century, built in the pioneer vernacular style. One such is at the corner of Stellys Cross Road and West Saanich Road. Their hipped-roof wraparound verandas are characteristic.

Another kilometre down the road are the buildings, totems and paintings of the Lauwelnew Tribal School. The art incorporates modern native life with older traditions and history. On the left beyond the village is the native cemetery, dating from the 1860s and still in use, where rough wooden crosses share space with ornate marble and a totem or two. At the centre of the graveyard is a memorial to several priests who served on the reserve, among them Louis Lootens, who came from Idaho and died in 1888.

Beyond the reserve on the left, Our Lady of the Assumption Catholic Church, built in 1894, overlooks Saanich Inlet. Holy Trinity Anglican Church, at the corner of Mills Road, was built in 1884 from lumber brought across Saanich

Inlet from a sawmill on the other side. The yew and oak trees by the church were brought from England and planted in 1937 to celebrate the coronation of King George VI.

West Saanich Road continues north to Lands End Road, which meets Highway 17 near the BC Ferries terminal. The building of the Swartz Bay terminal and the beginning of frequent ferry service between Vancouver Island and the mainland in 1959 had a major impact on the island, making it increasingly accessible for both people and freight.

Return to the highway headed south, then take the exit for McDonald Park Road. Continue on Resthaven Road to Harbour Road. Built in the early 1920s as a 14-room log house, the Latch, now an inn and restaurant, was extensively remodelled in the 1930s according to Samuel Maclure designs, as a summer residence for Lieutenant-Governor Walter Nichols.

The Sidney Museum, relocated from the waterfront to the lower floor of the Post Office building at Beacon Avenue and Fourth Street, displays the history of **SIDNEY** and the Saanich Peninsula. From the wharf at the foot of Beacon Avenue, you can see James Island, where 300 people lived between 1913 and 1970 while an explosives plant functioned on the island. Embedded in the sidewalk at the corner of Beacon and Second is a bolt that anchored the cable stays for a travelling crane used to move lumber. It's the last reminder of a sawmill that used to occupy this site. Check out Sidney as well for murals that relate to the history of the town and, on Fourth Street north of Beacon, vintage military equipment.

If you return to the highway and head south, then turn right (west) on Mt. Newton Cross Road, it will lead you to the Prairie Inn, a hostelry since 1859. The present frame pub building with wide verandas dates from 1893.

Just off Highway 17 on the way to Victoria (turn left—east—on Island View Road, then take an immediate left) is Heritage Acres, the display grounds of the Saanich Historical Artifacts Society, open daily in summer and mornings in winter. The displays include early farming equipment and tools and a fully functional model railroad, with engines, cars and tracks to scale. The railroad operates when club enthusiasts bring model railway rolling stock to the park. Enthusiasts also hold steam power events at various dates in summer and fall.

SOUTHERN GULF ISLANDS

Ferries for the southern Gulf Islands leave from Swartz Bay on Vancouver Island and from Tsawwassen on the mainland. A small ferry also connects Saltspring Island to Crofton.

The islands that lie between Vancouver Island and the mainland in the Gulf of Georgia share some history with Vancouver Island. As long as boats were more important than land transport, the pace of Gulf Island development paralleled—and sometimes exceeded—that of the larger island. But once roads were built on Vancouver Island, the Gulf Islands settled into the role that most inhabitants preferred, one of rural retreat, away from the mainstream of development (a role that's increasingly threatened as urbanites discover the joys of island living).

Many of the historic buildings on the islands date from 1880 to 1900, a time when settlers from a variety of countries and backgrounds were choosing to homestead on land cheaper than that nearer Victoria, though the soil was less promising. A number of these old farmhouses still stand, as do the community buildings so important to rural life.

The ferries that carry passengers to and from the islands are a major part of island history. Native canoes were the first boats to carry people to the islands. They were followed by sailing ships, rowboats and steamers. Private ferries served the islands until 1961, when the B.C. government bought the existing service and started its own runs. Each ferry that serves the islands today carries a plaque announcing when and where it was built.

Maps of each of the islands can be obtained from museums, infocentres or—probably the best bet—real estate offices.

On **SALTSPRING ISLAND**, the largest and most populated of the Gulf Islands, a petroglyph at Drummond Park near Fulford Harbour has been moved several times, first from the harbour itself, finally to its present site. Also on the island are more than 100 registered midden sites.

St. Paul's Roman Catholic Church (1880s) in Fulford Harbour resembles the old stone church, also known as the Butter Church, in the Cowichan Valley, and for good reason. A stained-glass window, the door and the bell all come from that church, brought by native canoe from Cowichan to the island, then by oxen-drawn stoneboat to Fulford Harbour.

One of those who built St. Paul's was William Naukana, whose grave lies east of the church, his name anglicized to Nowkin. Naukana was one of several hundred Kanakas—Hawaiian Islanders—brought to British Columbia by the Hudson's Bay Company in the 1840s and 1850s to work on HBC timber holdings and farms. Some of the Kanakas stayed when their contracts expired. The HBC gave this group Portland Island, a small island south of Saltspring. Naukana and others later settled on Saltspring as well as on Portland. Beside the church are graves of the Palua family, their name anglicized to Pallow. Some Kanaka descendants suggest that this church was once known as the Kanaka Church.

Near Ruckle Provincial Park is the Beaver Point School (1885), which is one of the oldest school buildings still standing in British Columbia. It is now a private preschool.

Henry Ruckle, who arrived on Saltspring in 1872, and his wife, Anna, acquired 192 hectares of farmland. Some of their farm buildings, including the farmhouse built circa 1876, can still be seen at Ruckle Park. They are not open to the public.

Saltspring attracted a great variety of settlers. Among them were Blacks who fled the United States in the 1850s and 1860s. Sylvia and Louis Stark and family arrived in British Columbia in 1858, among 600 freed slaves welcomed by Governor James Douglas. They pre-empted land on Saltspring in 1860. Sylvia Stark, who lived to the age of 105, is buried in the Ganges cemetery. Her father, Howard Estes, was killed fighting a forest fire in 1892 and is also buried in Ganges. Her mother, Hannah Estes, is buried in the pioneer cemetery near Victoria's Christ Church Cathedral.

The Bittancourt House, now on the Farmers' Institute grounds on Rainbow Road, was built in the 1880s by Portuguese settler Estalon Jose Bittancourt.

Mouat's Store (1914) in the village of Ganges is a landmark and a reminder of the pioneer family who came from the Shetland Islands to dominate Saltspring's commercial life. Thomas and Jane, the first of the family to arrive, farmed near St. Mary's Lake. Thomas died in 1898; Jane, who had 11 children, ran this store they had started in Ganges and a next-door boarding house called the Ganges Inn. Ganges, incidentally, takes its name from that of a Royal Navy ship. Also in Ganges are Mahon Hall (1902) and St. Mary's Church (1892).

The Saltspring Island Community Centre (1914) on the Fulford-Ganges Road was the island's first hospital, named Lady Minto Hospital for the wife of the then Governor General.

Community meeting places such as Central Hall (1896), where North End, Upper Ganges and Lower Ganges roads meet, were important in rural communities. This frame hall, built by the people of the hamlet of Central Settlement, now houses a cinema. St. Mark's Anglican Church, nearby on North End Road, was completed in 1889. The white house behind it was originally a boarding house, built in 1887; travellers were charged a dollar a night.

Once upon a time, there was only one **PENDER ISLAND**, with a narrow neck of land between Bedwell Harbour and Browning Harbour. The present separation results from a canal dredged in 1902, so that ships could move across the neck. As land transport became more important than sea travel, a bridge across the canal was built in 1955. Later excavations along the neck uncovered thousands of artifacts from native settlements dating back some 5,000 years, and the area was designated a provincial heritage site.

Most Pender Island residents live in a North Pender subdivision whose creation horrified long-time island residents. The subdivision precipitated the creation of the Islands Trust, the agency that oversees development or refusal of same on the Gulf Islands and is equally loved and hated by island residents.

Some evidence—mostly in the form of older houses—remains on the Penders of a pastoral or maritime past. The Corbett House (1902), on Corbett Road near Hope Bay, was home to Pender postmaster and storekeeper Robert Corbett and his wife, Isabel. The Grimmer House (1891), on Port Washington Road near the Port Washington wharf, was home to Washington and Elizabeth Grimmer (Port Washington is named for Washington Grimmer, thus avoiding the sobriquet Port Grimmer). Some trees remain from the orchard the Grimmers planted on their property, and the house has been restored to the way it looked in the 1930s.

The Pender cemetery on Bedwell Harbour Road contains the graves of many pioneers. The United Community Church (1906) on this same road near Hope Bay is the oldest standing church on the Penders. Nearby is old Pender Island Schoolhouse (1902), which is now a daycare centre.

The Pender Island Museum on South Otter Bay Road, in a 1908 homestead, is open on summer weekends.

Goldrushers heading to the Fraser River from Fort Victoria in 1858 found Miners Bay on **MAYNE ISLAND** a handy stopping place, halfway on their journey and the last refuge before the open waters of Georgia Strait. The Collinson residence (1892), now added to and serving as the Springwater Lodge, is an example of an 1890s farmhouse. The Plumper Pass Lockup (1896) was the headquarters for the outer Gulf Islands police until 1905. Its main room and two small cells now house the Mayne Island Museum. The island's first community hall (1900) on Fernhill Road is now the Mayne Island Agricultural Hall. The Church of St. Mary Magdalene (1897) stands above Miners Bay beside a pioneer cemetery; its font is made from beach stones.

Near Miners Bay on Village Bay Road is a 1910 house—now a restaurant—owned by the Nagata family. They were among 20 Japanese immigrant families who raised chickens and grew hothouse tomatoes and cucumbers in the 1920s and 1930s. The neat step-roofed, white farmhouse of the Kadonaga family at Horton Bay remains from those days. Their products bore the Island Brand label, from the Japanese Canadian hothouse cooperative. Like those of Japanese origin elsewhere on the islands, these families were exiled during World War II and their properties sold for a pittance. A Japanese garden in Dinner Bay Park, beautifully developed over the past decade, commemorates the Japanese Canadians who lived and worked on the island between 1900 and 1942. A plaque in the garden details their contributions. The garden is set to contain a replica of a Japanese charcoal kiln. These Gulf Islands kilns provided charcoal for the fishing industry in the early years of the 20th century.

The Active Pass Light Station at Georgina Point began operation in 1885. The original 13-metre square tower has been replaced by a higher beacon on a round pillar.

In the 1880s, Canadian Collieries acquired more than half of **GALIANO ISLAND**. Until recently, logging companies owned the land. MacMillan Bloedel's proposal to subdivide and sell off the property raised a storm on the islands and off, and some of the property was eventually acquired for parkland. Because so much of the land was owned by corporations, the landscape on Galiano looks a little different from that on the other southern Gulf Islands and historic buildings are rarer. A log house (1895) with hand-hewn logs neatly dovetailed at the corners stands on Porlier Pass Road near Retreat Cove. The North Galiano Community Hall (1927) on Porlier Pass Road north of Spotlight Cove was Galiano's second schoolhouse. One of the oldest buildings on Galiano is Finlay Murcheson's farmhouse (1882) on Sturdies Bay Road. A kitchen and an outside chimney have been added to the vertical-board house.

The guide now returns to Vancouver Island and continues north from Victoria on Highway 1.

VICTORIA TO NANAIMO

Highway 1 heads north out of Victoria along the east coast of Vancouver Island. Traces of history along this route are limited: the highway slices through the landscape distant from the earlier meandering roads that lead up-island, allowing the traveller to gain time but lose interest. History is more visible along these earlier roads.

Goldstream to Duncan

The first official trail to connect Victoria north to Cowichan Bay was built in 1861, though contemporary accounts suggest it was more a polite fiction than a reality. Described as a metre and a half wide, the Goldstream Trail was considerably narrower, poorly marked and close to unusable. In those days, efficient travel was by boat. Only in 1884 was the trail widened sufficiently to allow wagons.

Off the present-day highway at 1589 Millstream Road is the Caleb Pike homestead, settled as a sheep and cattle ranch by Pike in 1878. On-site are an 1883 house, an 1893 schoolhouse, a dairy building and a heritage orchard.

The highway crosses the Goldstream River, then continues on through Gold-stream Provincial Park. The river was named in 1863–64 when some 300 prospectors bushwhacked into the area after some minor gold discoveries. Prospector Peter Leech found more gold in the 1880s. Some shafts and tunnels remain from this era; they are visible from the Ridge Trail, which leads to Niagara Falls from a parking lot on the west side of the road in Goldstream Park. A cantilevered railway bridge built in 1912 is visible from the trail above the falls.

The river's original name, *Sawluctus*, the Coast Salish word for "fishing ground inside the arm," is verified every November when salmon return up the river in great numbers to spawn.

The region north of Goldstream posed challenges to road builders, who had to blast their way through rock ridges and build across streams along the Malahat Ridge. An early native name for the ridge was *Yaas*, "the home of a rainmaker," for if you point at the mountain, rain will fall. Of course, if you don't point at the mountain, rain will also fall. Though this highway has been widened and straightened a number of times since it first opened in 1911, raw rock cliffs along the way still show the effort required to cross the ridge.

Three roads lead from the highway to **SHAWNIGAN LAKE**. The southern-most forks left from the highway about 10 kilometres north of Goldstream park.

Shawnigan Lake's heritage is one of logging and tourism. Little remains of logging days, but the older buildings of Shawnigan Lake Resort, now the centre of a subdivision, originate from the days when Shawnigan was considered a relaxing vacation spot for Victorians. The Shawnigan Lake Museum, in the old fire hall near the four-way stop sign at the centre of the village, houses pioneer home and logging displays.

Shawnigan Lake School, off Shawnigan Lake Road north of the village, dates to 1916; its Virginia-creeper-covered older buildings are set amid gardens and flanked by newer classrooms and dormitories. Reflecting the British heritage of the area, the school is one of four private schools, past and present, in the Cowichan Valley. It now accepts both girls and boys. The Shawnigan Lake Girls' School has been a Baha'i centre for many years. Still active are the Brentwood Bay College School (1923) in Mill Bay and Queen Margaret's School (1921) in Duncan.

The last spike on the E&N railway was driven just south of Shawnigan Lake village; this line no longer carries freight, and the passenger service may or may not survive. A second line, built by Canadian National Railway, ran west of the lake. Now abandoned, it serves as the route for the Trans Canada Trail through this area. Worth seeing along this trail is the Kinsol Trestle, billed as one of the largest, highest trestles in the world. Unfortunately, you can't cross the trestle; local teens who thought it amusing to build a fire on the bridge have made sure of that. The trestle is increasingly unsafe in any case. Recent plans called for it to be torn down and a simpler bridge built in its place, but heritage enthusiasts protested, and it is now possible that the trestle will be preserved and restored. Trail builders have constructed a viewpoint so visitors can see the wooden supports and the river far below. To reach the Kinsol, take Shawnigan Lake Road, which goes around the lake to the point at the north end where Renfrew Road heads west. Follow Renfrew Road 1.4 kilometres to a parking area beside the trail, then cross the road and walk along the trail for about half an hour to the trestle.

The guide now returns to Highway 1 at the south end Shawnigan Lake turnoff.

North of the Malahat Summit, a road leads down towards the water and the old site of **BAMBERTON**. Bamberton lies across Saanich Inlet from Brentwood Bay and Butchart Gardens. A cement plant once operated on the Butchart site. In 1912, a new plant at Bamberton replaced the Butchart operation. The Bamberton plant closed in the 1970s. Since the 1990s, the site has been the subject of on-again, off-again development plans.

About seven kilometres north of the small community of Mill Bay, Cobble Hill Road, between Shawnigan Lake and Cobble Hill, veers back from the lake and crosses the highway to become the Cowichan Bay Road. To the left (west) is Cobble Hill, where residents commemorate the village's agricultural history in a fall fair that has been held every year for more than a century.

To the right, follow the road down into the waterfront settlement of **COWICHAN BAY**, long the home of the Cowichan First Nation and more

The Kinsol Trestle (near Shawnigan Lake), 38 metres high, 128 metres long, still stands as testimony to the railway builders' skills.

recently that of early Vancouver Island farmers. The Masthead Restaurant on the water side is in the old Columbia Hotel (circa 1868). Also on the water side is the Cowichan Bay Maritime Centre, run by the Wooden Boat Society (dedicated to small boats made of wood), with exhibits on local marine history.

North of this centre on the waterfront is a cairn commemorating the first group of settlers, 100 strong, who landed here on August 18, 1862, accompanied by Vancouver Island governor James Douglas. Farther along the road on the west side are two more commemorative markers. One, a cairn, notes that Yukon poet Robert Service lived and worked in the area. The other is a bench dedicated to the memory of the women who pioneered at Cowichan Bay.

At the junction of Cowichan Bay and Tzouhalem roads is the South Co-wichan Lawn Tennis Club, the last surviving trace of an era when ladies and gentlemen wielded wooden racquets, wore white flannel trousers or long white dresses and took tea on the lawn after the match. The club was founded in 1887 and is one of the oldest tennis clubs in the British Commonwealth, second only to Wimbledon.

Tzouhalem Road continues straight on through a Cowichan Indian reserve, past three churches with interesting history and/or architecture. The first and oldest, the old Stone Church, is atop a hill west of the road, and about a kilo-metre past the tennis club. Also known as the Butter Church, it was built by the Cowichan and a Victoria stonemason in 1864, paid for by the sale of butter produced by the small farm established nearby. Access to the church, its half-metre-thick stone walls still standing though the roof has long since fallen, is by permission of the Cowichan band, via a path near a small parking area on the west side of the road.

The road curves back towards Duncan. On the right (north) side is the church that replaced the church that replaced the Butter Church. The replace-ment church built in 1880 burned in 1900; the current white-painted, steepled St. Ann's Church was built at about that time. It is surrounded by a graveyard. West again is St. Peter's Quamichan, a frame Anglican church built by settlers in 1876 and still in use.

Near Highway 1 between Cowichan Bay Road and Duncan are two places of historical interest. At the first stoplight on Highway 1 north of Cowichan Bay Road, Koksilah Road leads west through what was an experiment in improving the lives of disadvantaged British children. Between 1935 and the early 1950s, boys and girls were sent from Britain to Prince of Wales Fairbridge Farm, where the girls learned to be domestics and the boys were trained as farm labourers. Some of the farm buildings are now private houses, mixed in with more modern dwellings; the farm chapel still stands.

Though the buildings at Whippletree Junction (on Highway 1, five kilometres north of the Cowichan turnoff) have all been moved here from somewhere else, some, such as two from Duncan's old Chinatown, are part of local history.

Duncan

The Cowichan natives have long lived along the banks of the Cowichan River. The Quw'utsun' Cultural and Convention Centre, beside the river west of the highway at the south end of Duncan (follow signs on the highway), re-creates the history and traditions of the coastal peoples in buildings, displays and presentations. Comeakin House, its roof supported by 20-metre-long cedar beams, is modelled after the Big Houses typical of the native peoples who have lived in this area for centuries. Built for Vancouver's Expo 86, it was dismantled, brought to Duncan and reassembled here. Cowichan artists work in the carving house and knitters demonstrate the making of a Cowichan sweater. (In the 19th century, Cowichan women took European knitting skills and married them to their own traditions of weaving.) A theatre presentation, longhouse feasts, interpretive dancing and an arts and crafts gallery are also features of the centre.

Native history and culture are on display throughout Duncan, which calls itself the City of Totems. A guide describing Duncan's more than 40 totem poles is available at the tourist infocentre; guided walks are also available in summer. The museum, housed in the restored E&N railway station at 120 Canada Avenue, presents turn-of-the-century artifacts of home, store, medical room and other locations. Duncan's City Hall, at 200 Craig Street, is a 1913 post office building complete with clock tower.

Two kilometres north of town, the BC Forest Discovery Centre (formerly the British Columbia Forestry Museum) runs a narrow-gauge railway with steam engines around its 40-hectare site. The open-air museum contains steam donkey engines used in logging, early logging trucks, a fire ranger's tower, a working sawmill and a blacksmith's shop, together with demonstrations of shake splitting, log sawing, bucking and papermaking.

Another kilometre north, Cowichan Lake Road (Highway 18) departs to the west. In the town of **LAKE COWICHAN**, 28 kilometres west, the Kaatza Station Museum (South Shore Road), housed in an E&N station, presents an outdoor railway display with 1918 caboose and two steam logging locomotives, a mural of life in the 1920s, a pioneer store, post office and school, and a re-created mining shaft.

33

Crofton/Chemainus

Northeast of Duncan, at Crofton, the Old School House Museum contains mining and refining displays, with re-creations of pioneer and smelter-town life. On the beach, slag heaps remain from a smelter that processed copper ore from nearby Mount Sicker between 1902 and 1908.

The Crofton road continues to Chemainus. You can also reach Chemainus by turning east from Highway 1, 26 kilometres north of Duncan. The first settlers arrived at Chemainus in the 1850s, seeking farmland not under the control of the Hudson's Bay Company. Chemainus claims it is the oldest deep-sea port on Canada's west coast. The first Chemainus sawmill began operations in 1862; the main mill closed in 1983. Murals depicting the history of the area are painted on almost every available Chemainus wall. Among the murals' subjects: logging, railroading and the town's Japanese heritage—Japanese Canadians were a significant minority in Chemainus until they were exiled from the coast and interned during World War II.

Chemainus also features a working water wheel, the Chemainus Valley Museum, a steam locomotive in Locomotive Park and St. Michael and All Angels Church (built 1891).

To reach Ladysmith, you can continue north on the back road or return to the highway and drive north.

Ladysmith

In 1900, James Dunsmuir, owner of coal mines in Extension to the north, decided to house his miners and their families in a new town away from the mines. He built Ladysmith, naming it when British forces relieved the besieged town of Ladysmith, Natal, on March 1, 1900, during the Boer War. Ladysmith streets named for British Boer War generals include Baden-Powell and Kitchener. Coal from Extension came to Ladysmith by rail and was shipped out from Ladysmith's harbour until the mines closed in the 1930s.

Near the southern entrance to Ladysmith, follow signs to Transfer Beach to view a steam donkey, weigh scales, a boom boat and a harpoon gun from the town's early days. At the infocentre and Chamber of Commerce you'll find a brochure that identifies other artifacts positioned along the main streets in a sort of outdoor museum. Also available is a heritage-walk brochure that guides the visitor to some 50 heritage buildings, most of them along First Avenue between Roberts and French streets, and on Gatacre, Roberts and Esplanade (the highway). Many of the buildings are marked by explanatory plaques.

At the corner of First and Gatacre is a novel collage of pioneer and industrial implements welded into an impressionistic picture of Ladysmith's history. Turn down Gatacre Street towards the water to visit the Black Nugget Museum, at 12 Gatacre Street, in a turn-of-the-century hotel building that began life in Wellington, north of Nanaimo; it was moved here in 1906. The restored barroom contains the original bar with polished brass foot rail.

Highway 1 north passes Nanaimo Airport about six kilometres north of Ladysmith. To reach what remains of the coal-mining town of Cassidy, built in the 1930s, go past the airport, turning west just beyond the bridge across the Nanaimo River onto Spruston Road, signposted to the Cassidy Speedway. The old coal mines are on your left. Morden Colliery Historic Provincial Park is east of the highway at the end of Morden Road; it contains the only coal-mining tipple remaining on the island (tipples were where mine cars were emptied of their coal). The tipple dates from 1912.

Many of the historic buildings of Ladysmith have been restored. The town Chamber of Commerce is housed in the former Masonic Temple building.

To reach the former coal-mining town of Extension, turn west from the highway onto Cranberry Road, at the Moose Hall, which is at the first traffic lights north of Cassidy. Follow Extension Road to its end (it bears right about three kilometres from the highway, so watch for signs). Named because it was considered an extension of the Wellington mines near Nanaimo, Extension has an unhappy history of mine disasters and labour strife. The mines operated from 1900 to the 1930s. Today, a few of the old miners' cottages are mixed in with new houses in front of piles of waste rock, ever declining as they are used for building and other purposes, coal tailings and sealed-off mine tunnels.

Not far from the community of Cedar, east of the highway and south of Nanaimo, are a few signs of one of British Columbia's ill-fated Utopian communities. The first of the New Agers, prophet Brother Twelve (more prosaically known as sea captain Edward Arthur Wilson) operated in the 1920s from the House of Mystery—located near the end of Nelson Road—and on nearby Valdes and De Courcy islands. The story and legend are well known in the area; Brother Twelve disappeared, not surprisingly, with the cash turned over to him by his followers.

Just south of Nanaimo, off Highway 1/19A, a sign marks Petroglyph Provincial Park, where trails lead to rock carvings thought to be up to 10,000 years old.

Nanaimo

Nanaimo takes its name from a Sne neymuxw term that translates to "people of many names"—many groups in this area formed an alliance for their own protection. As well as the petroglyphs at Petroglyph Park and at other locations near the city, shell middens on Newcastle Island, just offshore from downtown, remind us of these early residents.

In 1849, a Snu neymuxw who later became known as Coal Tyee brought a canoe-load of coal to show HBC officials at Fort Victoria. Four years later, the company sent men north to begin working the coal seams; in 1854, 24 miners from Staffordshire in England arrived with their wives and children and the coal industry began in earnest.

A number of reminders of Nanaimo's coal mines, which sustained the town from 1854 until World War II, remain. Among them are miners' cottages from the 1930s, small square houses that stand alongside Highway 1/Nicol Street at the south end of town. At the corner of Nicol Street and Esplanade, beside an early fire hall, a cairn marks the location of the Park Head Slope Mines, one of the first Nanaimo mines. If you walk a block west, across Victoria Road just past Cavan Street, you'll see a coal seam across the parking lot. At the corner of Bastion and Front streets is the Bastion, built by the Hudson's Bay Company in 1853 as protection for the houses and stores buildings that supported the mines.

The Nanaimo District Museum opened in a new home in the Port of Nanaimo Centre near the waterfront in 2008. Museum displays re-create old town, Chinatown and Snu neymuxw life and include a coal-mining tunnel exhibit. Maps of Nanaimo and a heritage guidebook are available from the museum or from Nanaimo infocentres. Though you can't tour them, tunnels from mining days criss-cross under Nanaimo streets and lead out under the water.

Pioneer Park, just north of downtown, on Comox Road at Wallace, contains the gravestones of some of Nanaimo's early residents. Among them was Ann Robinson, the wife of a mine manager, who arrived in 1854 aboard the *Princess*

By the 1870s, Nanaimo was already a 20-year-old town, sustained by its coal mines. (BCA A4422)

Royal, the ship that brought miners to Nanaimo. She died in childbirth.

Nanaimo's geography was altered by the mines. Terminal Avenue, now the route of Highway 1 through Nanaimo, was once a tidal ravine, a handy place for residents to go herring fishing. Mine workings were dumped into the ravine, and it eventually became a street and then a highway, still hemmed in by the cliffs that once faced the ravine. At Colliery Dam Park, at the south end of Wakesiah Avenue, dams from the mining era create two artificial lakes. You can reach the dams from the Nanaimo Parkway/Trailway, an 18-kilometre walking/cycling route that in places follows the roadbed of an old coal railway.

Interesting buildings in Nanaimo include the Nanaimo Courthouse, designed by Francis Rattenbury (1896) on Front Street; the Palace Hotel (1889) on Skinner Street; the Dakin and Rogers blocks (1909 and 1913), also on Skinner Street; the renovated Globe Hotel (1889) on Front Street, the city's oldest brick building; and the Occidental Hotel (1887) on Fitzwilliam above Richards Street, the oldest remaining building near the E&N rail tracks, completed between Victoria and Nanaimo in 1886. The Oxy was known as "the first and last stop" for train travellers. The third floor was added in 1917 when a new regulation decreed hotels must have 32 rooms in order to have a liquor licence.

Newcastle Island, just off Nanaimo's downtown, provides a wide-ranging history lesson. Foot passenger service runs from May to October, from Swy-a-lana Lagoon behind the arena. Native petroglyphs and shell middens testify to at least two native villages in the past, winter bases from which people hunted, fished and gathered food. Travellers will also see remains of a sandstone quarry on the island. In 1869, architects searched worldwide for the best sandstone for the San Francisco mint and found stone of sufficient quality on Newcastle. Sandstone from Newcastle was also used in the Nanaimo courthouse and other buildings; the quarry was worked from the 1870s to the 1930s. Incised into Newcastle rock are flat circles where pulp millstones were taken from the island in the 1900s. Near the north end of the island is the site of a herring saltery run from 1911 to 1941 by Japanese Canadians who also ran a ship-building and repair shop here. When they were expelled from the coast in 1942, their Newcastle possessions were sold for a low price or burned down. Near the ferry dock is a pavilion from the 1930s, when the island was a dine-and-dance destination for CPR cruise ships from Vancouver.

GABRIOLA ISLAND, also just offshore, has shell middens. At Petroglyph Park, some 50 petroglyphs date back to an unidentified people and era.

To Parksville and the West Coast

Highway 1 ends its island route at Nanaimo. Highway 19 continues north up-island. This newer island highway slices inland on a fast and direct route between Nanaimo and Campbell River, while the old highway, now named Highway 19A, follows the mainly oceanside route through long-established towns and villages. Unless otherwise mentioned, all directions between Nanaimo and Campbell River refer to 19A, the scenic seaside route.

Between Nanaimo and the Comox Valley, the strip of flat land between the mountains and the sea narrows, and settlements are perched at the water's edge. Agriculturalists were not impressed by this land, much of it sand and gravel. But, they reported in 1902, "there is excellent shooting and fishing around Parksville" and good hotel accommodation from Nanoose north. The region thrived then and continues to thrive today as a resort area and retirement haven.

Parksville

Heritage buildings from the Parksville area have been moved to Craig Heritage Park, just south of town. Among them are the French Creek Post Office (built 1886, first used as a post office in 1888), the Duncan McMillan log house (1885) and Knox United Church (1911). St. Ann's Anglican Church north of Parksville (west onto Pym Road, then right on Humphrey and right on Church Road) is a log building erected by 45 farmers at a work bee in 1894; oxen dragged the cedar logs for the church to the site. Also on the site is a 1930 cedar dugout canoe.

In Parksville itself, of interest are the E&N railway station and water tower, beside the tracks where they cross Highway 4A west of the centre of Parksville.

From the Parksville area, Highway 4 cuts west across the island to the Pacific coast.

New highway routes mean that the direct route to the west coast no longer passes Errington and Coombs. To reach them, continue north in Parksville on the seaside route, then turn left on Highway 4A signposted for west-coast places or take the Coombs exit from Highway 19.

The small villages and settlements west of Parksville reflect a British influence. **ERRINGTON**, south of the highway, is thought to take its name from a poem by Sir Walter Scott, who mentions the Northumberland village of Errington. The Englishman River and its falls commemorate an unnamed Englishman who drowned while trying to cross the river. **COOMBS**, with its craft shops, minigolf and restaurants, little resembles the staid settlement created by the Salvation Army in 1910 for 100 working-class English settlers from Leeds, Yorkshire. A barn or two from the old settlement still stands along the highway, and the Coombs General Store—though in a different building—dates from 1910.

As the highway winds along the south shore of Cameron Lake, travellers can look across to the north shore, to see trestles bridging streams and gullies. The trestles are part of the E&N railway line, built west to Port Alberni in 1911.

As historic houses represent a town as it used to be, so **CATHEDRAL GROVE**, in MacMillan Provincial Park west of Cameron Lake, represents the west-coast forests as they once were. These few hectares of land, with their virgin Douglas fir, western hemlock and western red cedar, form the only readily accessible grove of old-growth timber on an island where giant trees once clothed all but the alpine regions. The uniqueness of the grove emphasizes how rapidly the pace of logging increased when hand saws and horses gave way to power saws, railways and roads. The grove was donated to the province in 1944 by H. R. MacMillan, a former chief forester of British Columbia, who started the timber company H. R. MacMillan Export, the genesis of multinational MacMillan Bloedel, now part of Weyerhaeuser.

The very popularity of Cathedral Grove has threatened it. Many people stop to see the trees, wandering across the highway in the process. Plans were made to replace the existing parking lot with a new one, and cut down some trees in the process, but the battle over the changes is ongoing.

Long under restoration, the McLean Mill, west of Port Alberni, is a rare remaining example of the small lumber mills once so plentiful in British Columbia.

Port Alberni

Port Alberni began as Alberni, where nine men built a sawmill at the head of Alberni Inlet in 1860. The mill opened in 1861 with 70 employees. The company that ran the mill also operated four ships and traded with the native people for fish, fish oil and furs. The first sawmill in B.C. specifically designed to cut wood for export, the Alberni mill ran out of timber a few years later. In 1904, a new sawmill was built. And in 1947, a pulp and paper mill was established. As the mills go, so goes Port Alberni: mill shutdowns and closures have seriously threatened the city's economy.

The city's heritage is seen along the waterfront in Port Alberni's mills and rail lines. Next to the Alberni Harbour Quay, the 2-Spot Shay logging locomotive has been restored to working condition. The 2-Spot was built in 1912; for 40 years, it hauled logs, pushed crew cars and pulled stumps in the woods around Port Alberni. The locomotive was donated to the city in 1954, a year after the locomotive was retired.

A 1929 Baldwin logging locomotive runs in summer and on special occasions on the Alberni Pacific Railway between the restored railway station and the McLean Mill on the old Esquimalt and Nanaimo railway tracks (see below). Hikers and cyclists can follow the Log Train Trail, originally part of a rail logging operation, 20 kilometres from the outskirts of Port Alberni northwest through the valley, past the McLean Mill site. Trail maps are available from infocentres and historic sites.

Also at Harbour Quay, the *Lady Rose* leaves for island west-coast points. Built in Scotland in 1937, the ship was for years the only public transportation to logging camps and native villages along Alberni Inlet. The Maritime Discovery Centre, in a rebuilt lighthouse next to Harbour Quay, displays the maritime heritage of Alberni Inlet, Barclay Sound and the west coast of Vancouver Island.

The Alberni Valley Museum, at the Echo Centre, 4255 Wallace Street, has well-presented working displays of a waterwheel and steam engine, plus a good look at logging and maritime history and an extensive exhibit on Nuu-chahnulth traditions and history. A new museum that showcases heritage logging trucks and other industrial equipment is in the works.

Guided cultural and historical tours of First Nations heritage are available at Victoria Quay, from the Hupacasath nation.

A site just outside the city offers a fine opportunity to go back 60 years. To reach the McLean Mill National Historic Site, continue west on Highway 4, bypassing downtown and turning right at the bottom of the hill. Continue another few hundred metres and bear right on Beaver Creek Road. About 5.5 kilometres along this road, turn right on Smith Road, then continue across the railway tracks and onto gravel about three kilometres to the McLean Mill gate.

The lumber company that ran the McLean Mill was a three-generation family business in the Alberni Valley from 1925 to 1965. This steam-driven sawmill was built in 1925: it was little changed when it closed 40 years later. Abandoned for more than 25 years, its buildings gradually collapsing, it has now been restored. Visitors can view the mill, powerhouse, bunkhouses, cabins and other buildings that made up a self-contained mill site, as well as the machinery that has been brought back to life. Check with the Port Alberni Museum for site hours. A walking guide to the extensive site is available.

The West Coast

Two roads lead from Port Alberni to points on Barkley Sound: the highway west to Pacific Rim National Park and a part-paved, part-gravel road to Bamfield.

The Nuu-chah-nulth people have lived in villages around Barkley Sound for thousands of years; one native trade route led up Alberni Inlet to its head, then by trail overland to Qualicum Beach. Though the sound was and is important to its native residents, it was less so to new island settlers after the early days of exploration and fur trading. Like much of the deeply indented west coast of the island, it is difficult to reach by land.

Southwest of Port Alberni lies **BAMFIELD**, at the end of a dusty logging road. First settled in 1859, it was established in 1902 as the western terminus of the first trans-Pacific telegraph cable. The station was closed in 1959 when a connecting cable was laid to Port Alberni, but the site lives on as the Bamfield Marine Station, a research station owned by five western Canadian universities. The main building no longer stands, but the telegraph days are still evoked by various exhibits. A seaside boardwalk is a reminder of the time when boardwalks were the roads for most coastal communities.

Not far from Bamfield, the immensely popular West Coast Trail south to Port Renfrew begins. The first nine kilometres were once a supply route to the Pachena Point lighthouse (1907). A second trail leads from Bamfield to the Cape Beale lighthouse (1873). The lights averted many a shipwreck on the part of the coast known as the graveyard of the Pacific, but some ships were still driven onto the rocks by gales that blow up to 160 kilometres an hour. Along the trail are remains of ships wrecked between 1884 and 1984.

The West Coast Trail was built for linemen who strung and serviced the telegraph line (circa 1900) from Victoria to Cape Beale. The 1906 shipwreck of the *Valencia*, with 126 lives lost, prompted the improvement of the trail so that help could reach shipwreck survivors. It was little used once navigational aids made shipping safer. In 1973, Parks Canada began a reconstruction program, and the West Coast Trail eventually became part of Pacific Rim National Park.

Old-timers remember the muffler graveyard that used to be the road from Port Alberni to the west coast north of Barkley Sound. The new road, built in the

1970s, comes to a T-junction 93 kilometres west of Port Alberni: the intersecting road leads south to Ucluelet, north to Tofino. The clear-cut lands that are visible along Highway 4 and the road to Bamfield are among the most dramatic changes to landscape that the average traveller sees, and they have converted more than a few to the battle against this type of logging, and in fact against any logging of old-growth rainforest.

The Nuu-chah-nulth tradition of fishing Barkley Sound continues to the present day, though it is somewhat reduced as the fishing industry declines. UCLUELET, at the end of the sound, is home to a small fleet of seiners and trollers. Cannery buildings, now privately owned and posted with No Trespassing signs, can be seen across the inlet at Port Albion. The *Canadian Princess*, for 46 years the hydrographic service ship *William J. Stewart*, is moored in the harbour and serves as a floating hotel and restaurant. Amphritite Point lighthouse (1914) is beyond the town, overlooking Barkley Sound.

In Pacific Rim National Park, north of Ucluelet, Radar Hill marks the site of a World War II radar station. Tofino Airport started as a World War II military base. The only wartime incident on the west coast was the submarine shelling of Estevan Point lighthouse, erected in 1908–09 west of Gold River. The first white settlers homesteaded in the Long Beach area around 1900; their names show up at Chesterman and MacKenzie beaches and Grice Bay.

TOFINO, at the north end of the peninsula, was a Nuu-chah-nulth settlement long before Europeans arrived in the area. Meares Island, offshore across Browning Passage, is a traditional fishing, village and spiritual site for the Nuu-chah-nulth, who were at the forefront of a battle to have the island's forests preserved in the angry confrontations of the 1990s. Battles over the forest, this time setting environmentalists against First Nations, broke out again more recently in 2008.

The West Coast Maritime Museum/Whale Centre in Tofino presents artifacts from native and maritime history. A pamphlet mapping out a walking tour that follows Main Street along the waterfront, outlining the history of Tofino, is available from area infocentres. Among the highlights: the government wharf, first built in 1908; and the former Tofino Hotel, now the

Paddlers' Inn, where, legend has it, appendectomies were performed on the kitchen table in the days before Tofino had a hospital and the dentist set up shop in the lobby.

The guide now returns to Highway 19A, north of Parksville.

French Creek to Courtenay/Comox

For much of this stretch, the seaside route hugs the shoreline along the narrow strip of land between the Strait of Georgia and the Vancouver Island mountains. Farmers and miners were among the early non-native settlers here.

From **FRENCH CREEK**, a ferry leaves for **LASQUETI ISLAND**. Look for long-tailed wild sheep, probably descendants of early flocks raised by settlers who came here in 1875. The Teapot House, near the ferry terminal at False Bay, sports a teapot-shaped chimney; built in 1936, the house stands as a symbol of the islanders' individualistic nature. Some say a teapot was a bootlegger's symbol, and, say they, this house was once a bootlegger's. A second chimney was in the shape of a sugar bowl, but was probably modified. Perhaps an illicit baker once lived in the house.

At **QUALICUM BEACH**, north of Parksville, the local museum society has acted unconventionally: scorning the abandoned railway station, they have moved into a powerhouse built in 1929. To reach the museum, follow signs from the waterfront road. The E&N railway station (1914) with restored locomotive is nearby, beside the tracks. Above the station, on Fern Road West in the centre of the town, is the Old School House, built in 1912. The school operated for 40 years; the building was then occupied by the school board, then left empty and increasingly dilapidated. Residents saved the building, scheduled for demolition in 1986, and converted it to a gallery and art centre.

North of the Horne Lake Road intersection are interpretive signs detailing the history and traditions of the Qualicum First Nation. Cougar Smith Road, farther north, was named for a bounty hunter who is said to have shot a thousand cougars between 1890 and 1940.

The Qualicum Beach Museum is housed in an old powerhouse.

BOWSER, north of Qualicum Beach, was not named for the world's only canine bartender, who plied his trade in the town. (The dog served at the local inn, trained to carry a bottle of beer to the customer, bring the money to the bar and return the change. Or at least that's what *Ripley's Believe It or Not* reported.) The settlement is named instead for premier W. J. Bowser, a man not greatly loved in the area, since he ordered the troops in to quell a strike at nearby Cumberland.

Mud Bay, Deep Bay, Fanny Bay, Buckley Bay: some of the name derivations are obvious, but Fanny Bay has defeated even indefatigable name researchers.

The old school-house at Union Bay stands beside the highway in a row of historic buildings.

No one really knows who Fanny was—but everyone in town will be happy to tell you a story.

DENMAN AND HORNBY ISLANDS lie offshore from Buckley Bay. Though better known for their artists and artisans, the islands are worth exploring for evidence of their history. The Denman Island Museum is at 1111 Northwest Road. Also deserving a look are St. Saviour's Anglican Church (1914), the Denman Island United (Methodist when built in 1889) Church on Denman Road, the false-fronted Denman Island General Store (1910), a grave marker to the memory of early settler George Beadnell and shell middens along the shore.

A few old log and clapboard homes and barns exist on both islands. The Piercy barn (1909) is still in use, on Piercy Road, west of Northwest Road. On Hornby, the George Heatherbell barn (1895) on Shingle Spit Road went up in a two-island barn raising; the Slade house (1914) on Cape Gurney Crescent, at Whaling Station Bay, is an early log house.

Back on Vancouver Island, look for traces of coal mining history at **UNION BAY**. The original settlement around the coal mines at Cumberland was named Union, for the Union Coal Company. Coal from the mines was sent to Union Bay by rail, to be loaded onto freighters. Hills of waste from the coal docks, a few wharf pilings and the raised railbed remain from the days when several

48

This propellor was lost near Union Bay during World War II. It was raised from the sea bottom and placed at Union Bay in the late 1990s.

hundred men worked at the wharf, the coal washer, the coke ovens and the machine shops, supported by families and by hotels, stores, post office, church and school. The 1913 post office, the old jailhouse (1901), the 1915 schoolhouse, the 1906 Union Bay United Church and the 1911 master mechanic's house are on heritage row, beside the highway.

At **ROYSTON**, to the north, pilings still stretch into the water, flanked by the slowly disappearing wrecks of a lumber schooner, a tug and 13 other ships sunk to provide a breakwater. These docks marked the end of the Comox Logging and Railway Company line from the Comox Valley to the water. Logs were boomed here, then towed to Fraser Mills on the mainland to be milled. To reach the railway bed and the Royston wrecks, turn east on a side road about a kilometre north of Royston or turn east in Royston to reach the waterfront and follow Marine Drive to its north end. You can walk along the shore to the wrecks at low tide.

West from Royston, a road leads to **CUMBERLAND**, a coal-mining town that shows little sign today of a past that included fires, strikes, disastrous mine explosions and violence. The Cumberland mines were part of the Dunsmuir empire. Dunsmuir brought in Chinese, Japanese, Blacks, British, Welsh and other Europeans to work as miners for his mines. At its peak between 1900 and

The gravestones of Japanese Canadians who died at Cumberland have been set in a circle at the Japanese Cemetery, near the new highway that leads to the old coal-mining town.

1914, Cumberland housed 3,000 Chinese and 1,500 Japanese. Most of the Chinatown buildings were intentionally burned several decades ago. Only one remains: Jumbo's cabin, once an office of the Union Colliery Company, then a house for Chinese resident "Jumbo" Wong Gang. Chinese and Japanese cemeteries are both near the junction of Union and Cumberland roads.

The Cumberland Museum at 2680 Dunsmuir offers heritage tours of the town, as well as brochures with walking tours of the town and vicinity (also available at the infocentre). These maps chart locations for the Japanese townsite, Chinatown and the Black townsite and cairn, as well as various mines and pit heads and a cairn to the memory of the 295 men who died in mine disasters. Most of the sites are clustered around the road that leads to Comox Lake Park, off Dunsmuir and Sutton streets, at the old townsite of the original community. Signs mark many of Cumberland's historical landmarks. Follow the road to Comox Lake to see the sites of old mine shafts and of once-bustling Chinatown, which burned down and is now marked only by the roads that once formed its hub. Near the new highway, the old Chinese and Japanese cemeteries have been restored; the Japanese cemetery is particularly affecting.

Vintage aircraft are on display at the Comox Heritage Air Park.

The Cumberland Museum also presents a walk-through model of a coal mine and displays on the history of Cumberland, plus a collection of photos from glass plate negatives taken by Japanese Canadian photographer Senjiro Hayashi, who had a studio in Cumberland.

In the municipal cemetery is the grave of labour leader Ginger Goodwin. Part of the new inland highway near Cumberland was named Ginger Goodwin Way when the left-leaning New Democratic Party was in power. When the Liberals took over in 2001, the signs disappeared. No one has yet suggested renaming Dunsmuir Street, named for an equally controversial coal baron.

Courtenay/Comox

Once heavily forested, the Comox Valley was cleared by settlers who turned forests into farm fields from the 1860s on. The valley's economy centres on farming, fishing, logging, tourism/recreation and the armed forces base at Comox. Courtenay and Comox are the largest towns.

The history of the valley, including native and pioneer, is set out at the Courtenay and District Museum, downtown at Cliffe Avenue and Fourth Street. It is housed in the Native Sons of Canada Hall (1928), a massive vertical log structure. Also worth a look are the Courtenay House Hotel (1880s) in Lewis Park across the old bridge downtown; St. Andrew's Church (1870s); and the Sandwick Cairn, commemorating the arrival of the first white settlers in 1862. Check at the info-centre on the way into town for a map and locations. Also available are walking and driving heritage tour guides to areas throughout the Comox Valley.

Cross the river at the bridge (follow signs for Comox and Campbell River), then turn right at the end of the bridge and follow the harbour to Comox. The clapboard Lorne Hotel (1878), its wide veranda a landmark on Comox Avenue, is named for then Governor General the Marquis of Lorne. The Comox Archives and Museum is at 1729 Comox Avenue.

Farther along Comox Avenue at Filberg Road is Filberg Lodge and Park. The lodge and grounds were the home of logging entrepreneur Bob Filberg and his wife, Florence McCormack. The lodge, in English Arts and Crafts style, dates from about 1929. Buildings such as a root cellar and several barns share the grounds with more than 100 species of trees planted by Filberg. Embedded in the lodge's stone fireplace are a petroglyph, plus cannonballs fired nearby by the Royal Navy. The lodge grounds, open to the public, are the site of a tea house, art demonstrations and a yearly arts and crafts festival.

If you are visiting the Filberg Lodge, you can drive straight up Pritchard Road opposite the grounds to reach the Comox Air Force Museum and Heri-tage Air Park. Otherwise, take the road signposted to CFB Comox. The Canadi-an Forces Base at Comox was opened in 1942; it survives despite repeated threats to close it down. An outdoor display at the base includes five heritage aircraft (a DC3 Dakota, a CF-100 Canuck, a CF-101 Voodoo, a CF-104 Starfighter and a CP-107 Argus). The nearby museum houses a diorama of the base in the 1950s and exhibits on the history of the RCAF.

CAMPBELL RIVER/NORTH ISLAND

Beyond the Comox Valley, the coastal plain narrows once more. The area around **MERVILLE**, north of Comox, was one of the island's earliest logging clear-cuts, areas denuded before 1900. The government settled soldiers returning from World War I here in 1919, naming the new settlement for a French town where the Canadians had fought. At the Canadian Merville, they fought the land: land clearing left behind tree stumps, stones and poor soil that probably should have been reforested. A massive fire in 1922 wiped out much of the would-be farmers' investment. A local logging company was hauled into court and found responsible for the fire; claims for damages exceeded $125,000. Author Jack Hodgins's book *Broken Ground* contains a fictionalized account of this era.

At **BLACK CREEK,** two Mennonite churches bear witness to early Mennonite influence in the settlement.

Campbell River

The southern Kwakwaka'wakw were the first inhabitants of the Campbell River area, making good use of the salmon that later made the area famous. Stubs of the stake network that supported a native fish weir at the mouth of the Campbell River—at the north end of town near the float-plane base—are visible at very low tide. The Campbell River Museum at Fifth Avenue and Island Highway has marvellous displays of Kwakwaka'wakw history and traditions, along with other excellent north-island history displays. Unique is a life-size display on floathouse living. The Transitions Gallery at the museum focuses on the post-contact life of the native people, with a look at some painful topics such as residential schools and population loss.

Campbell River owes its existence to logging and fishing. Irish sportsman Sir Richard Musgrave, whose marriage to a Dunsmuir daughter was the social event of 1891 in Victoria, made the first reported tourist salmon-fishing trip to the area in 1896. Assisted by Kwakwaka'wakw guides in canoes, he hauled in a 30-kilo tyee salmon. The Tyee Club, made up of fishers who have caught large tyee, was formed in 1925.

The Haig-Brown House, at 2250 Campbell River Road, was the home of famed outdoor writer and conservationist Roderick Haig-Brown and his wife, Ann, from 1936 to 1975. The designated historic site includes both the house and eight hectares of forest and farmland.

The move from sea-based to land-based transportation reversed the relative importance of Campbell River and Quadra Island. Once far busier than "The River," **QUADRA ISLAND** (reached by ferry from Campbell River) is more

Campbell River's showpiece museum, on the Island Highway at the south end of town, presents exhibits on logging, fishing, coastal life and First Nations culture and history.

peaceful now. Beside its winding roads is evidence of each step in its history. At the south end of the island, two new buildings re-create the oldest part of island history. The museum at Cape Mudge village has reopened as the Nuyumabales Cultural Centre, with exhibits and totem poles. The museum houses the pot-latch collection of masks, headdresses, coppers and other objects confiscated by the Canadian government in 1922 and reclaimed in 1979. The museum's beam structure echoes the traditional Big House; its shape, in the spiral form of a snail, reflects the evolution of Kwagiulth culture. A canoe shed on the waterfront protects a canoe carved in 2004, the first to be carved in a hundred years. Also at Cape Mudge, native traditions are continued in the Tsa-Kwa-Luten Lodge, a native-run resort. The main foyer and lounge are in Big House design; the lodge features native food, art and cultural activities. Cape Mudge has been a native village site for more than 2,000 years; the Lekwiltok Kwakwaka'wakw estab-lished their winter village at the cape about 200 years ago.

Loggers and settlers came to the island in the 1880s; fish cannery buildings at Quathiaski Cove date from circa 1904. Cape Mudge lighthouse has flashed its warnings to ships entering Discovery Passage since 1898. Also on the island: Quadra Island United Church (1931); petroglyphs on a number of island beach-es, especially near Cape Mudge; Heriot Bay Inn, established in 1894 to serve water-borne traffic (parts of the present building date from 1916); April Point Lodge, a tourist resort established in the 1950s, on a site formerly occupied by a colony of handliners (five-cents-a-pound independent fishermen).

Rebecca Spit, on the north shore of Quadra, was a pioneer picnic ground. Fault lines visible at the north end of the spit show where a hectare of land sank into the sea after a 1946 earthquake. You can hike to ruins of the Lucky Jim Mine, where miners blasted out copper and gold ore from 1903 to 1910 (check locally for a map).

Whaletown, on **CORTES ISLAND**, a ferry ride from Quadra, was the site of a whaling station established in the 1870s. But whaling predates the station: the native name for the bay was *teck-tum*, "sharpening place"; natives butchered whales here. There are petrolyphs on the rock wall of the entrance to Gorge Harbour.

The Cortes Island Museum is in the old Manson's Landing store.

Highway 28 West

Highway 28 leads from the north side of Campbell River to the west coast, through Strathcona Provincial Park, established in 1911. North of the first third of the highway are Upper and Lower Campbell lakes, which were turned into one 80-kilometre-long body of water with adjoining Buttle Lake by a series of dams built between 1949 and 1955 to provide power for the island.

GOLD RIVER, inland from the end of Muchalat Inlet on the west coast, was born in 1965, an instant town to house the employees of the Tahsis Company's pulp mill on the inlet. Gold River was celebrated as Canada's first all-electric town and the first to have all-underground wiring. This pleasant town was carefully built at a distance from the mill. The mill, however, was almost built directly on top of a Nuu-chah-nulth village.

The MV *Uchuck III* leaves from the head of Muchalat Inlet for a trip to Nootka Sound and up Tahsis Inlet. Nootka Sound was the site of the historic meeting between Captain James Cook, RN, and the Mowachaht of Yuquot (also known as Friendly Cove). Cook's account of that event showed the meeting of two equal groups who traded goods in a friendly spirit. Cook and his crew acquired furs, lumber, food and feed for their animals in return for any metal items they were willing to part with. Native tour guides offer guided visits to the island.

Depending on demand, the *Uchuck* also visits the tiny logging camps, floating and onshore, along the sounds and inlets it traverses. The ship calls at Kyuquot Sound, where an attempt to reverse history continues. Eighteenth-century European traders wiped out the sea otters that lived in these waters, profiting from their thick, silky pelts, which brought astonishing rewards in China at the time. Biologists now think they have succeeded in re-establishing a small sea otter population in the sound.

TAHSIS, at the end of a dusty and challenging road from Gold River, predates Gold River. The Mowachaht wintered here every year for hundreds of years; in the 1940s, a floating logging camp, then a permanent onshore camp, was established. Sawmills were also established, then expanded in the 1950s and a village built. Like other mill towns whose mills have closed, Tahsis now leads a threatened existence. A museum in the infocentre depicts Nuu-chah-nulth culture and area history.

North Island

Back on the east coast of the island, Highway 19 continues north from Campbell River.

This highway, opened in 1979, cuts inland through forest and logged areas with very little settlement in the rugged land between Kelsey Bay and Port McNeill. Logging, mining and fishing have long been the mainstays of the north island, though some people made ill-fated attempts to farm some small stretches along the coast.

The most famous landmark north of Campbell River is an absent one: in 1958, a massive explosion billed as the world's largest non-nuclear blast removed Ripple Rock from Seymour Narrows. The rock was a navigational hazard that claimed more than 20 ships and over a hundred lives.

For years ferries to Prince Rupert began their northward trip at **KELSEY BAY**. When the highway was extended to Port Hardy, the ferry terminal was moved north.

WOSS, halfway between Kelsey Bay and Port McNeill, is on a trade route through the Nimpkish Valley. The route linked east and west coasts of the north island and was used for hundreds of years by native peoples. A network of logging roads, some active (therefore with restricted use), honeycombs the valley. A steam locomotive that once hauled logs along rail tracks to the booming grounds at tidewater is on display at Woss.

ZEBALLOS is at the head of Zeballos Inlet, a dusty 21 kilometres west of the highway. Originally a native settlement, Zeballos sprang into prominence in 1929 when traces of gold were found and claims staked. By 1938, mining companies had found a good quantity of gold and Zeballos became a boom town. Five years later, it fell asleep again. The Zeballos Museum is on Maquinna Avenue.

TELEGRAPH COVE, at the end of a side road that leaves the highway where it meets the coast again, was established in 1911–12 when the Canadian government was building a telegraph line from Campbell River to the north end of the island. By 1922, A. M. Wastell had bought most of the land around the cove and established a chum salmon saltery with Japanese investors. The saltery didn't last but Wastell's son Fred continued to run a sawmill; his house still stands at the end of the boardwalk that runs the length of the settlement. The sawmill and an assortment of houses on pilings hearken back several decades in the village's life.

Port McNeill is a logging community established in 1937; from here a ferry goes to Alert Bay and Malcolm Island (Sointula).

North Island Kwakwaka'wakw and Nuu-chah-nulth have lived along the coast for thousands of years; archaeological studies date first residents to 8,000 years ago. But the Kwakwaka'wakw settlement at **ALERT BAY**, on Cormorant Island, is more recent. Nimpkish Valley natives came here in the 1870s to work at a cannery established by white entrepreneurs. They brought ancient potlatching traditions with them; Alert Bay natives were at the centre of the confiscation in 1921 and later return of important potlatch artifacts. A number of those artifacts, returned in 1979, are displayed at the U'Mista

The streetscape in Alert Bay after the turn of the 20th century still presented a picture of native art and heritage. (BCA B7602)

Cultural Centre and Museum. *U'Mista* translates to "return of something valuable." On the Alert Bay Nimpkish reserve are a 53-metre-tall totem pole, a Big House (the 1963 building burned down in 1999 and was replaced) and a cemetery with carved memorial poles. Visitors should keep to the walkway outside the cemetery unless they have permission from the band to enter the graveyard.

Other buildings of historic interest at Alert Bay are Christ Church (1879), prefabricated in England, with one window portraying 100 years of history on the island; old cannery buildings along the waterfront; Namgis House (1929), formerly St. Michael's Residential School, which replaced an 1894 school; and the Nimpkish Hotel (1920), originally erected on reserve lands, but barged to the village because no liquor licences were allowed on the reserve. The museum in the municipal hall contains photographic exhibits of the island's heritage. Heritage brochures are available at the infocentre.

At the turn of the century, new settlers moved by boat to northern Vancouver Island. Most were drawn by fanciful advertisements promising amenities that didn't exist: railways, grain elevators, stores, houses. But some settlers were attracted by the isolation of the north island. Among them were Finns who came to **MALCOLM ISLAND** to found **SOINTULA** in 1901. Most were miners and their families from Nanaimo, disgusted by the unsafe conditions and poor treatment meted out in the Dunsmuir mines. The Sointula Co-op Store (founded in 1905, present store built in 1953), the Finnish Museum in the old school building on First Street next to the tennis courts, Finnish books in the library, Finnish names in the phone book, Finnish country architecture in the red and white cottages, gravestones in the cemetery south of the ferry dock and a certain hardiness of spirit remain from the Kalevan Kansa company days when the colony tried to make co-operative socialism work. Though debt, fire and philosophical divisions doomed the colony, many settlers stayed on after it dissolved.

PORT ALICE, southwest of Port McNeill, was the first instant town incorporated in B.C., in 1965. A variety of companies operated pulp and paper mills here from 1918 on; the townsite was moved from beside the mill to its present location in the 1960s. St. Paul's Anglican Church (1927) is one of the few churches in the world located in the middle of a golf course. The course was set out in 1927; it has survived four floods and mudslides.

FORT RUPERT, near **PORT HARDY**, was one of the earliest white settlements on Vancouver Island. Only a stone chimney and fireplace remain of the fort built to protect coal miners in 1849. The coal was of poor quality, and the mines were quickly abandoned.

Coal was also the basis of **COAL HARBOUR**, southwest of Port Hardy, founded in the 1880s, but here too the poor quality of the coal brought quick closure of the mine. The community supported a whaling station until 1967 and an RCAF base during World War II. A number of military buildings remain from war days. A harpoon gun displayed near the centre of the village comes from whaling days. The six-metre-long jawbone of a blue whale, removed for restoration a decade ago, is now back in place. The remains of a World War II telegraph line still border Holberg Inlet.

Danish immigrants were convinced at the turn of the century that **CAPE SCOTT**, at the northern tip of the island, would provide fertile farming land. Isolation, the cost of sending produce to market and the stormy weather at Cape Scott drove most of the 200 settlers away, but remains of their farms can still be seen in Cape Scott Provincial Park. One Cape Scott settler planted his garden with trees and shrubs from around the world; newer residents are recultivating the garden. A map showing the route to the Ronning garden, which is on a restored section of the San Josef wagon road, is available at the infocentre. The garden contains century-old twin monkey puzzle trees.

Settlers abandoning Cape Scott founded **HOLBERG** and found it little more to their liking. In 1942, logging contractors built a floating logging camp here, with houses, a fire hall, pool hall, bunkhouse and more. The town was moved ashore in 1956.

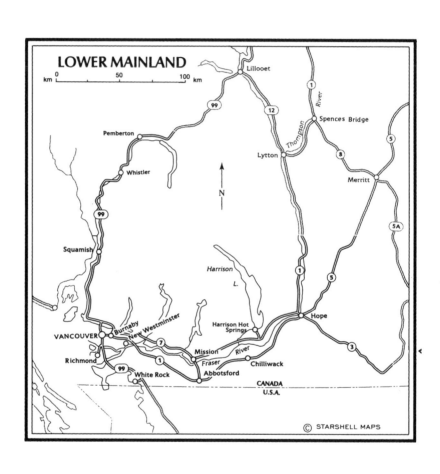

LOWER MAINLAND

km 0   50   100 km

Lillooet

99

12

Thompson River

Spences Bridge

1

5

Pemberton

Lytton

8

Merritt

Whistler

N

5A

99

Squamish

Harrison L.

1

5

Hope

Burnaby

New Westminster

Harrison Hot Springs

VANCOUVER

7

Mission

Fraser River

Chilliwack

3

Richmond

1

99

White Rock

Abbotsford

CANADA
U.S.A.

© STARSHELL MAPS

LOWER MAINLAND

A visitor to the Pacific Northwest in the mid-19th century would have supposed that the area we now call the Lower Mainland had everything stacked against it. In an era of sailing ships, the estuary of the Fraser River, muddy, multi-channelled and treacherous, was uninviting. Even when steam took over from sail, the area seemed to have little to recommend it: the Lower Mainland simply was not on the route from anywhere to anywhere.

Strategically, the region was vulnerable. The Royal Engineers insisted the capital of the new colony of British Columbia should be established on the north side of the Fraser River, not on the south bank where, presumably, it could be readily attacked by American invaders. But even this site would be difficult to defend.

The Lower Mainland seemed an agricultural dead end. Though the silt washed down the river for eons had built up fertile land, the soil was often waterlogged and the river valley susceptible to flooding; mosquitoes abounded in the sloughs and marshes, and heavy forests choked the land. No panegyrist wrote paeans suggesting that the valley of the Fraser River would contain a mighty economic centre.

Fast forward to the 21st century. Vancouver dominates the province's economy. The Lower Mainland—from the mouth of the Fraser to the eastern end of the Fraser Valley at Hope, from the mountains in the north to the American border in the south—holds more than half the total population of British Columbia. Apart from the natural features of river and mountain, the region bears little resemblance to what it was as recently as the 1880s. Cities have been built, swamps drained, riverbanks dyked, farms and industry established, suburbs created and forests levelled. Major highways arrow through every part of the region, and roads and streets criss-cross almost every section. The story of the Lower Mainland in the last 130 years is a story of major change fuelled by transportation and technology and inspired by its mild climate and natural beauty.

The Halq'emeylem-speaking people of the valley, most part of the Sto:lo nation, were very much peoples of the great river that cuts through their territories. For many centuries, a vast abundance of salmon passed along the river on their way to spawning grounds as distant as the Interior plateau and the north. Though the region provided other resources, salmon were the greatest, and most villages were built along the banks of the river.

In the 1860s, when Victoria and the Cariboo were booming, newcomers hurried up the river, eager to reach the goldfields. Few saw the region's potential: the best they could say was that it was relatively easy to paddle up the wide river or go up by steamboat. Would-be farmers and ranchers were more tempted by Vancouver Island or the bunchgrass plateaus and valleys of the Interior. It was too difficult to clear or drain fields in the Fraser Valley, there were few settlers to buy farm products and there was no easy way existed to get them to market. Only a few farmers cleared the brush and battled with the waterlogged soil.

Colonial authorities chose the site of New Westminster, on the north bank of the river, as the mainland's first capital. But when Frederick Seymour, new governor of the colony, arrived in 1865, he could only conclude that the waning of the gold rush had blighted the town. It was, he declared, "played out."

Residents were not prepared to give up. Newspaper editor John Robson, later elected premier, announced that "in less than a year, New Westminster, traduced and deceived by a jealous and grasping neighbour [Victoria], will be the centre of . . . great systems . . . which must speedily make her worthy to be the great capital of an important colony and the great centre of commerce on the British Pacific." Robson was inspired by the building of a telegraph line to New Westminster, on the route of the Russian-American telegraph. But the telegraph project was abandoned and Victoria won the battle to be the capital of the combined colonies.

That battle was only a sideshow. In the 1880s, the magnates of the CPR chose the shores of Burrard Inlet, barely touched by native settlement and by a sawmill and a small cluster of businesses, as the terminus for the railway. Vancouver was built and burned down and built again in brick and stone in 1886. From then on, the city had no rival as a centre of population and commerce in British Columbia. Vancouver thrived and grew through the rest of the 1880s and the early 1890s, took a breather in the mini-depression of the mid-1890s then moved ahead once more at the turn of the century. Well before World War I, it was clear that Vancouver would dominate the economic life of British Columbia. That dominance has never since been challenged.

The city became a magnet for immigrants. Vancouver's Chinatown passed Victoria's in size and influence. Japanese immigrants came to work in the canneries and developed their own centres in Vancouver. Sikh immigrants came to the province to work in the lumber industry, echoing their work in India, and they established homes in Vancouver. Every ethnic group that came to British Columbia chose an area of the city as its base.

In the valley south of the Fraser River, a different story unfolded. Native peoples steered clear of the swamps near present-day Abbotsford and Chilliwack and made only hunting and fishing forays into the bush from their villages on the main rivers. Though some hardy souls pioneered on this land in the 1860s and after, it was not at first a favoured site for settlement.

Present-day residents can testify to the power of the Fraser River when, swollen with snow melt, it breaks through the dykes built over the last hundred years to contain it. And you need only drive through the valley when winter rains lie in lakes on the ground to imagine the difficulties farmers had with the heavy and slow-draining (but fertile) soil of the region.

The swampy land posed other problems. Charles Wilson, secretary to the commission that surveyed the international boundary between 1858 and 1862, wrote graphic descriptions of his mosquito-tormented time in the valley. "Pray do not think," he wrote, "that I am inventing stories to amuse you, as however incredible, they are perfectly true. My hands . . . have been so swollen and stiff that I could hardly bend my joints . . . Even when wearing kid gloves the bites through the needle holes in the seams were sufficient to produce this." He also wrote of a mule, which, once packed, had to be led into a circle of fires to protect it from insects; two mules were blinded and six horses so covered with sores that they were turned out on the prairie to fend for themselves. Mosquitoes thronged on the tents to the point that Wilson could scarcely see the canvas. Lack of sleep and irritation exhausted the men and made them long for the winters, which they spent—thus reinforcing a new Canadian custom—in Victoria.

From 1883 to 1885, the CPR built a line north of the river, avoiding the marshy ground and the other trials of the land to the south, and villages grew up along the north bank. But farmers could not forever overlook the fertility of the soils deposited by the river over thousands of years. From the 1890s on, determined efforts were made to dyke the area from Ladner south and east. In the early 20th century, swamps, sloughs and shallow lakes were drained, brush cleared and farms created from tidewater to where the valley narrowed and the river emerged from the Fraser Canyon.

With the valley's floods and standing water tamed, its potential became readily apparent. New railways and roads provided easy means of transporting milk and butter, fruits and vegetables to the markets of a growing Vancouver. The fertile fields attracted diverse groups. Japanese Canadian farmers dominated small-fruit growing around Abbotsford. When Canadians of Japanese descent were exiled from the coast in 1942, Mennonites took over many of their farms. Chinese immigrants worked and oversaw many of the valley market gardens.

North of the river, loggers and sawmill workers lived in growing towns along the Fraser's edge. North of Burrard Inlet, middle- and upper-class residents eagerly bought houses in new developments. Along Howe Sound, miners worked the rock faces of Britannia. Farther inland, farmers discovered the Pemberton Valley.

Out in the rest of the province, logging and sawmilling dominated some interior cities, while mining continued to be the mainstay for others. In Vancouver and its far-flung suburbs, primary-resource industries became less and less important. The swings in commodity prices, the exhaustion of ore bodies—events that dictated the life or death of other communities—were here felt second-hand. The strategic importance of its location, its position as the economic centre of the province and the allure of its climate and natural attractions assured that the Lower Mainland would continue to be the pre-eminent player in British Columbia.

———— ◆ ————

Vancouver

Vancouver presents the richest historical tapestry in the province, and no guide can hope to include every evidence of its past. The following suggests areas, buildings and cityscapes of interest but is far from exhaustive. It concentrates on the period from 1867 to 1914, during which Vancouver was transformed from a few muddy roads and clusters of shacks on the edge of a dense forest into a city of stone, glass and brick.

Downtown

Neither the First Nations nor the early explorers were much impressed by the south shore of Burrard Inlet, which lacked salmon streams and anchorages adequate for sailing ships. But subsequent settlers saw the advantages of the heavily

In 1912, Vancouverites turned out in force to see the Duke of Connaught at the downtown courthouse square. (BCA G255)

wooded shore and protected harbour and set up sawmills and began lumbering and farming in the area.

Vancouver's oldest remaining building was built just east of the present downtown area (bordered by False Creek, English Bay and Burrard Inlet). Edward Stamp erected the Hastings Mill at the foot of present-day Dunlevy Street in 1865, producing sawn lumber and spars for markets around the shores of the Pacific, and for Britain. The Hastings Mill Store was built that same year. In 1930, no longer in use, it was floated down the inlet and around Stanley Park to its present location at the foot of Alma Street. It is now a museum.

The original Hastings Mill offices are long gone, but offices built in 1905 still stand on Dunlevy, west of the railway tracks. When port expansion forced closure of the mill in 1929, the National Harbours Board took over the building. In 1973, it became home to a seaman's mission and club. Three granite sculptures near the building mark the centenary of Hastings Mill.

GASTOWN was the first settlement on the downtown peninsula. It took its name from Gassy Jack Deighton, a talkative man who opened a saloon at the corner of present-day Water and Carrall streets, convinced—and he was right—that employees of the Hastings Mill would walk the rough trail to the saloon for the sake of a drink. Though his hotel is long gone, Gassy Jack is remembered in a statue at his old corner.

The building of Canadian Pacific Railway tracks to tidewater at Burrard Inlet marked a new era in British Columbia history and the real beginnings of Vancouver as a port city. Wharves and warehouses were built near "the end of steel," as were hotels, flophouses, stores and houses. These first buildings, almost all wooden, had barely been thrown up when fire razed the site in the summer of 1886, destroying 800 buildings and killing 13 people. The devastation led to a decree that all new buildings except sheds and privies must be of brick and stone. Much of the post-1886 business district has survived. Because the city centre moved west, the old buildings were not torn down for redevelopment, and the Gastown revitalization movement and campaign against freeways through downtown ensured that the area retained its turn-of-the-century look. In its heritage conservation program section, the City of Vancouver website provides a detailed walking tour of this area, as well as tours of Chinatown, Yaletown and Shaughnessy.

The best way to get a feel for this oldest part of Vancouver is to walk the streets, looking for the characteristic arched windows, curved roof lines, bay windows and decorated cornices of 1880s and 1890s buildings. The well-documented problems of the Downtown Eastside may give you pause, but this area near the harbour had long been a gathering ground for upcoast loggers looking to carouse, and for lost souls wending their way west to the end of the road.

One history-seekers' route is along Alexander Street from Main Street west to Water Street, then along Water through restored Gastown to Cordova, east on Cordova two blocks, then north on Carrall back to Water.

Not surprisingly, most of the 1880s and 1890s buildings on this route started life as hotels, warehouses or business premises. At 2 Water Street, the Byrnes Block (1886–87) housed business offices and the plush Alhambra Hotel; the Grand Hotel (1890) at 26 Water competed with the Terminus Hotel (1886) at 30 Water until both were put to other uses. The Tremont Hotel (1888) at 208 Carrall operates now as the King's Hotel. Thomas Dunn's hardware store (1889) occupied premises at 8 West Cordova, with a variety of business, fraternal and religious organizations upstairs. Much quieter now than it was in 1886 is the second Ferguson Block at 6 Powell Street. Then, it housed the CPR land office; the phrase "a land-office business" dates from the time in the early 1800s when American land offices allocating homesteads to would-be settlers were so busy that people had to be turned away.

For building its 23 kilometres of track from tidewater at Port Moody to Burrard Inlet at Vancouver, the CPR received a grant of 2,400 hectares in the downtown area, much of which they sold to eager buyers in the 1880s. The company dampened speculators' fervour by insisting on one-third down and full payment within a year and by giving rebates to purchasers who built within a year. Nonetheless, real estate agents outnumbered grocers in early Vancouver, and land prices doubled, tripled, rose as much as 1,000 percent in the first five years.

The railway was, of course, at the centre of this development. Just west of Gastown, at 601 West Cordova Street, the Canadian Pacific Railway station

The old CPR roundhouse (circa 1912) on Pacific Boulevard in the False Creek area is today the centrepiece of a community centre.

(1912–14) is the third CPR station in the city, by far the most grandiose with its columns and spacious pilastered waiting rooms. Passenger trains rolled into the station until the 1970s, when VIA Rail chose the Canadian National Railways station as its terminus. The nicely restored CPR station is now the SeaBus and SkyTrain terminal.

Also renovated and restored is the CPR roundhouse, complete with tracks and turntable, located at Davie and Pacific streets. Now a community centre, it also houses Engine 374, which pulled the first passenger train into Vancouver on May 23, 1887.

Early immigrants usually made their first homes on the Downtown Eastside. Though Chinese Canadians now live throughout the Lower Mainland, Vancouver's **CHINATOWN** still occupies Pender and parallel streets east and west of Main. Anyone who ventures into Chinatown, especially on a Sunday morning, is transported into a timeless world where black-garbed elderly women prod vegetables and argue prices with store owners, where—despite efforts of regulations-bound health inspectors—bronzed ducks still hang in barbecue shop windows, where herbalists suggest age-old remedies for age-old complaints. Recessed balconies on the Chinese Benevolent Association buildings (1909) at 108 East Pender, the Mon Keang Chinese school (1921) at 123 East Pender and the Chin Wing Chum Society building (1925) at 160 East Pender show strong links with traditional Chinese architecture; such balconies are not found in San

Francisco's Chinatown. Part of the Wing Sang Building, now under renovation, at 51 to 67 East Pender (look for the date 1889 on the facade) is the oldest structure in Chinatown. Yip Sang, who emigrated to Canada in the 1880s, was a merchant, labour contractor and philanthropist who presided over his several families here and was often to be seen in his later years by the stove at the front of his building.

Its historic importance is limited but the Sam Kee building at 8 West Pender deserves recognition as an example of an immigrant victory over city bureaucracy. Chang Toy, like many Chinese Canadians an immigrant from Guangdon province, came to British Columbia in 1874 and started the Sam Kee Company in the 1880s, trading to the Cariboo goldfields and in Vancouver. He exported canned and salt fish to the Orient and got involved in logging and sawmilling. Unhappy because the city expropriated part of his property but refused to pay, Toy built this 1.8-metre-wide, two-storey building, reputedly the narrowest commercial building in the world, in 1913. It had communal baths under the sidewalk in the basement. The city's reaction is not recorded.

Anti-Asian racism often focused on the highly visible buildings and people of Chinatown. Japanese immigrants tried to learn from the Chinese experience: though Powell Street was home to many Japanese Canadian houses and businesses, the building facades were intentionally nondescript. The Vancouver Buddhist Church (1906) at 220 Jackson Street, for example, bears little sign of its Japanese heritage. Though it began as a church, it was converted to government offices after Canadians of Japanese descent were banished to the interior of the province in 1942, then returned to church use when some of those internees returned to Vancouver and were joined by new Japanese immigrants.

Nearby **STRATHCONA** was Vancouver's first residential district. Once the area to the west of Granville was developed, better-off homeowners moved west, and the east side became known as the workingman's district. Preserved in Strathcona are both some of the fine houses of the wealthy and some of the small workers'-cottages, though most of these have fallen to the wreckers. Check out the 500-, 700- and 800-blocks of Hawks and East Keefer for heritage row housing and single-family homes.

At the turn of the century, American steel king Andrew Carnegie pledged millions to build libraries in North American cities. East side and west side battled to be the location of Vancouver's library. The east side won the battle and the Carnegie Library was built at the now infamous corner of Hastings and Main. Then the west side had its turn: the Carnegie building became, and still is, a community centre, and a main library was built at Robson and Burrard. Times change: a new main library now occupies a new building closer to east than to west.

The commercial district spilled west along Hastings, then up Granville Street. The CPR built its first Hotel Vancouver and an opera house near the corner of Georgia and Granville streets in 1887. The results of a building boom that lasted until Word War I are evident on a number of streets. Between Granville and Hamilton on West Hastings and Pender are buildings that testify to Vancouver's growing commercial importance: the Canadian Bank of Commerce building (1906–08) at 640 West Hastings; the Royal Bank of Canada building (1903) at 404 West Hastings; and the BC Permanent Loan Building (1907) at 330 West Pender. The Imperial Trust Company, later the Dominion Trust Company, built the Dominion Building, a 13-storey skyscraper, in 1908–10, but having a new building didn't solve the company's financial woes: Dominion collapsed in 1914. The federal government took an appropriately bureaucratic amount of time (1905–10) to erect a post office building at 757 West Hastings. That building is part of the Sinclair Centre, four restored heritage facades linked by a glass-roofed court. Also part of the centre are the Winch Building, a 1908–9 palazzo built for a salmon-canning tycoon; the 1935–39 Federal Building; and the 1911–13 customs examining warehouse. Merchants and businessmen also built in the busy area: the Rogers Building at 470 Granville dates to 1911–12, the Hudson's Bay Company store at Georgia and Granville to 1913, the Standard Building at 510 West Hastings—then the second-tallest building in Vancouver—to 1915.

YALETOWN, in the area of Mainland, Homer and Hamilton streets, is a warehouse district that has been revitalized and now is occupied by upmarket cafés, offices and condominiums. Most of the warehouses were built between 1909 and 1913. They are four to six storeys high, with freight elevators inside. The front of the building was usually located at the top of any slope it occupied; the loading bays were at the back, downhill and wide enough for unloading boxcars that arrived on the tracks that used to run along these streets. The streets have been one-way for many years, a move made necessary to accommodate the wide railcars. The buildings at 1152 Mainland (1913) and 1140 to 1150 Hamilton (1912) are examples of these warehouses.

In the 1890s, as now, few moneyed people wished to live on the doorstep of industry and commerce. By the mid-1890s, Vancouver money had moved to homes on Blueblood Alley, on and west of Georgia Street, and into the newly fashionable West End between Georgia Street and English Bay. Apartment and commercial buildings soon lowered the tone of the **WEST END**, and the wealthy sought other places to live. Single-family homes were divided into suites, and others were torn down and apartment buildings erected in their place. These in turn were torn down after World War II and high-rises built. Walking the West End, however, still provides some insight into turn-of-the-century change.

If you stay away from main thoroughfares such as Denman and Davie, and zigzag along residential blocks, you'll come upon a surprising number of older houses and low-rise apartment buildings. Take a look, for example, at the 1100-block Comox for middle-class homes, the 1100- and 1000-block Nelson for older apartments and, in the 1300-block Comox, beautiful renovated and restored frame houses from between 1907 and 1911. Gabriola, the mansion designed by Samuel Maclure for sugar magnate B. T. Rogers using stone from Gabriola Island, is at 1531 Davie Street. The mansion had B.C.'s first full concrete basement, 17 fireplaces, a conservatory, a gazebo and a porte cochère—presumably to protect Rogers's electric car. One jaunt in this car saw Rogers hauled into court: for driving along a bicycle path, he was fined five dollars—a punishment he probably chose over the alternative, 10 days in jail.

Barclay Heritage Square, fronting 1400-block Barclay Street, includes nine heritage homes. One is the Roedde House, built circa 1892 for Gustav and Matilda Roedde. Gustav, a German immigrant, was Vancouver's first bookbinder. The house's distinctive turret was built so that Matilda could look out over English Bay as she had over the North Sea from her German home. The Roedde House contains a small museum. Also in Barclay Square is Barclay Manor, built in 1904

A number of the city's older residences have been preserved in the West End's Barclay Square.

as a residence for the manager of a Gastown hotel who did not care to live where he worked. And a West End tour wouldn't be complete without a walk along English Bay, past the Alexandra Park bandstand at 1700-block Beach Avenue, where brass bands played from 1914 on for the enjoyment of those who strolled along the promenade. Not far away (1154 Gilford at Beach) is the Sylvia Hotel, built in 1912 as an apartment building and named for the owner's daughter. The suites at the Sylvia were converted to hotel rooms in the 1930s, which accounts for some of the odd-shaped rooms and the blocked-off dumbwaiters—and for the character that distinguishes the hotel. Beyond the Sylvia is the entrance to Stanley Park, the cultivated wilderness on downtown's doorstep.

The park owes its existence to a battle that never happened. In 1859, when colonial authorities feared an attack from the expansionist United States, they set aside much of today's park as a military reserve: troops stationed here on the heights could see and scuttle any attack on the fledgling colony. The attack never came, but the reserve remained in place. It included the site of Khwaykhway, a village where later excavations found middens up to 2.5 metres deep.

The park, leased from the federal government, was formally opened in September 1888. The natives were ordered out of their houses, material from the middens was used to surface park roads and, after smallpox broke out, native and white settlers' houses were burned. Squatters, both native and white, lived in the park until they were turned out by court order in the 1920s. Only one Squamish woman was permitted to stay, after she proved the necessary 60 years' occupancy.

Over the years, other areas have been tacked on to the park, to bring it to its present size of 405 hectares. Within the park are a number of historic sites and monuments, among them a memorial to Japanese Canadians who fought in World War I, the Stanley Park Pavilion built in 1911, the Nine O'Clock Gun (installed in 1894 to provide accurate time for ships' captains), the Brockton Point totem poles and a memorial fountain to poet Pauline Johnson. The seawall that circles the park was built mainly between 1912 and the 1930s, though the final stone was not laid until 1971. The devastation wrought by a winter storm in December 2006 is a reminder that nature, too, can create huge change.

Outside Downtown

Pity the rich; they just can't get away from the rest. As the West End filled with apartment renters, the affluent hastened across the Granville Street Bridge (1909) to the new CPR subdivision of Shaughnessy. Scornful of straight lines, Shaughnessy's designers plotted curving streets between lots that ranged from a tenth to six-tenths of a hectare. Close to 30 of the original Shaughnessy mansions remain (some divided into rental suites). A walk or drive along Marguerite, Matthews, Osler, The Crescent, Marpole and Angus between King Edward and 16th reveals the imposing columns, porte cochères, curving windows and decorative woodwork that pre-war money bought.

Though times have changed, the divisions between Vancouver's working-class east side and moneyed west side remain a constant. Driving through Vancouver's west side south of False Creek, from Kitsilano to Kerrisdale to Point Grey, the traveller will see a variety of houses designed for middle and upper income levels. Those pre-1930 Kitsilano houses that have escaped the developer's bulldozer were built after the art deco–style Burrard Street Bridge across False Creek was completed in 1932 and streetcars ran west for the middle class, including clerical workers. Point Grey was a ritzier region: the earliest remaining houses here date from the 1930s.

One road carries a reminder of much earlier times: Southwest Marine Drive, from the University of British Columbia to the Arthur Laing Bridge, follows the route of a trail trodden first in 1863 from New Westminster to Point Grey. Below the road is the Musqueam reserve, the traditional home of the Musqueam First Nation. The Great Fraser Midden, on the north shore of the Fraser opposite the beginning of the river's Middle Arm, holds deposits up to five metres deep and 3,000 years old. Musqueam villages were located all along the North Arm near the river's mouth.

Those interested in Vancouver's immigrant history can see evidence—though ever-diminishing as many groups meld into the Vancouver mosaic—of various ethnic groups along the city's streets. Though the earliest Greek immigrants arrived in B.C. in the 1850s, most Greek immigrants came after World War II. In Vancouver, they chose to build restaurants, stores and other community centres along Broadway from Macdonald Street west. Alessandro Malaspina, on a sailing expedition for Spain in the late 18th century, was the first Italian in these regions and Carlo Bossi made a modest fortune in 1850s Victoria, but Italians, too, immigrated mostly after World War II. Little Italy in Vancouver grew up around Commercial Drive between Broadway and Hastings. Sikhs and other immigrants from India had a painful passage to this province; rejected and turned back to India in the early years of the century, they did not immigrate in great numbers until after 1945. They, too, created a commercial centre that brought echoes of their homeland, on Main Street south of 41st Avenue.

A number of museums present information on the history of Vancouver and area. The Vancouver Museum, at 1100 Chestnut Street, has permanent and visiting exhibits on Vancouver's history and Canada's native people, with particular focus on the 19th century. The Vancouver Maritime Museum has been housed nearby at the foot of Cypress Street for many years, but it is slated to close in 2009, to be replaced by a National Maritime Centre for the Pacific and Arctic in North Vancouver. Discussions continue on how the museum's collection, owned by the City of Vancouver, can be housed at the new centre. The University of British Columbia Museum of Anthropology, off Northwest Marine Drive on the UBC campus, presents displays on British Columbia native history and culture, among them a re-created Haida village, a gallery of northwest coast jewellery, research collections and totem and mortuary poles. The Vancouver Police Centennial Museum, which headlines itself as "a place of mystery, history and intrigue," is aptly housed in the old city morgue at 240 East Cordova Street. And a train museum, a sport-fishing museum and a model ship museum can be found on Granville Island at 1502 Duranlean Street.

North Shore/Howe Sound/Whistler Pemberton Valley

Today, there are three main ways to cross Burrard Inlet: two bridges and a harbour ferry. In the early days of settlement, native people used canoes to cross between north and south shores. The first non-native settlers went by canoe or rowboat from the north shore to the head of a rough trail that led to New Westminster. A steam ferry replaced the rowboat in 1866; however, it exploded at the wharf in 1871. A variety of ferries did duty on the inlet in following years, including the *Senator*, with a pleasant stateroom for lady passengers, a less pleasant deck room for males. A car ferry motored between the foot of Lonsdale Avenue in North Vancouver and the Vancouver waterfront until 1958.

As industry developed and people moved to the north shore, the first bridge across the inlet was built at Second Narrows, between the east end of Vancouver and North Vancouver. It was completed in 1925, 15 years after it was first planned. Rail and car traffic shared the bridge, with a lift span in the centre that could be opened to allow marine traffic to pass. Four years and four ship-bridge collisions later, the bridge collapsed. It was replaced in 1934. In 1958, a new bridge was under construction when it collapsed, killing 18 workers. A rebuilt bridge opened in 1960. Though usually referred to as the Second Narrows bridge, its official name is the Ironworkers Memorial Bridge, to commemorate those who lost their lives in bridge construction here.

At the west end of the inlet, the Lions Gate Bridge, that most familiar of Vancouver landmarks, spans First Narrows from Stanley Park to the north shore's Marine Drive. The Guinness family who financed the British Properties land development in West Vancouver also financed the bridge. Opened in

November 1938, it was the longest suspension bridge in the British Empire. Two steel towers support the two 40-centimetre-wide cables that hold aloft the 450-metre clear span. Deck widening in 2001 frustrated commuters but left the basic bridge design untouched.

The Squamish people continue to live on the north shore on four reserves near the waterfront. The mouth of the Capilano River was long a native meeting place, especially during salmon-spawning season; fishers still cluster here each year. Chief Snatt chose a site for the Vancouver area's first church in present-day North Vancouver, a location where natives gathered to roast and dry wild ducks. The small church, St. Paul's Mission Church, was built in 1866 at the behest of French Oblate fathers. A second, the basis of the present St. Paul's Indian Catholic Church (424 West Esplanade), replaced it in 1884. The church dedication took place on a warm and windy June day in 1886. As people gathered, their eyes were drawn to the clouds of smoke rising from the south shore: Vancouver was burning. A second tower was added to the church in 1910 and the church was remodelled. The two towers were an official landmark on charts of the Vancouver harbour. At Cates Park, on the Dollarton Highway at Roche Point, are reminders of native history: totem poles and a 15-metre canoe built by Chief Henry Peter George in 1921. Appropriately, the canoe is near the entrance to Indian Arm, named by early explorers for the native people they met while charting Burrard Inlet. Canoe and kayak tours leave from the Tsleil-Waututh lands here; guides tell the cultural history of the Burrard Inlet and Indian Arm.

North Vancouver

The north shore of Burrard Inlet attracted non-native interest before the south shore. In 1862, two New Westminster residents saw potential riches in the cedar and Douglas fir that lined the sharp slopes of the north shore mountains and built Pioneer Mills on the inlet. The mill failed, as did the next attempt at sawmilling. Then American immigrant Sewell Prescott Moody, more often known as "Sue," took over the site, and Moodyville was born. It grew quickly, with the first school on the inlet and the first electric lighting system north of San Francisco. Once the CPR tracks reached the south shore of the inlet, however, Moodyville waned and the mill closed in 1901. Nothing remains except the names Moody Avenue and Moodyville Park.

North Vancouver, split into city and district, followed a rocky economic road as settlers discovered how difficult it was to make a living on the mountain slopes. Much of the land they pre-empted was returned to the district in the 1890s, and absentee landlords took over large tracts. A boom in 1900 buoyed the area, and docks, mills and shipyards opened along the waterfront. Then the Depression destroyed the new prosperity, and both city and district declared bankruptcy. World War II brought new work for shipyards and a return to affluent times.

Lonsdale Avenue, North Vancouver's main north-south street, was once a skid road for logs on their way to the inlet. The docks contain some reminders of early development: now disused, the shipyards in the 200-block East Esplanade date to 1906. The site will be the location of the National Maritime Centre for the Pacific and Arctic to be built at the foot of Lonsdale.

Lower Lonsdale was the second centre of settlement on the north shore. Among the attractions are the original Bank of Hamilton building (1910), now the Canadian Imperial Bank of Commerce at 92 Lonsdale, and the Aberdeen Block (1910) at 78 Lonsdale. The Aberdeen Block was once city hall; at one time it contained the office of the company that ran the electric streetcars that climbed North Vancouver streets. In the 1990s, fire destroyed the old-fashioned hardware store—it still sold nails by the pound—that had occupied the building since 1912.

West Vancouver

Unable to lure industry because of its steep slopes and lack of a harbour, West Vancouver council in 1925 declared the municipality an industry-free zone. The only services allowed within its boundaries would be those such as restaurants and stores. Lots had to be at least 50 feet wide in the eastern part of West Van, 75 feet in the west.

The gamble succeeded. By making a virtue of necessity, West Vancouver soared while North Vancouver sank. British investors led by the Guinness family saw potential for an exclusive residential area and developed, British Properties,

77

above what is now the Upper Levels Highway. They banned undesirables from owning property in the development; when the covenant was struck down, unwritten rules kept out non-whites and non-Christians until after World War II. Large lots, lavish houses and winding private streets are a reminder of the dream of exclusivity.

The Upper Levels Highway replaced Marine Drive as the main road to Howe Sound, but Marine Drive still provides a pleasant meander through the older areas of West Vancouver. Along the way, at Lighthouse Park, is the Point Atkinson Lighthouse (1911–12), which replaced a lighthouse built in 1874. Other buildings in the park also date to the same era as this hexagonal tower.

Horseshoe Bay to Squamish

Ferries have run from the Vancouver area to Nanaimo on Vancouver Island for decades. Canadian Pacific Steamships sailed from Vancouver harbour, and Black Ball Ferries from Horseshoe Bay, at the entrance to Howe Sound. In 1961, the province bought out Black Ball and began operations between Horseshoe Bay and Nanaimo's Departure Bay and between Horseshoe Bay and Langdale on the Sunshine Coast. The ferry terminal now dominates Horseshoe Bay.

Above the town run the tracks of the railway that for years went from "nowhere to nowhere"—from Squamish at the head of Howe Sound to Quesnel in the Cariboo. Few respected the PGE train enough to call it by its real name, the Pacific Great Eastern; instead, passengers nicknamed it the Prince George Eventually or the Please Go Easy. Then, in the early 1950s, the line was finally extended from Squamish to North Vancouver (much to the dismay of West Vancouverites, through whose backyards the track ran) and from Quesnel to Prince George.

Travellers who take the train or follow the cliff-hugging highway from Horseshoe Bay to Squamish can appreciate the reasons for the delay. The cliffs are scarred by rock slides, mudslides have necessitated the rebuilding of communities, and the highway and rail tracks are squeezed together on a frequently narrow ledge between cliff and sound. Many millions are being spent to improve the highway before the 2010 Olympics, but rock slides are an ever-present danger in this difficult terrain.

In the late 1920s and early 1930s, Britannia Mine at **BRITANNIA BEACH,** 33 kilometres beyond Horseshoe Bay, produced more copper than any other mine in the British Empire. The mine has a troubled history: rock slides, fires, floods and mining accidents took many lives before Britannia closed in 1974, victim of depressed prices for copper and a dwindling ore body. The mine buildings and tunnels now house the British Columbia Museum of Mining and have been declared a National Historic Site. Features include the gravity-fed concentrator that clings to the side of the vertical cliff, underground tours by train into the mine tunnel, rock and mineral displays and working displays of mining equipment.

The town of **SQUAMISH** lies at the head of Howe Sound. As befits a town where for decades the PGE began, Squamish is the site of the West Coast Railway Heritage Park, with more than 65 pieces of heritage railway rolling stock, including CPR locomotive 4069 and an open observation car, plus a large collection of railway memorabilia. The PGE car repair shop, probably built circa 1915 and one of just three structures remaining from early PGE days, has been moved to the museum site.

The Squamish Valley Museum is on Second Avenue, with displays of pioneer and First Nations history.

Whistler and the Pemberton Valley

Beyond Squamish, Highway 99 cuts into the Coast Mountains past Garibaldi Park, which takes its name from Garibaldi Mountain. One story has it that an Italian sailor on a survey ship named the mountain for Italian patriot Giuseppi Garibaldi because it was Garibaldi's birthday when the sailor saw the mountain. Whistler Mountain, beyond Garibaldi, is the site of a destination ski resort.

In 2008, the two First Nations that share this region opened the Skwxwú7mesh Lil'wat7úl (Squamish Lil'wat) Cultural Centre in the Upper Village at Whistler, in a three-storey building designed to evoke a traditional longhouse and pit house. Inside are canoes (including an ocean-going war canoe carved from a single cedar tree), spindle whorls and cultural displays. A stand-alone longhouse and pit house are under construction.

Highway 99 leads on to the Pemberton Valley, a broad fertile reach between steep mountains. Early settlers joined the Mount Currie Lil'wat people in this valley in the 1880s. The Pemberton Museum, at 7424 Prospect Street, includes two houses from the native communities of Mount Currie and D'Arcy and a later-settler's house.

Beyond Pemberton, Highway 99 (formerly known as the Duffey Lake Road) continues through the Mount Currie reserve, across the Lillooet River and on to Lillooet. During the gold rush, between 1858 and 1860, prospectors followed Lillooet Lake and Lillooet River, then turned north along the Douglas Trail towards Anderson Lake. The road to D'Arcy on Anderson Lake is paved; the road beyond that, above Anderson Lake, is only for adventurers who have strong stomachs and strong vehicles. The Hurley River Road, from the north end of the Pemberton Valley, leads to the old gold mining towns of Bridge River country. (The Hurley, however, is closed in the winter. For more on this area, see the Bridge River section in Chapter Six, The Interior Plateau.)

The gravel Lillooet Lake Road follows the shore of Lillooet Lake south, then parallels the route of the first gold-seekers' trail. Some portions of that heritage trail have been cleared. To find one such, follow the road south past 18 Mile Creek bridge, then look carefully on the right side for a tiny sign that indicates the trail's location. On the way south, you'll see the sign for St. Agnes Hot Springs (also known as Skookumchuck Hot Springs). These springs, long used by the Lil'wat, were named for a daughter of colonial governor James Douglas; the springs at Harrison were initially named for her sister, Alice.

The Church of the Holy Cross at Skatin (the village formerly known as Skookumchuck) was built by the native people here between 1895 and 1906. Money they earned from trapping went to buy the Italian stained-glass windows. This beautiful Gothic-style church with a finely carved altar has fallen into disrepair, and is considered one of the most threatened of Canada's official National Historic Sites. A campaign is under way to raise sufficient money to restore the church.

Port Douglas, at the end of the road on the shore of Little Harrison Lake, was the water terminus for 1859 goldrushers, the beginning of the overland trail. A cairn commemorates the site of the short-lived town.

North of the Fraser, West of the Pitt

The guide now returns to the Vancouver area.

North of the Fraser, east and south of Vancouver proper, lie the municipalities of Burnaby, New Westminster, Port Moody, Coquitlam, Richmond and the district of Coquitlam. Together with Vancouver proper, they make up the heavily populated urban area.

Burnaby

Between the waterfront settlements of Hastings and New Westminster, Burnaby was late to develop. Robert Burnaby, for whom the municipality is named, was secretary to Royal Engineers Colonel R. C. Moody. Burnaby claimed land at the head of False Creek in 1860 but lost it when a different claim was declared legal in 1862.

By 1900, only 400 people lived on the more than 10,000 hectares that had been incorporated in 1892 as the municipality of Burnaby. But the pressure of expanding population—and the building of roads east from Vancouver—brought a post-1900 expansion.

The Burnaby Village Museum, on Deer Lake Avenue off Sperling Avenue, south of Canada Way, re-creates a 1925-era village in more than 30 buildings and outdoor displays, and features a 1912 carousel as well as a Chinese herbalist's shop and a blacksmith's shop. The Museum of Archaeology and Ethnology, at Simon Fraser University on Burnaby Mountain, has displays of Northwest Coast art and life.

New Westminster

New Westminster was the first major town on the Fraser, built as the capital of British Columbia in 1859. Since then, it has had its ups and downs. It lost out to Victoria as political capital—and to Vancouver as economic capital—of the province. But it rebounded as sawmills and fish canneries were established along the Fraser. The boom died in the 1890s; floods washed out the rail lines in 1893–4, and a massive fire in 1898 destroyed many houses and almost every building in the business area along the waterfront. One of the few remaining, at 411 Columbia Street, was built in 1892 by the Burr family and now houses the Met Hotel.

The city grew again, though slowly. By 1912, the *Columbian* newspaper was proclaiming New Westminster "the Montreal of the Pacific" and forecasting a great future. War brought another bust, postwar another boom, Depression a bust and World War II and the following years another boom. The city's history of boom and bust—and the effect of fire and flood—is visible in its streets.

The earliest remaining building is Irving House, at 302 Royal Avenue. William Irving ran a Fraser River passenger and freight fleet that became the nucleus of the CPR steamships coastal service; he survived a boiler explosion on a competitor's ship that killed eight passengers. He had this house built in 1865 by ex–Royal Engineers, high on a hill overlooking the river, in Gothic revival style with a steep roof and pointed gables. Irving imported marble fireplaces from England and a mahogany staircase from Scotland. Irving House is now a museum, next door to the New Westminster Museum.

New Westminster's waterfront has always been critical to its economy. Successive generations have had buildings torn down and rebuilt, but some evidence remains of the past. The infocentre near Westminster Quay is housed in a 1905 prefabricated house of a type shipped all through British Columbia in the 1900s.

A 23-sign informative walk along the boardwalk begins at the Fraser River Discovery Centre. Busts and plaques by the quay commemorate explorer Simon Fraser and the Royal Engineers. Near these plaques is berthed the *Samson V*, the last steam-powered sternwheeler to operate on the Fraser, in a tradition that began with the HBC ship *Beaver*, the first steam-powered ship to enter the Fraser, in 1836. Built in 1937, the *Samson V* was retired in 1980 and is now a maritime museum. The original *Samson* started its career as a snag-puller on the river in 1883.

The original home of St. Andrew's Presbyterian Church (1863) at 321 Carnarvon is a board and batten building that was demoted to church hall in 1889, when parishioners built a new brick church.

Two structures dominated New Westminster for decades. Almost nothing

One of the few buildings to escape New Westminster's great fire in 1898 now houses the Met Hotel on Columbia Street.

now remains of the old B.C. Penitentiary buildings on Columbia Street, beside the original townsite occupied by the Royal Engineers. But the Pattullo Bridge still leads across the Fraser from New Westminster, though a fire in early 2009 closed the bridge for two weeks and created traffic chaos. The first bridge (1904) linking New Westminster to the south bank was a two-storey span. The top level was for wagons, horses and pedestrians; on the bottom were rail tracks and motor vehicles. The second and present Pattullo Bridge opened in 1937.

New Westminster's military history is preserved in the Royal Westminster Regiment museum at the Armoury, at 530 Queens Avenue. And the city maintains a heritage inventory accessible at the library. The library's website lists these buildings, with descriptions of the most significant.

Port Moody/Coquitlam

Port Moody looked forward to a great future in 1886 when the railway tracks reached tidewater here. The extension of the tracks to Vancouver's harbour put an end to that kind of dreaming; like other neighbouring communities, Port Moody is now primarily residential.

The port's most cherished heritage building is the 1905 railway station at 2734 Murray Street; it replaced the first station, built in 1885. The station no longer serves railway passengers: passenger service to PoMo ended in 1945, freight service in 1976, though trains still pass through on their way elsewhere. The station, like so many others in B.C., is now a museum. The City Hall, at 2425 St. John's Street, is worth a look, as is the building at 2227 St. John's Street. This street, the grand main street of town, was supposed to be named for John Murray, a man who at one point owned half the town, but his son, John Jr., inadvertently wrote *St. John* instead of *John St.* on the map. A Royal Engineer who somehow acquired large amounts of land, John Sr. was reputed to be no saint. Ask at the library or museum to see the list of Port Moody's 55 designated heritage buildings.

The easternmost communities on the Fraser and Pitt rivers' north shores, Coquitlam and Port Coquitlam still stand at the edge of forest and mountain. Pity the first residents—*Coquitlam* comes from the Halq'emeylem word meaning "stinking of fish slime." The Coquitlam, starving in a winter famine, had sold themselves into slavery with the Kwantlen. Since one of their jobs was to kill fish, they were often covered with its slime. (An alternate explanation suggests the word means "little red fish" and refers to a type of salmon.)

Within the District of Coquitlam lies British Columbia's oldest francophone settlement, Maillardville. Voyageurs from Quebec were among the first white men to enter British Columbia. Quebecois and French settlers arrived on the coast with the gold rush. Maillardville was settled in 1909 by Quebecois who moved west to work in lumber mills. The area bordered by Brunette, Schoolhouse, Rochester and Blue Mountain streets constitutes old Maillardville. Notre Dame de Lourdes church and rectory at 830 Laval Square, the priest's house at 828 Laval Square and the school at 1432 Brunette Avenue are part of that francophone heritage. Each year in March a Maillardville committee organizes a Festival du Bois to celebrate the town's past as a home for sawmill workers. Heritage Square, at 1120 Brunette, contains Ryan House and the Mackin House Museum (1909), the Fraser Mills CPR station and an arts centre and music school.

Richmond

Richmond lies across the North Arm of the Fraser from Vancouver, on islands formed by silt carried downstream by the Fraser year after year. The rich soil brought by flood and falling water created ideal farmland. By the mid-1860s, farmers had moved onto many of the islands at the river's mouth, among them Lulu Island, named by Royal Engineer Colonel Moody for Miss Lulu Sweet, an actress in a theatrical company that visited New Westminster in the early 1860s. Later settlers claimed land on Sea, Mitchell, Twigg and Deadman islands, which together make up the municipality of Richmond.

Evidence of their work, albeit expanded and reconstructed, is visible in the network of dykes that block the river and the sea from Richmond's fields. You can walk the dykes at the western end of Steveston Highway, or beside Dyke Road, along the south arm of the Fraser, at the south end of No. 2, 3 or 4 roads.

"Even with comparatively careless cultivation," wrote a commentator in the 1882 *B.C. Directory*, "enormous yields are realized, and an accurate statement of what the land will do in this respect, would sound like romance." Such accounts were, indeed, usually romance, but in this case the author spoke the truth. Though housing developments have spread over former farmland not protected by the Agricultural Land Reserve, Richmond market gardeners still produce— and sell at stands along Steveston Highway—vegetables and small fruits such as cranberries, blueberries and strawberries.

One of the few remaining early farmhouses is the London farmhouse (1882) at 6511 Dyke Road, preserved with its surrounding fields as a historic site.

The Gulf of Georgia Cannery in Steveston, now a National Historic Site, recalls an era when salmon fishing dominated the Fraser mouth.

Immigrant brothers Charles and William London bought 80 hectares of land here and operated a store, post office and wharf.

Richmond's other historically important industry, fishing, is on display at Steveston, at the south edge of Richmond. To reach Steveston, follow the Steveston Highway west and watch for signs.

A walking-tour brochure, as well as good maps and displays at the old post office/museum building, guide visitors. The whole town is a pleasant step back in time. One of Steveston's main historic features is the century-old Gulf of Georgia Cannery, once the second-largest cannery in British Columbia. Cans of salmon and herring came off the lines here until 1946; the plant was used for processing herring until 1979. The cannery is a National Historic Site, with displays and exhibits including a self-guided canning-line exhibit. Nearby BC Packers' Imperial Cannery barely managed to celebrate its hundredth birthday. It opened in 1893, closed in 1992.

Another heritage site, the former Britannia Shipyard and Cannery, circa 1889, contains the oldest remaining structure on the Fraser River. It has nine heritage buildings on a three-hectare site.

At 12004 No. 1 Road is the old telephone exchange building; the first telephone in the area was connected to the general store here in 1891, whence a messenger would deliver messages for ten cents.

FRASER VALLEY: SOUTH OF THE RIVER

From Richmond, Highway 99 leads south to the border with the United States. A network of roads criss-cross the Fraser Valley south of the river between Georgia Strait and the Cascade Mountains. Straight and somewhat arbitrary lines divide this part of the valley into the municipalities of Delta, White Rock, Surrey, Langley District, Langley City, Abbotsford and Chilliwack. Everywhere in the valley, farming seems to be fighting a losing battle with housing developments as Vancouver spills into the flat lands to the south and east of the main metropolitan area. If farming does lose out, the loss will be ironic: farmers and other settlers fought ongoing battles with heavy soil, sloughs and frequent floods before they could take full advantage of the fertile valley soil.

Delta

For many centuries, the Tsawwassen camped along the shores of the delta during the summer, fishing for salmon and sturgeon and digging for clams and other shellfish, hunting deer and gathering roots and berries—wisely preferring to leave the swampy interior alone.

The first white settler arrived in 1859; several more families, including the Ladners, pre-empted land in the 1860s. Since no overland transportation routes existed, they, too, preferred land near the river. The municipality of Delta was incorporated in 1879, some years before Vancouver. Today's town of **LADNER** had its beginnings in Ladners' Landing, where a post office, wharf and government warehouse were built. Ladner grew as farmers pre-empted, cleared and drained land farther inland over the years, and because fishermen chose it as a home port for the rich salmon runs. By the 1870s, several canneries were processing fish along Ladner's shores. Native men fished the Fraser; native women worked in the canneries. Other cannery workers were Chinese, Norwegian, Finnish, Greek, Basque and Croatian immigrants. A small, mainly Croatian, community was established at Port Guichon, near present-day Port Guichon Park at the west end of Ladner.

But the river gave and the river took away. Floods and extreme high water in the 1890s silted up the deep channel of the river near Ladner and scoured a

Autumn rains serve as a reminder that the heavy, waterlogged soils of the Fraser delta challenged would-be farmers in the days before dykes and drainage.

new channel close to the opposite shore. Steveston prospered; Ladner languished. Present-day Ladner is separated from the river by marshes and islands of river silt.

Evidence of Delta's history is apparent at a number of sites around Ladner. The Delta Museum and Archives is housed at 4858 Delta Street in Ladner, in a 1912 building where displays include Coast Salish artifacts; information on historic buildings is available. Look also for special exhibits each year, perhaps on the history of dyking of the river or of the area's food culture. Staff offer guided walking tours of the town during the summer; check with them for historical cruises of the Fraser River and other innovative offerings. Though it was largely Chinese labour that built Ladner Trunk Road, still a major artery (Highway 10) in Delta, no sign remains of Ladner's once-thriving Chinatown. Ladner Trunk Road is much improved from early days, when it was recorded as "not generally practicable except for droving cattle, for ox sleighs and for gum-booted pedestrians."

Much of the Ladner-Tsawwassen urban area has been overtaken by development. Townhouses, apartments and housing subdivisions make it difficult to see the area's early history in the landscape. But travel Ladner's River Road from the town towards Westham Island, and a different picture emerges. On the river side, a high dyke guards against floods. Early dykes in Delta were built by landowners, but the 1890s flooding convinced the municipal government to build dykes along all of Delta's shores in 1895 and 1896. Between dyke and river are still some remains of old cannery and dock buildings, and a small fishing fleet still ties up at Ladner's docks. On the land side, the occasional farmhouse dating from before 1900 has been lovingly preserved, and weathered and sometimes listing barns in a variety of styles remain. Turn right over the Westham Island bridge, a picturesque swing span built in 1912, and the landscape becomes completely rural, with farmhouses and barns both heritage and new and geese feasting on stubble in the fields in autumn and winter.

One of the most impressive historic buildings in Delta is an adopted one. The Burr family built Burrvilla in Richmond in 1906. It was almost torn down in the 1980s but was rescued after public outcry. One of the conditions of the reprieve was that it be moved: it was moved, though a low telephone cable blocked the way and the house and moving truck spent a night by the side of the road.

Today, well restored and furnished with items such as the 11-leaved dining table that seats 28, it is the centrepiece of the Deas Island Regional Park. (Take Highway 17 north across Highway 99, then follow the signs to the park.) Also in the park and open to visitors are a 1909 heritage school and the Delta Agricultural Hall (1894).

From the park on Deas Island, travellers can look across the Gravesend Reach of the Fraser River to Richmond—but they can't see a linking bridge. Ferries carried traffic from Ladner to Woodward's Landing—in present-day Richmond—from 1913 to 1959. Repeatedly, Ladnerites petitioned for a bridge. In the 1930s, a contract was signed; when the provincial government changed, it was cancelled. Construction started on the Deas Island tunnel in 1956. Residents who were excited by the prospect that the tunnel could handle 700 cars an hour, compared to the 70 transported by ferry, could not anticipate the long lineups at the tunnel's south end in the mornings, at its north end in the evenings.

White Rock and Surrey

To the south at 13723 Crescent Road are the restored buildings of the old Stewart farmstead on the Nikomekl River. To reach Elgin Heritage Park, go south on Highway 99 to the Crescent Road–White Rock exit, then follow signs. The Stewart family settled here in the 1880s; the house and pole barn have been restored to a turn-of-the-century look. At the site are exhibits on marine heritage, particularly fishing and boat building, and heritage gardens and an orchard. Also in the park is the Hooser Weaving Centre, where traditional spinning and weaving techniques are demonstrated in summer.

White Rock, with its kilometres of beach, has been a holiday destination for decades; rail tours from the United States and from Vancouver were advertised soon after 1900. The Great Northern (now Burlington Northern) railway tracks still run beside the beach, between the ocean and the road, and the city's 467-metre pier arrows out across the water. Built in 1914, the pier saved ship passengers from getting their feet wet. It was extended in 1915, turned over to the municipality in 1977 and rebuilt; it now serves not ships, but the legions of strollers who use the waterfront walk. Just south of the pier is the massive rock—originally limed white by bird droppings, now painted a brighter white—that gave the city its name. Not far from the pier, at 14970 Marine Drive, the 1913 Great Northern Railway Station houses an art centre and the museum.

White Rock carves a small rectangle out of Surrey, the second-largest municipality in B.C. In pre-modern times, most native groups confined their visits to Surrey to times when fishing, hunting or berry-picking beckoned. And settlers were not at first attracted by the marshes and virtually impenetrable brush known as hardhack that covered the low ground, or by the dense forests of fir and cedar that clothed the rare high ground. Some people did pre-empt land in the 1860s, once surveys were complete, but they were absentee landlords—the first, though far from the last, of Surrey's land speculators.

As elsewhere in this area, settlements grew with draining, dyking and the building of roads and railways. The traveller driving east today along one of the through roads—though not Highways 1A, 10 or 99A, which are flanked by strip development and choked with traffic—will come upon various signs of the region's history.

The Surrey Museum is located at spiffy new digs by Highway 10 (17710 56A Avenue) in Heritage Square. The museum explores, through new exhibits, the life of the First Nations people of the area, pioneer settlements, farming and more modern history. A temporary exhibition gallery presents changing exhibits from around the world. Check out, too, the Hooser Textile Studio and Library, with programs and displays that demonstrate spinning, weaving and fibre arts; the studio is named for Honey Hooser, and celebrates her 50 years of weaving in Surrey. A pioneer cabin and a World War I cenotaph are also in Heritage Square.

A series of storyboards at historic sites throughout Surrey details the history of each site. Check with the museum or online for a map of the sites. The museum also offers a brochure with a driving tour and a book portraying Surrey's historic buildings, but the casual traveller will spot older houses and barns without much difficulty. These include the 1912 Surrey Municipal Hall at 17675 – 56th Avenue, which now houses the community archives; and the two-storey house at the corner of 54th Avenue and 184th Street, which was built in 1911 for the Robert Dougal Mackenzie family.

CLOVERDALE prospered when tracks were laid on the New Westminster Southern Railway from the American border to Brownsville, opposite New Westminster, and a second railway built from the Ladner area to Cloverdale. Downtown Cloverdale is still an attractive, low-rise town, with a variety of buildings dating back to 1891 that form a quintessential small-town landscape. A walking-tour brochure is available from the Surrey Museum (see above).

If you follow 176th Street north and turn right just before the freeway on 97th Avenue, then left on 177A Street, you'll find Anniedale School, the simplest possible one-room schoolhouse where children learned their lessons between 1891 and 1954. It was moved here from the original site on Townline Road (96th Avenue).

The Aldergrove Telephone Museum and Archives, at 3190 – 271st Street in Aldergrove, is in a 1910 prefabricated BC Mills building; it contains a variety of historic telephone equipment.

Fort Langley/Langley

Continue north on 176th across the freeway, turn right on 96th Avenue, then left on Allard Crescent to reach the site of the first Fort Langley. (There were three.) If you take a side trip into Derby Reach Regional Park, you can—if you ignore the people fishing from the river's bank—see the river as those first fur traders saw it, high and brown in late fall, winter and spring, shrinking down past the sandbars in summer. Farther along Allard Crescent is a plaque, simply presented and surrounded by picket fencing, commemorating the fort's original location. Near here was the proposed site of Derby, the town that never was. James Douglas picked this site as the capital for the new colony of British Columbia but New Westminster was chosen instead. For a number of years, once the land speculators gave up, only a church and a few houses marked Derby's dreams; then even the church was moved, to Port Hammond across the river.

The first Fort Langley was built near the mouth of the Salmon River in 1827. The second was built in 1838–39 a few miles upstream; it burned to the ground in 1840. The third fort was built just upriver that same year, on the present site, and is now a National Historic Site. Though only the storehouse remains from the 1840s, careful reconstruction and restoration have made Fort Langley a good re-creation of the days when it was the centre of Hudson's Bay Company operations on the coast. Displays of barrel making, blacksmithing and other 19th-century arts take place in summer months. The first government of British Columbia was officially proclaimed here on November 19, 1859; each year, the provincial cabinet meets at Fort Langley on November 19.

The fort takes its name from Thomas Langley, a governor of the HBC. McMillan Island is named for the founder and first chief factor at the fort, James McMillan. Stave Lake and River, across the Fraser, are named for the staves cut by cooper William Cromarty for the barrels used to export dried salmon to the Hawaiian Islands and England.

McMillan Island lies below Fort Langley. It is the home of the Kwantlen people, part of the Sto:lo nation. When the fort was built, the Kwantlen moved to the island from traditional summer and winter villages downstream. The Church of the Holy Redeemer, a traditional, white, high-steepled chapel, was built at the turn of the century by natives working for Oblate fathers from St. Mary's Mission across the river at Mission. Logs for the church were rafted down to the New Westminster mill to be sawn into planks; payment for the milling was made in logs.

The town of Fort Langley grew up around the fort; most of its historic buildings date from years after the closing of Fort Langley in 1886. Information on the period houses and other buildings is available at the Langley Centennial Museum at Mavis and King streets. The CNR station near the riverfront dates from 1915; tenants in the 1911 Coronation Block at 9048 Glover Road have ranged from a butcher to a druggist to a veterinarian to an art gallery. The Fort Langley cemetery, with graves that date back to 1882, is on Glover Road.

Exhibits at the Langley Centennial Museum show pre-contact life among the Sto:lo and early settler exhibits. The British Columbia Farm Machinery and Agricultural Museum next door is well located: the first farm on the mainland was developed around the fur-trading fort. Exhibits at the farm museum include a working sawmill and the province's first crop-dusting plane, a Tiger Moth.

Glover Road out of Fort Langley leads across the freeway and back to the

City of Langley. A cairn at the corner of Glover and Telegraph Trail commemorates the massive but futile 1860s effort to build a telegraph connecting North America and Europe via British Columbia, the Yukon, Alaska, Siberia and Russia. Old barns on 80th Avenue preserve the rural character of this area; floodgates on some of the east-west roads off 176th testify that winter rains can still inundate parts of the valley.

The Canadian Museum of Flight at the Langley Airport (at Hangar No. 3 at 5333 – 216th Street) site houses some two dozen aircraft, from a 1937 WACO Cabin to a Tiger Moth and a Harvard; seven planes have been restored to flying status by the museum's volunteers.

At the corner of 216th and Milner is the restored Milner United Church, built in 1886. Continue on 216th Street across Highway 1A to **MURRAYVILLE**. Sharon United Church, with an old horse trough with water spout still working, is near the corner of 216th and 48th. Also at this corner is the Travellers Hotel, built in 1887 and restored to its original function. Nearby on Old Yale Road are the Murrayville School (1911) and two houses built circa 1907.

Various roads head south to Boundary Road, sometimes known as Zero Avenue. It parallels, usually no more than a few metres away, the border between Canada and the United States. Cenotaph-shaped boundary markers serve as mileposts; east of the Highway 13 border crossing, two roads—one Canadian, one American—run together, separated only by a wide ditch.

The broad prairie between the river and the boundary narrows now, edged by the Coast and Cascade mountains. To the north are the triplet communities of Abbotsford, Clearbrook and Matsqui, once separate settlements but now effectively one entity.

Abbotsford/Clearbrook/Matsqui

The Trethewey House at 2313 Ware Street, south of South Fraser Way in Clearbrook, is a farmhouse built in the 1920s from fir processed in a nearby sawmill on Mill Lake. It now houses the MSA (Matsqui-Sumas-Abbotsford) Museum and archives, with displays of Sto:lo traditions, and lumbering, pioneer and agricultural development. Not far distant (north on Highway 11 through Abbotsford, east on Clayburn Road) is the former brick-making town of **CLAYBURN**, founded in 1905. Yellow and red brick from Clayburn ovens was used for coke ovens as far east as Crowsnest Pass in the Rockies, and throughout the valley for houses and commercial buildings. Clay mining—in underground shafts sunk in the clay beds—and brick making at Clayburn began around 1905. It thrived through the pre-war building boom, survived a war and a depression and continued up and down until the 1960s. By no means a ghost town, Clayburn still contains buildings related to its brick-making days, including the restored red brick Clayburn Church, a number of brick makers' cottages and the old general store/post office.

A time-travelling Fraser Valley resident from even 30 years ago might find this part of the valley almost unrecognizable. The growing population of the Lower Mainland has sprawled into the area, transforming farm fields into housing developments linked to Vancouver by freeways that slice through rural neighbourhoods. Abbotsford area farmers now feel compelled to print brochures explaining how farming and subdivisions can co-exist. Yet the herds of dairy cows grazing on green pasture and the fields of berries that brought Abbotsford the title "Raspberry Capital of the World" are themselves the result of a massive change in the landscape.

River diversion, draining and dykes transformed much of the land between Abbotsford and Chilliwack from mosquito-infested swamp and oft-inundated flood plain to fertile farmland. At one time, Sumas Lake covered more than 6,000 hectares of valley land east of Abbotsford. In the early 1920s, dykes were built, the lake bed drained and a pump station built to keep the area dry. The Barrowtown Pump Station is the second station; built in 1985 for $25 million, it replaced the earlier station built in 1923. To reach the station, take Exit 106 on Highway 1 north to North Parallel Road, then follow the signs. Several plaques and cairns explain the history of the land-draining project.

The Vedder Canal was part of the project. The Chilliwack River was diverted into the canal, its waters contained within the canal banks so that spring floods would no longer cover the low-lying farms in the area.

Some of the first settlers on Sumas Prairie were Mennonites, invited to take up land by the first owners of the reclaimed flood plain. Like the Doukhobors who settled farther east, the Mennonites were not popular as settlers. Their determination to live by their own economic and social rules, their pacifism and the fact that their devotion to hard work and communal effort made them richer than neighbouring farmers made others resent them.

That unpopularity kept Mennonites on the move. Their arrival in British Columbia was part of a continued hegira that saw many move from the Netherlands to Poland to Russia to North America to South America and back to North America again. Mennonites settling in the Fraser Valley in the 1930s founded the settlements of Yarrow, Greendale and Vedder Crossing and farmed the fields nearby. Early experiments in growing vegetables failed; when the Mennonite farmers switched to small fruits, they succeeded. Along with Japanese Canadian farmers, they were the main raspberry growers in the area. After Canadians of Japanese descent were banished from the valley in World War II, Mennonites dominated small-fruit farming between Abbotsford and Chilliwack. Mennonite names and institutions are still widespread in the area: the Abbotsford area alone has close to 20 Mennonite churches, a seniors' home, a hospital for the chronically ill and several Mennonite schools. Mennonites have much to do with the prevailing conservative, Christian tenor of the valley's politics. Yarrow, one of the first Mennonite communities, south of Highway 1 near the Vedder Canal, is still a pleasantly rural community with simple white-painted houses and two Mennonite churches.

Not far away, on Old Yale Road, sometimes known as Majuba Hill Road, is a sign commemorating the old Yale wagon road and marking the start of several kilometres of hiking trail along this pioneer route through the Fraser Valley. Understandably, it runs along ground higher than the reclaimed farm fields.

VEDDER CROSSING, another community founded by the Mennonites, is now a service centre for Canadian Forces Base Chilliwack and the home of the Canadian Military Engineers Museum. The museum documents the work of military engineers from Placentia Bay in Newfoundland to Fort Rodd Hill in Victoria, from the 18th to the 20th century. The surrounding park contains equipment used by engineers at various times and replica log cabins of a type that an 1860s military engineer might have used.

Chilliwack

This area has been home to native peoples for thousands of years; the present-day city of Chilliwack is surrounded by First Nations reserves. The name *Chilliwack* is a local word; it means "going back upstream," a reference to the original homes of the Chilliwack (Ts'elxwiqw) people.

Yale Road from New Westminster to Yale, completed in 1875, was the making of Chilliwack; though, to begin with, mud in the rainy seasons and dust in the summer meant that the road would still be secondary to the steamboats that plied the Fraser. The intersection where Highway 1A/Yale Road crosses Wellington Avenue and Young Street is known as Five Corners; as early as the 1870s, it was the site of a blacksmith shop, hotel, public school and church. One of the few National Historic Sites in the valley is close by: Chilliwack's museum is now housed in its old City Hall (45820 Spadina), a stately 1912 building with columns and ornate detailing underlining the status residents saw ahead for Chilliwack.

East of Chilliwack the valley narrows, and road and rail north and south of the Fraser run together in the cleft between the mountain ranges. All lead to Hope, the town founded as a fur-trading post and vastly expanded in the gold rush. For information on Hope, see the Hope section later in this chapter.

FRASER VALLEY: NORTH OF THE RIVER

South of the Fraser, a number of highways lead through the valley between Vancouver and Chilliwack. North of the Fraser, the mountains crowd closer to the river, leaving only a narrow strip for settlement and for one major east-west road: Highway 7, also known as the Lougheed.

Maple Ridge and Area

This part of the guide begins at the Pitt River bridge on Highway 7.

The area north of the Fraser and east of the Pitt River promised good soil, but only after World War II did people solve problems of flooding. Postwar Dutch immigrants, led by Dr. Jan Blom, drained and dyked the area known as Pitt Polder, north of the Lougheed Highway and Pitt Meadows, then settled in to grow berries, bulbs and other produce. Today, a cairn on Neaves Road north of the Alouette River bridge commemorates that achievement. Only the occasional Dutch-style barn or house in the wide flat fields below the dykes, and some of the names on mailboxes or businesses, suggest the area's Dutch settlers.

Settlers who sought farmland came to **PITT MEADOWS** itself in 1873 but the town wasn't incorporated until 1914. Like many a small pioneer community, Pitt Meadows made do with one church building that served all residents, regardless of denomination. The United and Baptist churches still share this building at Harris and Ford roads. The Pitt Meadows Museum at 12294 Harris Road is in a former general store that has been in its present location since 1908. The museum society is working towards opening to the public the Hoffmann & Son machine shop and ditching business. Check for a walking tour of the Harris Road area.

The Katzie people live now on a reserve at the foot of Bonson Road in Pitt Meadows, along the river that has traditionally supplied them with salmon and a transportation route. They were the first residents of the area around **HANEY** and **MAPLE RIDGE**. Artifacts reflecting their history and other displays such as the history of Finnish and Japanese settlers are on display at the Maple Ridge Museum at 22520 – 116th Avenue. The museum, housed in the 1907 manager's house for Haney Brick and Tile, is at one end of a Fraser River Heritage Walk, a paved walkway that begins at the refurbished Port Haney wharf. Thomas Haney came to the north shore in 1876, bought land here and established, among other things, a brickworks that used blue clay dug from nearby deposits. The Port Haney Brick Company, later to become Haney Brick and Tile, used Chinese and native labourers, among others; the brickyard closed in 1977.

Haney House, at 11612 – 224th Street, was built in 1878 for Thomas and Annie Haney. The walking-tour route also includes a post office, several bank buildings, a church, a telephone office and, across the street from each other, a blacksmith shop that served local farmers and a garage and Ford cars agency that took over from a livery stable. Building dates range from 1906 to the 1930s.

The river served early residents well as a transportation route. As elsewhere, the coming of railway and roads changed the north shore's focus from water to land, but the logging industry continued to make use of both. The Abernethy and Lougheed Lumber Company, in the 1920s one of the largest logging companies in the province, brought logs down to the river booming grounds at the mouth of Kanaka Creek in **WHONNOCK**. Mills and log booms near Whonnock and Ruskin are reminders of those earlier logging days.

RUSKIN is named for writer John Ruskin, a strong supporter of the co-operative ideal in 19th-century England. The Canadian Co-operative Society opened a sawmill at Ruskin in 1897 and members of the co-op built the town. But co-operation eventually foundered. The mill went bankrupt in 1898.

Bits and pieces of the original Dewdney Trunk Road still show up on area maps, escaping the Fraser Valley trend of replacing street names with numbers. The road was surveyed by Edgar Dewdney, who came to British Columbia in 1859; he was best known for supervising, along with Walter Moberly, the building of the Dewdney Trail from Fort Hope to the Kootenays. On Dewdney Trunk Road is the Stave Falls Power House, where a historic gallery goes back to an earlier era of electric power, featuring a 1912 generating station and stories behind its construction and operation.

Mission

The Lougheed Highway crosses the Stave River beyond Ruskin and runs into Mission, a town of 35,000 that celebrated its centennial in 1992. Living here long before 1892 were the Sto:lo. Displays that detail their lives before and after contact are at the Mission Museum, at 33201 Second Avenue, along with other displays on area history. The museum is housed in a prefabricated 1907 structure that served as the Bank of Commerce building in early Mission. Later Sto:lo history and general information are presented at Fraser River Heritage Park just east of downtown Mission. The park includes Toti:lthet Centre, a First Nations learning centre and trade school.

Toti:lthet is housed on the grounds of the mission that gave the town its name. The first Oblate mission to the native people was established on the riverbank here in 1861, with a school for native and white children. The Sisters of St. Ann added a convent and girls' school to St. Mary's Mission in 1868. In 1892, the same year that the district of Mission was incorporated, the Grotto of Our Lady of Lourdes was consecrated with hundreds of natives participating. Times change: by the late 1950s, educators were questioning what many natives had always disliked—the religious residential school. Most of the buildings of the mission and school were demolished in 1965.

A reconstruction of the Grotto of Our Lady of Lourdes is on a walking tour of the park, as is a bell tower built in 2000 to house an 1875 bell.

The hill high above the town attracted another religious group. In 1957, monks of the Benedictine order established Westminster Abbey, a monastery, retreat and church with a bell tower visible for many kilometres.

A map highlighting Mission's historic buildings, which date from 1896 to 1940, hangs at the entrance to the Mission Museum, housed in a 1909 bank building at 33201 Second Avenue. Most of the buildings are on First, Second or Third Avenue, between Birch and Welton streets.

When developers began clearing land around a huge rock east of Mission, a Sto:lo archaeologist found artifacts such as pebble tools that date back as much

By the 1860s, the lives of First Nations people had undergone great change. This Fraser Valley group was called on to pose for the photographer in an attitude of prayer. (BCA E4419)

A child investigates the rabbit hutch at the Kilby Historic Site, near the junction of the Harrison and Fraser rivers, where Acton Kilby operated a general store in the since-vanished community of Harrison Mills.

as 9,000 years. The rock, known as Xa:ytem, the Transformer Stone or Hatzic Rock, is the centrepiece for the Xa:ytem Longhouse Interpretive Centre (35037 Lougheed Highway), where Sto:lo history, traditions and culture are featured. This is the place where, according to Sto:lo tradition, Xa:ls transformed three leaders into stone for not sharing the gifts given by the Creator; their life force is contained within the rock.

From Mission east, the mountains crowd closely to the road, and what farm fields there are lie between the road and the river. The CPR laid tracks north of the river in the 1880s, preferring this route to one through the marshier ground south of the river. The station of **HARRISON MILLS** was built at a point where people could easily cross the river. Passengers and freight did so directly by boat from Harrison Mills to the settlement at Chilliwack. A score of residents established a store and post, telegraph and express offices, building them on pilings connected by boardwalks to escape the almost yearly Fraser floods. Harrison Mills acquired its name from the sawmills in the neighbourhood and its prosperity from the steamer service that replaced the canoe-ferry, carrying people and farm produce from Chilliwack to the CPR station. When a new railway was built along the south bank of the Fraser, Harrison Mills declined.

Today, Acton Kilby's general store, restored as a historic site, serves as a reminder of Harrison's best days. The store was once a temperance hotel, built on pilings and linked to the railway station by a ramp to its second storey. Thomas Kilby converted it to a general store in 1910. Acton and Jessie Kilby took over in 1928, when Thomas died, and ran the store until they were in their eighties. Travellers can visit the store/hotel/post office and horse barn, south of the Lougheed near the eastern end of the Harrison River bridge. Those who wander away from the historic site will glimpse ruins of old buildings in the woods and the pilings of old docks in the river.

The river served as the first step after the Fraser River on one of the earliest routes to the Cariboo goldfields. In 1858, James Douglas not only persuaded men to work on a new route, he also persuaded them to pay for the privilege (the $25 they put up was to be refunded in goods at trailhead when they had completed their work) by convincing them that they would be the first into the gold-bearing country. Would-be miners went by boat up the Harrison River and Harrison Lake, then overland along the Lillooet River, then by boat and trail on to Lillooet. See page 80 for the Pemberton section of this chapter for more details.

Harrison Hot Springs

Legend has it that the hot springs on Harrison Lake were discovered when a miner fell into the lake right here and was delighted to find himself not frozen, but warmed—but this legend overlooks the fact that native people frequented these waters for thousands of years and that the native name for the lake means "hot water."

When the railway was built along the Fraser, entrepreneurs soon took advantage of the springs, building the first resort in 1886—the St. Alice Hotel, complete with bathhouse. Fire destroyed that hotel in 1920; the present hotel opened in 1926. The owners acquired rights to the hot springs at that time, with the proviso that a flow of not less than four gallons (about 18 litres) a minute from the spring should be available to the public, free, between 6 a.m. and 5 p.m. every day. The public still has access, but there is now an admission charge to the public pool. During World War II, the hotel served as a casualty retraining centre and as a convalescent home for women in the armed forces. Since the war, other hotels, motels and restaurants have been built at Harrison.

Just east on Highway 7, **AGASSIZ** is often overlooked in the rush to Harrison. Named "Ferny Coombe" by its first land pre-emptor, Lewis Agassiz, it was renamed when the CPR came through. It's the site of a federal agricultural research station founded in 1888. Agassiz's museum, in a wooden 1893 railway station, has been moved to the research station grounds at 6947 Lougheed Highway. A row of false-fronted small-town stores near the railway track preserves a turn-of-the-century feeling.

Some 15 kilometres east of Agassiz is the Wahlean Rest Area, with illustrated panels detailing the heritage of the Sto:lo people.

The highway east of Agassiz is a relatively new one, dating from the 1970s. It follows the river through the ever-narrowing valley to Highway 1, just north of Hope.

HOPE AND THE FRASER CANYON
Hope

Hope lies at the point where the Fraser River makes a right-angle turn, tumbling free from the canyon to the north and flowing westward through the Fraser Valley. At Hope, old and new transportation routes come together. The old native, fur-trading and government trails ended at Hope; modern Highways 1, 7, 3 and 5 intersect at or near the town.

Fort Hope was founded as a Hudson's Bay Company post in 1849, a stop on an all-British route between Fort Langley and Fort Kamloops, but it remained a small, quiet outpost until 1858 and the gold rush. Miners working their way upstream stopped at Hope for provisions, a rest and a moment to decide how they would get all the way to the Cariboo. Reminders of those gold-rush days, including a gold-ore concentrator, are displayed in the Hope Museum, on Water Avenue beside Highway 1. Hope's Christ Church, built in 1861, is said to be the oldest church in the province still at its original site, a block off Highway 1 on Fraser Avenue. The Fort Hope cairn, at Highway 1 and Wallace Street, marks the founding of the fort.

Hope's most interesting historic site comes from a later era. Follow signs in town to Kawkawa Lake Road and bear right on Othello Road to Coquihalla Canyon Provincial Recreation Area, where you will find a series of railway tunnels built against all odds. Engineer Andrew McCullough, surveying for a railway route after 1910, sought one through the Coquihalla River gorge to link sections of the Kettle Valley Railway that was to connect the West Kootenay to the coast. McCullough rigged a wicker basket with ropes and cables to swing out over the gorge, then made a decision to blast four tunnels through the rock walls of the canyon. The tunnels were built but floods plagued the line. Opened in 1916, it was closed in 1959 and was officially abandoned in 1961. Similar weather still poses problems, so the area is officially closed in winter. But a walk through the Othello-Quintette tunnels when water seeps down the rock and drips on the railbed or when snow lies heavy on the ground would probably show McCullough's achievement much more vividly than a sunny stroll. Hope marks the beginning of the Kettle Valley Railway, now a hiking and biking trail.

Gardens in the centre of town next to the town hall are dedicated to Japanese Canadians interned during World War II. Tashme, one camp that housed the internees, is located at Sunshine Valley, beyond the Hope Slide east of Hope. In 1965, a minor earthquake sent 46 million cubic metres of rock and debris, half a mountainside, spilling over the Hope-Princeton Highway. The huge scar from that slide, now greening, is still visible.

Cariboo gold-rush prospectors turned north at Hope, up the Fraser to the head of navigation at Yale and the trails that led to the goldfields. They were far from the first to use trails in this area. Most fur-trade and gold-rush trails followed paths the native peoples used for hunting, fishing or trading. Some 38 kilometres of the Hudson's Bay Company brigade trail, in use from about 1849 to 1859, have been declared a historic trail. For access points to the trail, check with the Hope infocentre.

Along the Fraser north of Hope, gold panners still occasionally work the sandbars revealed as the river falls in summer. One such location is Emory Bar, rich enough in 1858 to sustain a town of 500 gold seekers. As elsewhere on the river, the spasm of activity soon ended and miners moved on to other claims;

also as elsewhere, Chinese miners moved in to clean up what more impatient men had missed. During the Depression, the provincial government held training camps here, teaching placer mining, wilderness survival and first aid.

At low water, travellers can see a large sandbar 2.5 kilometres below Yale on the east bank of the river. Hill's Bar was the richest of the Fraser River bars; more than $2 million in gold was washed from the sand in just a year or two.

Yale

Yale was the head of navigation on the Fraser. Ahead lay the steep walls and turbulent waters of the canyon—and, after 1864, the Cariboo Road. In 1858, adventurer David Higgins described gold-rush Yale as "the busiest and the worst town in the colony," filled with both the god-fearing and the god-ignoring: gamblers, ruffians, drinkers, turncoats, highwaymen, thieves, murderers and painted women. A correspondent from the *London Times* suggested Yale was "so unsavoury—so exactly like its inhabitants . . . that we could not pitch our tents in or near it."

Today's Yale is much quieter, though proud of its gold-rush history. It is well worth an exploratory stop. The pioneer cemetery a few minutes south of town, below the highway on the east, was established in 1858; headstones date

In the 1880s, Yale was a wide-awake town as railway construction crews flooded in. The proprietor of Yale's 80-room California Hotel poses here with his family in front of his house. (BCA A3607)

back to 1862. One marks the resting place of one of the first white men born in Yale. In-town historic spots include St. John the Divine Church (circa 1859), restored to its original appearance in 2001; a national monument dedicated to Chinese railway workers employed in building the CPR and other lines; a national monument to the building of the Cariboo Wagon Road that started at Yale; a commemorative plaque for Barnard's Express (a stagecoach and freight service between Yale and the goldfields); and the Yale museum, in an 1868 house, with displays on native, gold-rush and railway history. Museum staff conduct walking tours of Yale.

In the river at Yale is Lady Franklin Rock. The wife of Arctic explorer Sir John Franklin, Jane Franklin travelled through the area in 1861, as part of a world tour.

The first suspension bridge at **ALEXANDRA**, 22 kilometres north of Yale, took the Cariboo Wagon Road across the Fraser Canyon; it opened in 1863. A second bridge that replaced the first in 1926 rests on the old bridge abutments. That bridge can still be seen from Alexandra Bridge Provincial Park, as can some remnants of the original Cariboo Road east of the bridge. Access to a 13-kilometre part of the Hudson's Bay brigade trail is from a clearing about 300 metres north of Alexandra Lodge.

The **FRASER CANYON** awed explorer Simon Fraser, who declared, notwithstanding the native trails and ladders visible on its walls, that no man should pass this way. The Hell's Gate Fishway Viewpoint 27 kilometres north of Yale is probably the best free vantage point, though it is increasingly difficult to see the canyon without resorting to the commercial air tram that crosses above the turbulent water. The canyon provided a major challenge to builders of both the Cariboo Road and the two railways that cling to its rocky walls. Travellers who look down upon the railway tracks can easily see why.

Beyond Hell's Gate, Highway 1 leaves the Fraser Canyon and enters the Interior plateau (see Chapter Six).

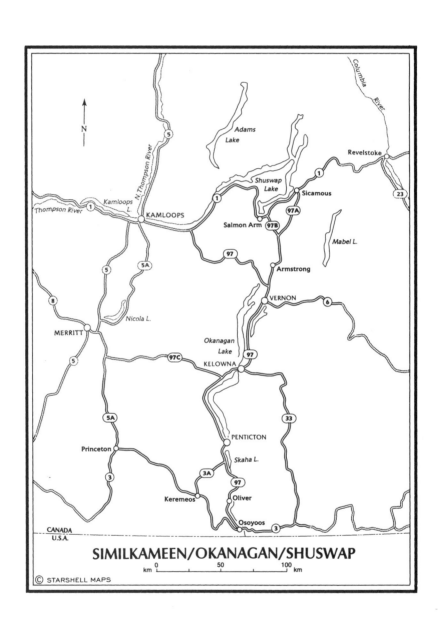

SIMILKAMEEN/OKANAGAN/SHUSWAP

km 0   50   100   km

© STARSHELL MAPS

SIMILKAMEEN/OKANAGAN/ SHUSWAP

Though the scale of recent development might surprise them, those who arrived in the sunny valleys of south-central British Columbia a hundred years ago would today find much that is familiar. Why would they be astonished that thousands of refugees from Prairie winters and crowded Ontario cities—and, indeed, from B.C.'s Lower Mainland—have found happy haven in the Okanagan, the Similkameen and the Shuswap? Land promoters at the turn of the century were already quite convinced that sunny skies, a moderate climate, blue lakes and fertile soil added up to Eden.

The sighting of the promised land is a theme that runs through the history of this region, a long rectangle lying halfway between the Rockies and the coast and stretching some 250 kilometres north from the United States border. Though the native people left us no written tracts proclaiming the virtues of the land they lived in for thousands of years before whites arrived (and perhaps they were the only residents not to wax eloquent in print), their stories and songs reveal their love for this land.

More than in any other area of interior British Columbia, the history of the Okanagan is a history of changing land use. From the relatively untouched land when the First Nations were in sole occupancy, the valley has been successively transformed by ranchers, orchardists, viniculturists and urban dwellers who hanker after large suburban or rural properties and who treasure hours spent on the golf course.

The valleys of the Similkameen, Okanagan and Shuswap were long the territories of native groups that bore those names. They fished in the rivers, hunted over the hills and traded at sites on the Similkameen and where Okanagan Lake narrows.

They first met white newcomers in the Okanagan Valley, which centres on the Okanagan River and on a string of narrow, north-south lakes. The valley runs from well below the American border to the low height of land that separates the Columbia River system from the basin of the Fraser River. A hundred and sixty years ago, explorers and fur traders who made their way north from the Columbia were delighted with the pasture promised by thick green grass that grew, they claimed, as high as a man's waist. Those traders used native routes for their brigade trail that led from the Columbia along the lakes and overland to Fort Kamloops.

The same grass that fed the brigades' horses in the 1850s attracted ranchers to the north end of the Okanagan. Here, express transportation companies that served the Cariboo wintered their horses while, farther south, pioneer ranchers raised cattle to feed the Cariboo miners. At first, the newcomers shared the land with the First Nations people: several parts of the valley were declared commonages, where all could pasture their animals.

Twenty years later, the coming of the railway and an efficient lake-boat system put an end to that communal use. The commonages were opened to preemption, and land speculators moved in, inspired by the promise they saw in the warm sunshine, dry weather, fertile soil and creeks and lakes of hill and valley.

Those energetic land promoters liberally interpreted that promise. "In order to be poor in the Okanagan," one truism ran, "you have to waste an awful lot of time and money." A story in *Westward Ho* magazine, following close upon a three-page exhortation to be a "self-winding man," was headlined "Another Eden Discovered in the West" and sang a paean to the business acumen, climate and conditions to be found in the Okanagan.

You would discover, proclaimed the article, none of the rough class inevitably drawn to mining districts. "Fruit growing does not attract the lazy man, and this district is peopled with a good class of well-educated and desireable settlers," it announced. The same magazine later ran an article entitled "Farming as a Cure to Insanity."

A promotion by the Central Okanagan Land and Orchard Company, selling land near Kelowna, reiterated the theme. Okanagan settlers, it said, were intelligent, educated and cultured English and Canadians. Water for the orchards was guaranteed, there was neither scrub nor rocks, the land was as level as the Prairies and the area was perfect for all fruits. "Can you," it asked rhetorically, "earn $3,000 a year as easily in any other way?"

The promises were bolstered in the Okanagan and Shuswap by relatively easy access to transportation. Like the Okanagan, the Shuswap is an area centred on rivers and lakes, but the waterways here drain to the Thompson and then to the Fraser, and this land gets more rain and is more heavily treed than the semi-desert Okanagan. The east-west valley was the logical route for the Canadian Pacific Railway. The last spike on the CPR was driven in 1885 at Craigellachie, just east of the Shuswap, and the towns of Sicamous and Salmon Arm took their life from the railway. In 1892, the CPR built south to Okanagan Landing and the ranching centre of Vernon, and established a shipyard where sternwheelers and tugs were built to serve the lakes.

Despite promises of ready markets on the Prairies and in the mining camps of the Boundary and Kootenays, of fertile soil and reliable irrigation that would ensure perfect orchards and of easy pickings (though not, of course, for the lazy), Okanagan orchards were not particularly successful until the development of disease-, weather- and pest-resistant species, and the establishment of reliable irrigation systems, in the 1920s. It took time for the Okanagan slogan "Intelligent men no longer pray for rain—they pay for it" to become a reality.

Meanwhile, the Similkameen Valley to the west was enjoying a boom of its own. The Similkameen River rises high in the Cascade Mountains east of Hope. Fed by scores of mountain creeks, it corkscrews down the mountains, then flows, wide, shallow and rapid, through a broad valley to the Okanagan River in Washington State. For the first half of its length, it cuts through mineral-rich rocks.

In the 1860s, when gold was discovered in the Boundary and the East Kootenay, Governor James Douglas feared American prospectors would take over the gold-bearing regions. He ordered a trail built from Hope east; the Dewdney Trail, the first official non-native east-west route, led miners through the Similkameen. From the 1890s to the 1930s, miners hacked at coal seams and copper ore near Princeton. With no little irony considering the conditions under which hardrock and coal miners worked, a turn-of-the-century brochure lauds the Similkameen climate as "dry and extremely healthful, being recommended for those suffering from consumption and lung diseases."

After the mines started operations, the Kettle Valley Railway was built across the southern Interior from Hope to the Okanagan, and several rail lines speared north from the United States, taking away ore to smelters and bringing in supplies.

In 1902, a Shuswap rancher wrote, "Nor is the place deficient in attractions for the tourist. Fish and game are plentiful, while nature has distributed her gifts with a lavish hand. The beauty of the surrounding hills, covered as they are with a velvety carpet of green, combined with the delightful scenery around the lake, produce an effect which cannot fail to arrest the attention of the beauty-loving eye." Hoping to develop tourism, the CPR built a hotel at Sicamous in the 1880s. Over the next decades, both the Okanagan and Shuswap became known as places where travellers could happily enjoy themselves.

That trend accelerated after World War II as Canada switched from steel rails to rubber tires. The Trans-Canada Highway through the Shuswap, the Hope-Princeton Highway connecting the Similkameen directly to the coast and the growth in Okanagan highways made the region seem much closer to both coast and Prairies. The pleasant climate and scenery attracted an increasing number of vacationers. Prairie people seeking escape from long cold winters retired in the valleys. So many came in the 1950s that Penticton named streets for Moose Jaw, Edmonton and Calgary, and a Kelowna radio station broadcast a program of Prairie news every day. An equivalent boom in the Similkameen, despite its being a less accessible area and lacking the long lakes of the Okanagan and Shuswap, arrived several decades later, and is now well under way.

In the 1980s and 1990s, development shifted again, this time to the Okanagan cities, which experienced rapid growth, and to the countryside, where orchards and open land were converted to subdivisions, country estates and vineyards. By the end of the 20th century, the southern Okanagan/Similkameen's dry grasslands landscape was considered among the most threatened in Canada, as hectares of bunchgrass and antelope-brush disappeared under lawns, asphalt and vines.

Though the language of present-day real estate promoters is somewhat more restrained than that of their early 1900s counterparts, the message hasn't changed. "This is paradise," they proclaim, and the influx of people that still goes on seems to bear them out.

————◆————

THE SIMILKAMEEN

In Manning Park east of Hope, 1,356-metre Allison Pass marks the division between the coast and the interior of the province. On one side, heavy rain or snow and tall coastal evergreens, ferns and salal; on the other, sunshine and scant precipitation, ponderosa pines and rabbit brush. The Similkameen region lies just east of the Cascade Mountains, on either side of the Similkameen River that flows down to join the Okanogan River south of the border with the United States.

This section of the guide begins on Highway 3 east of Hope, at Allison Pass in Manning Provincial Park.

The original Dewdney Trail followed a route farther north than the present highway from Hope to what is now Princeton. In the 1860s, pioneer rancher John Fall Allison hacked a rough trail through this pass and brought his wife, Susan, to homestead near present-day Princeton.

About 11 kilometres east of Sunday Summit, beyond Allison Pass, the mines of Copper Mountain are visible across the Similkameen River. An Okanagan native whose name was not recorded discovered the copper deposits in the early 1880s. Informed of the discovery by a friend, prospector Robert Allan "Volcanic" Brown—sometimes known as Crazy Brown—staked the area shortly thereafter, and began developing a mine. Brown is a British Columbia legend. Some years earlier, he had discovered what he considered to be the motherlode on a mountain by the north fork of the Kettle River in the Boundary region. Brown prepared to develop a mine and a town, but according to his own precepts. There would be no room for those scourges of modern life—churches, schools and banks. Railroads would converge from north, south, east and west to serve his utopia, and all who lived there would be rich and happy. Alas, his mountain produced neither gold nor silver, and Volcanic City was never more than an untested dream.

Older and perhaps wiser when he staked claims on Copper Mountain, Brown contented himself with selling out for a fair fortune and buying himself a set of gold teeth to celebrate. Some years later, he disappeared while prospecting in the Lower Mainland near Pitt Lake.

The town of Copper Mountain—also known as Allenby—around the mine that produced more than 2,500 million kilograms of copper between 1920 and 1957 has been virtually eradicated by strip mining on the site. Access is via Princeton; check at the local travel infocentre or the museum.

Just after the road hairpins across Whipsaw Creek (named for the old and back-breaking method of sawing lumber), a sign near the kilometre 112 marker points out the beginning of a 26-kilometre stretch of historic Hope Trail, the precursor of the Dewdney Trail.

Princeton

The highway follows a long, steep grade down into Princeton, renamed unimaginatively for the Prince of Wales when he visited Canada in the 1860s—even though he never made it anywhere near Princeton. The original First Nations settlement near here was called *Yak-Tulam*, anglicized to *Tulameen*, the Similkameen word for "red earth." First Nations people travelled here from as far away as Oregon and the Prairies to trade for this red ochre, much prized for ceremonial uses such as rock paintings and face decoration. White settlers changed the name to Vermilion Forks and Princeton's main street is called Vermilion Avenue. Red ochre can still be seen near the corner of Bridge and Fenchurch streets.

Storefronts downtown have been given a frontier look, and coal-car planters are set out along main streets. St. Paul's United Church and the courthouse date from the early settlement era. The Princeton and District Museum on Vermilion Avenue has an excellent fossil collection, as well as exhibits relating to First Nations, Chinese, mining and farming history. Check here for self-guided ghost-town tours and a historical walk.

The area around Princeton is honeycombed with mining tunnels, old placer sites and the remains of once-bustling mining towns, most of them built to serve coal or copper mines that tapped into the mineral seams that underlie the region. The mines and towns that once were the busiest are to the north, along the Tulameen River. To reach them, cross the Similkameen on Bridge Street, then turn left at the T-junction and follow Tulameen Avenue towards Coalmont and Tulameen. You'll see more ochre bluffs along this route.

About 15 kilometres along this road is **COALMONT**, once publicized, like so many others, as "the City of Destiny." Like so many others, it wasn't. Coal from Blakeburn, up the hill, the largest of the area's coal mines, was shipped via aerial tramway to Coalmont, then moved on by rail. When Blakeburn died, Coalmont went to sleep, though it has now been somewhat reawakened with the popularity of the Kettle Valley and Trans Canada Trail routes. The Coalmont Hotel, nicely though not overly renovated, was built in 1912.

GRANITE CITY (go straight on at the Coalmont Hotel, then follow Blakeburn Road about two kilometres to the Granite Creek road sign near the river) was born in 1885 when prospector Johnny Chance found gold nuggets in the creek. News of his find brought the usual ragtag assembly into the valley. Three hundred whites and a hundred Chinese immigrants arrived by the following spring, and some suggest that in 1886, Granite City was the fourth-largest town in British Columbia. Three years later the gold was gone, and so were those who sought it. Platinum was apparently found with the gold here, but miners threw it out since it had no known value. Legends persist of a platinum cache buried somewhere in the old townsite. Today, all that remains of Granite City are sagging boards and the marks of frenetic digging for the cache and for old bottles.

Follow Blakeburn Road up the steep hill beyond Granite City to the site of **BLAKEBURN**. On August 13, 1930, also known as Black Wednesday, an explosion in the No. 4 mine killed 45 workers. The town never recovered. A 1950s open-pit mine has destroyed most traces of Blakeburn, though you can still see the remnants of some buildings and of the towers that supported the aerial tramway.

Blakeburn Road also leads to the Kettle Valley Railway and Trans Canada trails, increasingly popular with hikers, bicyclists and snowmobilers. Beyond Granite City, watch for logging trucks and warning signs.

The guide now returns to Princeton.

Follow Highway 5A from Princeton across the Similkameen River, branch right on the Old Hedley Road, then bear left onto the Princeton-Summerland Road to follow a section of the Kettle Valley Railway route. To keep the grade below 2.2 percent, the rails swooped up in four wide loops from the Allison Creek Valley. Though the rails are long gone, the route of the railbed remains clear. It's now part of the Kettle Valley Trail. Motorists will find a scenic, part-paved, part-gravel, often washboarded, sometimes twisty back road that is best travelled in dry weather. It is 92 kilometres from Princeton to Summerland.

The Old Hedley Road runs close to the original route of the Dewdney Trail and is flanked by the remains of the first Hedley-Princeton Road, built in 1901. Since the cliffs rise precipitously above the river, it is difficult to see the old cribbing above. Better viewpoints are located on Highway 3 across the river. But this route north of the river is, though gravel, pleasantly quiet, winding through ponderosa pine, bunchgrass and rock slides.

The flats on the north side of the Similkameen were the location of Similkameen village sites, campsites and burial places. Smallpox cut Similkameen numbers in half in the mid-1800s. Plains and Similkameen natives traded at a site where the Old Hedley Road rejoins Highway 3. More than 50 sets of pictographs were inscribed along the north bank of the river, but some have been destroyed or defaced by vandals.

The Similkameen called a place in the hills east of Princeton *Snaza'ist,* "the striped rock place." Rock paintings, culturally modified trees and other evidence of long occupation have been found at the Snaza'ist village site. The striped rocks attracted prospectors in the 1890s and resulted in two major mines. Nickel Plate operated from 1905 to 1956, with a tally of $47 million in gold removed, and Mascot, a smaller claim in the middle of Nickel Plate, from 1934 on. Gold claims are still active in the area.

The ruins of Nickel Plate and Mascot perch on the rocks high above the town of **HEDLEY**, where travellers can see the remains of a three-kilometre aerial tramway and of Mascot Mine buildings 1,200 metres up on Lookout Mountain. The Upper Similkameen Indian band takes visitors by bus up the treacherous road to the site for three-hour tours through the old buildings and the mine site. Be warned: there are 500 steps in the various staircases. Tours start at the Snaza'ist Discovery Centre (which contains exhibits on the life of the Similkameen people), from mid-May through mid-October on the weekends, plus Thursdays and Fridays in summer.

Though fires in 1956 and 1957 destroyed much of the original town of Hedley, some historic buildings have been restored. Stop at the Hedley Heritage Museum for information (or to take a look at the mountain through a telescope), or ask in the village. Outdoor displays at the museum include an ore car and a section of flume; inside are displays of Hedley's history. Look for Grace United Church, which dates from 1903, and the pioneer cemetery just east of town.

About four kilometres east of Hedley, the restored St. Anne's Catholic Church is to the right of the road on Similkameen land. Entrance is by permission of the band.

Highway 3 continues along the river towards Keremeos. Five kilometres before that town, the Ashnola River Road branches south towards Cathedral Lakes Provincial Park, through an old wooden covered bridge of a type rare in British Columbia. The bridge conveyed traffic on the Vancouver, Victoria and Eastern Railway (VV&E) that speared north in 1907 as part of the Great Northern (Burlington Northern) Railway.

The name *Ashnola* is thought to be a version of *Acnu'lox*, a First Nations village here. A number of village and burial sites are in the vicinity.

Keremeos

The town of **KEREMEOS** has been in three different locations. Old Keremeos was about three kilometres north of the present site and Keremeos Centre just south of that. Both sites lost out when the Great Northern Railway followed a route through the present townsite. The fruit stands—fewer now than in the past— at the entrance to Keremeos indicate part of the town's history. Fruit growing began here in 1910 and thenceforth sustained the town. The South Similkameen Museum is in a former provincial police office and jail at Sixth Avenue and Sixth Street.

No one has ever proved it true or false, but a fine story suggests that Spanish soldiers ventured this far north in the middle of the 18th century. They are said to have camped near Keremeos until battles broke out between them and the natives. The soldiers killed many natives, then retreated—oddly—north, taking prisoners with them. They returned from putative camps somewhere near Kelowna the next spring and were ambushed near Keremeos. No Spaniard was left living. Their burial place, known as Spanish Mound, is said to be somewhere just northeast of Keremeos.

Is it more than a story? No records exist of any such invasion. But pictographs near Keremeos show men mounted on horses, and native stories tell of white-faced men who wore metal clothing. Weapons unlike others found in the area, the remains of an old log building found in 1863 near Kelowna and turquoise found near Okanagan Falls lend some credence to the account.

A kilometre north of Keremeos, Upper Bench Road branches east to pass the Keremeos Grist Mill, probably the only pioneer gristmill west of Ontario that still has its operating machinery and building more or less intact.

Barrington Price, pioneer rancher and trader, built the mill in 1877. At first, he installed a Barford Perkins Improved Corn Grinder but soon moved on to the Louisville Patent New Process grinding machinery that used a rolling stone cylinder instead of the traditional grindstones. Modern health-food advocates will groan to realize that this advance made white flour possible. The mill, which operated until the 1890s, is a historic site and has been nicely restored, with heritage wheat growing behind the mill and a garden in accordance with a diary written by a visitor in 1894–95. The gardens contain a number of heritage varieties of flowers, vegetables and fruit trees.

Upper Bench Road continues east, following the Dewdney Trail route; road builders took the trail along this bench to avoid the swampy land below.

THE OKANAGAN

East of Keremeos, Highways 3 and 3A leave the Similkameen and enter the Okanagan, a long north-south valley centred on the Okanagan River and a string of lakes.

Highway 3 dips south to enter the Okanagan through Richter Pass, near the United States border. The pass is named for Francis Xavier Richter, who left Bohemia for America at age 16, served as a scout in the American Civil War, escaped from Apaches who had captured him, sought gold in California and on the Columbia River, then ended up in the Similkameen, lured by reports of good cattle-grazing land. He settled near present-day Keremeos, where he ran 1,500 head of cattle on more than 4,000 hectares of land. In 1897, he established the first commercial orchard in the area. He died in 1910.

Osoyoos and Area

Spotted Lake (visible from Highway 3, 3.9 kilometres west of Osoyoos) was a healing place for Okanagan First Nations who lived nearby. The high concentration of Epsom salts, magnesium and other trace minerals in the mud relieved aches and pains. The salts could cure or help kill: during World War I, Chinese labourers skimmed salts from the lake to be shipped to munitions factories. The lake is privately owned and can be viewed only from the highway.

So-yoos is the Okanagan word for "gathered together," a reference to a native village south of the current town. David Stuart, travelling for the Pacific Fur Company in 1811, camped at the sandspit that cuts almost across Osoyoos Lake. A store was established at Osoyoos when the HBC abandoned Fort Okanogan in the U.S. The spit is now the site of Haynes Provincial Park, named for rancher John Carmichael Haynes. Haynes came through this area while travelling as a government gold commissioner and fell in love with it. He saw little joy from

This general store and gas station near Osoyoos, probably photographed in the early 1930s, is a classic example of the rural all-purpose store. (BCA C852)

this love: his first wife died when she was only 22, and Haynes himself died suddenly at 57. After his death, the house and ranch were foreclosed on.

Travellers entering Osoyoos today might look for some Spanish connection, since the town has adopted a Spanish theme expressed in quasi-Spanish architecture. But the theme has everything to do with modern tourism and nothing to do with history. History is on display at the Osoyoos Museum in the community park, with exhibits on First Nations, the irrigation system and the British Columbia Provincial Police. (Haynes was a member of this force, established in 1858.) Also at the park is an 1891 log schoolhouse.

The Nk'Mip Desert Cultural Centre, at 1000 Rancher Creek Road, is a project of the Okanagan First Nations that provides an insight into the land and the Okanagan world of legend. A Voices of the Past Pithouse transports the visitor to what life was like in a traditional winter home.

At Osoyoos, Highways 3 and 97 cross. Highway 3 continues east out of the Okanagan up Anarchist Mountain, named for a postmaster whose radical views cost him his job and who took up ranching on this hill. Follow Highway 97 north through the Okanagan Valley. About four kilometres north, a cairn east of the highway on 176th Street, opposite the Osoyoos cemetery, marks the site of the first colonial customs post in the Okanagan, opened in 1861 to deal with cattle drives coming north to new British Columbia ranches.

The Osoyoos Oxbows, which are bends in the river about 7.5 kilometres north of Osoyoos (take Road 22 east), show what the landscape used to look like before canals and flood control transformed the Okanagan River to a straight, controlled channel. Look for marshes, water, meadows and grassland. Continue on this road to see an old barn on stone foundations and a house from the Haynes Ranch. The road bears left through the Inkaneep Indian reserve, a traditional tribal gathering place. Circular depressions from winter pit houses and pictographs denote the sites of prehistoric villages. Ask at the band office for permission to see these sites, early trails and the remains at Inkaneep village of what was one of the oldest churches in B.C.

Oliver

The town of **OLIVER**, 20 kilometres north of Osoyoos, is a relative newcomer in the Okanagan, incorporated only in 1945. In 1919, provincial premier John Oliver backed a very expensive scheme to irrigate this area and have returning World War I servicemen and their families settle here. Irrigation was completed between 1920 and 1924. Water was carried from lakes in the hills by means of a 50-kilometre, concrete-lined ditch built by hand in 3.5-metre sections, and a siphon tube that stretched across the valley and under the present site of Oliver. Sections of the ditch and of wooden irrigation flumes are still visible along the highway and on the hillsides, and a disused irrigation canal disappears underground in the centre of the town. Oliver was once known as the "Cantaloupe Capital of Canada," but that title has presumably passed to some other community, since farmers here no longer grow the orange-fleshed melons.

The town museum at 9728 – 356th Street is housed in a jailhouse moved from the former mining town of Fairview; look for exhibits on irrigation, agriculture and mining. The Oliver Community Centre and infocentre are housed in the 1923 CPR station east of Highway 97 at the north end of town. A map of a heritage walking tour is available online or from the Oliver Chamber of Commerce infocentre.

To reach the **FAIRVIEW** site, follow 350th Avenue (Fairview Road) west from the centre of Oliver, crossing an irrigation canal, to 149th Street. Fairview once had the usual quota of hotels and bars, houses and stores; it flourished from 1888 to 1906. The huge wooden vats built for the mine mill are said to have had other uses. One was the site of town dances while the other, known as the Methodist Tub, was reserved for more sedate pastimes, such as refined parlour games.

But now all that marks the site of Fairview are display boards, some gravestones and an iron cross where the Presbyterian church, now moved to Okanagan Falls and serving as a United church, used to stand.

OKANAGAN FALLS, north of Oliver, is now misnamed. A dam built to control flooding in the valley transformed the falls to gentle rapids. This settlement was once known as Dogtown (*Skaha*, the name of the nearby lake, is Shuswap for "dog"), and a dog it initially was. Heavily promoted as yet another Eden and the hub of the Okanagan, it never prospered as other valley settlements did. The museum here is housed in the 1909 Bassett House, a prefabricated residence ordered through the Eaton's catalogue, shipped in pieces via rail, sternwheeler and horse-drawn wagon and assembled on-site.

Just to the north is **KALEDEN**, the winning name in a contest for a townsite laid out in 1909. "Kal" comes from the Greek *kalos*, "beautiful," and "Eden" is self-explanatory. The Grand Kaleden Hotel was built in 1912; today, it is just a fascinating skeleton. The 1912 general store has been converted into a bistro.

Penticton and North

Skaha Lake was once part of Okanagan Lake, but silt from creeks on either side of the lake created a delta that eventually separated the two. Penticton is built on that delta. Now a quintessential resort town with beaches, motels, restaurants and amusements, Penticton was first settled by the Okanagan First Nations, became at the turn of the century a service centre for ranchers and then expanded as part of the tree-fruit boom.

The first train on the Kettle Valley line into the Penticton area in 1912 was the signal for a land boom. Some 22 real estate companies went quickly to work, selling lots laid out with hope in the 1890s. In little more than a year, Penticton changed from a small village serving the few surrounding ranches and orchards to a busy town.

The KVR swung through Penticton, then continued east. At the lakeshore, goods and passengers transferred to lake boats to head north. Canadian Pacific had started a lake-boat service in 1893, connecting its Okanagan Landing/ Sicamous branch line with Okanagan settlements. Between then and 1972, nine sternwheelers and tugs plied the lakes. The sternwheeler SS *Sicamous* and the tug SS *Naramata* alone remain. The *Sicamous*, built at Okanagan Landing in 1914, was the largest sternwheeler on the lake, with room for 500 passengers and a fine dining lounge. In those days, when dollars were hard to come by and time even more precious for orchardist families, a trip on the *Sicamous* was the yearly vacation for many in the valley. As roads improved and people switched from rail to cars, the *Sicamous* did duty mainly as a freighter, carrying fruit from valley orchards to the CPR line. But the boat worked less and less, and was finally retired in 1937.

Eventually, the City of Penticton bought the sternwheeler, but it went through some hard times, semi-preserved and semi-rotting. Beached by the lakeshore at Okanagan Inland Marine Heritage Park, it is being restored, a lengthy and painstaking process. There's also a working KVR model here, as well as the *Naramata* (launched in 1914, more recently shipped south from Okanagan Landing), the stern saloon of the SS *Okanagan* (1907) and Canadian National Tug No. 6, all being restored.

Also in Penticton is the R. N. Atkinson Museum (785 Main Street), with collections of Okanagan First Nations history, early settler artifacts, militaria and natural history. A monument to Andrew McCulloch, of KVR fame, stands in Gyro Park. The Leir House, at 220 Manor Park Avenue, built in 1927 and a fine example of an upper-class residence, houses the Penticton and District Community Arts Council and other arts-related organizations.

A road angling northeast from the east side of Penticton leads to Naramata, a small community on the east shore of the lake, founded, as were Summerland and Peachland, by promoter John Moore Robinson. Robinson first thought to call the town Brighton Beach, but his belief in spiritualism dictated otherwise. At a séance, he heard the word *naramatah* spoken through a medium by a dead Sioux chief; the name of the chief's wife, it meant "Smile of Manitou." For

J. M., it was a message. He so named his new town. It became his favourite of the towns he founded: he moved to Naramata in 1907 and died there in 1943.

Robinson built the Hotel Naramata in 1908. It has now been restored, rather luxuriously, as the 12-room Naramata Heritage Inn and Spa. The Naramata Museum is in the old fire hall on Robinson Street; check out the mural on the side of the fire hall, a copy of a 1910 poster. Just northeast of the village, the Kettle Valley Railway bed curves away on its run towards Kelowna: there is good walking and biking here. If you are more of a driver than a walker, follow the not-so-great-gravel North Naramata Road 19 kilometres to Chute Lake (some old KVR buildings remain at Chute Lake Resort), and drive from there along the railbed for a further 17 kilometres to the Bellview Creek bridge, which is definitely not for motor vehicles.

To go north up the Okanagan Valley from Penticton, take Highway 97. The Pacific Agri-Food Research Centre is just south of Summerland. The station was opened in 1914 to try to improve forage, grain, vegetable, flower and tobacco crops and to increase yields of poultry, sheep, pigs, bees and fruit. Staff used horses to work the 160 hectares until 1946, when the first tractors were bought. Over the years, staff have found cures for serious apple and cherry diseases; developed, among others, the Spartan variety of apples; vastly improved storage procedures for apples and pears; and worked on many other advances that have improved agriculture in the valley and elsewhere. The heritage gardens at the station, started in 1914, and the original superintendent's house, are open to the public in July and August.

The impressive Trout Creek KVR bridge is visible from the grounds of the research centre. In 1911, engineers on the KVR decided the railway must bypass Summerland since the deep canyon of Trout Creek lay between tracks and town. Residents protested vigorously and won the day: the KVR crossed the creek on the highest bridge along the entire route, on a trestle 188 metres long and 73 metres high. Timber for the trestle approaches to the steel bridge was cut at a local sawmill opened for just this purpose.

The Kettle Valley Steam Train uses the revitalized KVR right-of-way. A 1912 steam locomotive pulls 1950s passenger coaches and open-air cars on a

10-kilometre stretch from Prairie Valley Station, off Prairie Valley Road west of Summerland, May to October. The train crosses the Trout Creek bridge.

The benches above **SUMMERLAND** were reserved as a commonage for whites and natives until 1889, when the area was opened to individual ownership. In 1906, J. M. Robinson subdivided the land and advertised yet another "heaven on earth, with summer weather forever." Summerland's museum (9521 Wharton, next to the library) contains early settlement artifacts, KVR artifacts and displays including a scale model of the railway, plus a 15-metre mural that traces the past from pre-contact to modern times. The museum or infocentre can provide information on historic sites and buildings, including stone St. Stephen's Church (1909).

PEACHLAND was the first of entrepreneur Robinson's promotions. Like many another turn-of-the-century immigrant, Robinson came seeking gold and stayed for gold of another sort. He arrived in British Columbia from Manitoba in 1897 and quickly found that prospecting was a disappointment. Travelling along the Okanagan lakeshore, he stopped at an isolated homestead and tasted homegrown peaches of such sweetness that he immediately declared the land's potential. He claimed benchland above the lake, subdivided it into four-hectare lots and put the lots on sale as—what else?—a new Eden. Though, to be fair, this was Robinson's *first* new Eden.

Peachland's museum is in a former Baptist church, an eight-sided wooden building dating from 1910. In it, among other displays, are photographs showing the development of orchard land in the area and another scale model of the KVR.

In about 1817, North West Company fur trader Alexander Ross was at the Rivière de Jacques near present-day Peachland when Shuswap Chief Short Legs was carried into camp badly mauled by a bear. Ross cut off flapping parts of Short Leg's scalp and tried to dress the wound. The chief's skull was also fractured; eight days later, Ross extracted a five-centimetre piece of bone plus several smaller pieces through holes in the skull. The wound closed and healed, except for a small spot "about the size of an English shilling." Short Legs was again on horseback, hunting, six weeks later. Trepanier Creek and the hamlet of Trepanier are named for this wilderness attempt at skull surgery.

John Fall Allison and Susan Allison arrived on the shores of Okanagan Lake in the 1870s to take up ranching on land John Allison claimed near present-day **WESTBANK**. "I led a perfectly idyllic life at this time," wrote Susan, extolling the time spent fishing, idling on boats and trying to keep their pet deer from swimming out and tipping the boat. She mentions five "neighbours" on a long stretch of lake and suggests that the area was rapidly getting settled—a concern all too familiar to modern Okanaganites. Westbank grew when land promoter Ulysses G. Grant, nephew of the Civil War general, bought and subdivided the land into orchard and town lots. The Westbank Museum, near the infocentre, is at 2736 Lower Glenrosa.

Kelowna and Area

Just before the bridge to Kelowna, a cairn at the eastern edge of Westside commemorates the brigades that often camped here overnight. The Hudson's Bay brigade trail went past the native settlement on Siwash Point, at the narrowest point on the lake, a traditional crossing place for natives, then whites. But the horses could not swim the lake here, so the trail continued up the west side of the lake. To see some of the remaining trail, follow Westside Road (turn west at the traffic lights south of the bridge across Okanagan Lake).

The brigade trail followed older native trails along Okanagan Lake. Company employees took furs from Fort St. James and the northern district by boat to Alexandria, on the Fraser. They continued by horse brigade to Fort Kamloops, where herds of horses were pastured, then overland to Okanagan Lake, the Okanagan River and Fort Okanogan. There, the brigade switched to boats once more for the final mile to Fort Vancouver on the Columbia River. On the return journey, they brought supplies and trade goods back into the country. The Vernon branch of the Okanagan Historical Society has done an excellent job of tracing the route of the trail, used between 1826 and 1847; you may be able to find a booklet that describes the route and what can be seen of it today. Some portions of the old trail are marked by pieces of white metal nailed to trees and by the occasional aluminum marker.

One of the more interesting sections of the trail crawled along the edge

of Mauvais Rocher, about half a kilometre north of Deighton Road, 25.6 kilometres north of Highway 97 near Nahun. At Nahun also are the remains of the steamer landing from the days before road and rail, when boats served the lakeside communities. Besides this historic evidence, Westside Road provides a pleasant drive—though the curving narrow stretches may not be to everyone's taste—along the quiet side of Okanagan Lake.

The new five-lane floating bridge that crosses Okanagan Lake between Westside and Kelowna is the successor to a bridge and to boats that used to cross the narrows. Okanagan natives used canoes; later settlers tried crossing by rowboats, their horses swimming behind. In 1885, a small barge that could carry up to five horses became the first commercial boat at the crossing; if the not-so-seaworthy barge ran into trouble, the horses were pushed overboard to swim for shore. In 1904, a steam launch took over service, followed by a variety of boats and scows, culminating in the 15-car MV *Kelowna-Westbank* in 1927. By 1950, four shuttle boats ferried traffic across the lake. Traffic continued to grow and the government, headed by Kelowna resident Premier W. A. C. Bennett, decided to build a bridge.

The first floating bridge—necessary because the lake reaches a depth of up to 60 metres here—was opened in 1958. A bottleneck as Kelowna and its traffic grew, it was replaced in 2008.

Eight buildings— four from this now-tranquil site and four historic buildings moved here from elsewhere—sit amid trees at Kelowna's Pandosy Mission.

126

The original fur-trader's settlement here was across the lake from the native village. August Gillard, one of the first white settlers, was a big, dark, rough and heavily bearded man who lived in a half-shanty, half-underground dwelling. Perhaps Kelowna's name came from the Okanagan word for grizzly bear, applied to this uncouth settler. Or perhaps it predated Gillard, for a village with a similar name existed here long before Gillard arrived.

Black bear there may have been in the area, but perhaps black robes had a greater impact on the region. Oblate priest Charles Pandosy and two student priests arrived here in 1859. They camped for the winter 30 kilometres north, where they ate moss, roots, berries and even their own horses to keep from starving. In the spring, they moved south. In the fall, they established a permanent mission on Mission Creek. That mission is now a historic site. To reach it, turn south off Highway 97 at Orchard Park Shopping Centre onto Benvoulin Road and drive four kilometres. The original Oblate chapel, built of hand-hewn logs and handmade nails, still stands, as do several other mission buildings. Also on the site are the McDougall and Chretien early settlers' houses, moved here from their original site near Kelowna.

Along the way at 2279 Benvoulin Road is Benvoulin Heritage Church, an 1892 Gothic Revival Presbyterian church nicely restored, with xeriscaped gardens that show how Okanagan residents can garden without using much water. Benvoulin Heritage Park also contains an 1890s house moved to this site.

The restoration of Brents Grist Mill (1871) at the corner of Leckie Road and Dilworth Drive is now under way. It's considered to be the oldest surviving gristmill in the province.

A heritage driving-tour brochure is available from infocentres or the Okanagan Heritage Museum at 470 Queensway. The museum includes displays of Okanagan First Nations history and a replica of a pioneer Chinese grocery store and an 1860s trading post.

Among the historical highlights in downtown Kelowna are brick buildings along the first three blocks of Bernard Avenue, turn-of-the-century homes along Abbott Street, later and more modest homes on Laurier Avenue, the Cathedral Church of St. Michael and All Angels (1913, built of local stone) and the 1927 railway station.

Between 1904 and 1914, thousands of benchland hectares were irrigated by flumes and ditches that brought water from the hills, and orchards were planted. The Laurel Packinghouse, built in 1917 of locally made brick, is downtown at 1305 Ellis Street. The BC Orchard Industry Museum and the BC Wine Museum in this building contain displays of irrigation, fruit picking, pruning, packing, processing and shipping, as well as a small display on the much newer Okanagan industry of winemaking. The valley's transitions from pristine hills to ranches to orchards to vineyards are all evident at the museums.

Nearby is the Okanagan Military Museum at 1424 Ellis, in the Memorial Arena building.

Guisachan House (south from Highway 97 on Gordon Drive, right on Cameron Road) was home in the 1890s to Lord and Lady Aberdeen. He was Governor General of Canada from 1893 to 1898. The Aberdeens bought the surrounding ranch sight unseen, then turned it over to Ishbel Aberdeen's brother to manage. They arrived by boat one moonlit night and walked the few kilometres to the ranch; in her book *Through Canada with a Kodak*, Lady Aberdeen pays tribute to the beauty of the spot. Convinced the future of the Okanagan lay with orchards, Lord Aberdeen subdivided some of the land here and at Coldstream Ranch to the north, and was the first to plant a commercial orchard. That the orchard failed and had to be torn out does not detract from Aberdeen's foresight. In 1893, the CPR named its first Okanagan steamboat the *Aberdeen*. The one-hectare Edwardian gardens here, established by later resident Elaine Cameron, have been restored to their 1920s splendour, with displays of journals and photos of the time. Also on the property are the McDougall House (1886), built by a First Nations patriarch, and a milk shed. Both were moved here when they were threatened by development.

To see some of the original orchard land, turn off Highway 97 north of the city centre onto Gordon Road, then turn left onto KLO Road (named for the development company the Kelowna Land and Orchard Company). Orchard land lies below KLO Road; to reach good viewpoints, turn onto McCulloch Road or follow East Kelowna Road off KLO Road. Along this route you will also see landscape change: some orchards have been overtaken by housing developments, while bulldozers have ripped out others for golf courses, leaving just a narrow screen of trees.

Railway buffs can rejoin the Kettle Valley Railway route near here, to walk or cycle one of its more interesting sections. Several routes are possible. On weekends and at other times when logging roads are open to the public, and if you don't mind gravel, turn from KLO Road onto McCulloch Road at the East Kelowna Community Hall. In about seven kilometres, cross the KLO Creek bridge and a kilometre later, turn right at a road that directs you towards Myra Forest Service Road. Follow this road to a parking lot; park and walk about 15 minutes to the first trestle. It's 12 kilometres one way to see this part of the line.

Twelve of the justly famous trestles of Myra Canyon were destroyed by a wildfire that swept through the area and into Kelowna's outskirts in 2003; though it was first thought that the trestles could not be rebuilt, the governments did come through with sufficient money for the huge job and, in 2008, the last nails were hammered into the restored trestles. Myra Canyon is a National Historic Site. Though a direct line from Penticton to Midway would have been much shorter, the steep terrain between the two towns dictated that the rails follow this long loop north, then south again along the Kettle River.

Two other routes lead you to the KVR. Take KLO Road to McCulloch, McCulloch to June Springs, which becomes Little White Forestry Road—a rough route. About four kilometres farther on, turn left and park: the rail route is in front of you. Or, follow Lakeshore Road south along the east side of Okanagan Lake to Chute Lake Road; turn left on Hedeman, then right on Gillard Forest Service Road. Some 8.5 kilometres on, you'll see the KVR route at a major intersection. Turn right to head for the Chute Lake Resort, left for four kilometres for more tunnels and trestles.

Highway 33 runs east, then south from Kelowna, through areas that were once farms but are increasingly suburbs of the city, towards Rock Creek on the edge of the Boundary country. Halfway to Rock Creek are **CARMI**, a short-lived mining town, and **BEAVERDELL**, where the owners of the Beaverdell Hotel (perhaps once a brothel) boast that the hotel contains B.C.'s oldest pub in continuous operation—which must make for some very tired bartenders.

Back at Highway 97, north of Kelowna, the road leaves Okanagan Lake and parallels Wood and Kalamalka lakes on its way to Vernon.

Just before Wood Lake is **WINFIELD**, where the Lake Country Museum at Winfield has displays of area history. Wood and Kalamalka lakes were once known as *Chelootsoos*, "long lake cut in the middle." A canal built in 1908 cuts through the narrow neck of land between the lakes.

Thirty-seven years before Japanese Canadians were considered aliens in this land, the small Okanagan town of **OYAMA** was named for Prince Iwao Oyama, the Japanese field marshal who captured Port Arthur in the first Sino-Japanese War, and who was commander of Manchuria in the Russo-Japanese War.

Vernon and Area

From Vernon, follow 25th Avenue south to Okanagan Landing, the terminus of a CPR branch line that linked Okanagan Lake to the main line at Sicamous in 1892. From the 1880s, various boats churned along the lake between fledgling settlements and ranches. Captain D. T. Shorts, his name noted in Shorts Creek, was one of the first to start a lake service, rowing or sailing various boats on nine-day return trips along the lake. In 1886, he launched a kerosene-powered boat, borrowing, or so legend has it, enough kerosene at every stop along the way to complete his trip. Perhaps it was the people at these stops who convinced him to convert his boat into a wood-burner. Shorts ran the *Jubilee* for two years; she sank in ice in 1889. Competitors launched their own services, and Shorts responded with the steamer *Penticton*. But his days on the lake were numbered. On May 22, 1893, when the rail line to Vernon was opened, the steamer *Aberdeen* was launched from the new CPR shipyard at Okanagan Landing. Until the 1920s, when the railway was extended to Kelowna, Okanagan Landing was the main port in the north end of the valley.

The steel-hulled tug *Naramata*, which ended her working life in 1967, was beached at Okanagan Landing for some years; the tug is now being restored on the Penticton lakeshore (see page 121). At the landing, the railway station is being renovated as part of a new community hall. But the landing is no longer a separate town: in 1993, it joined Vernon.

Like many another B.C. community, Vernon was founded by those who came to mine and then stayed to farm. Forbes and Charles Vernon pre-empted 400 hectares of bunchgrass lands in 1864 and started the first ranch in the area. Not long after, the owners of Barnard's Express freight and stage line, working in the Cariboo, bought a ranch near here, called it the B. X. and raised and wintered horses for their stagecoaches and wagons. Barnard Avenue in downtown Vernon is named for these early ranchers.

The Greater Vernon Museum and Archives is in the Civic Centre complex

Turn-of-the-century houses on Vernon's East Hill remain from the days when the city was the economic centre of the Okanagan Valley.

at 3009 – 32nd Avenue; ask for a walking-tour guide here and for information on 27 murals throughout the downtown that describe the city's past. In downtown Vernon, a walk along 30th (Barnard) Avenue between 34th and 27th streets passes a number of historic buildings. They include a commercial building at 3309 – 30th, one of the oldest buildings on the avenue and Vernon's original post office from 1892 to 1991; an 1894 building at 3124 – 30th that has an anvil symbol to represent its original use as a hardware store; a former jeweller's store at 3122 – 30th built in 1894; the 1912 Union Bank building at 3025 – 30th; the 1911 post office at 3001 – 30th; the Kalamalka Hotel at 3004 – 30th; and the Vernon courthouse, at 3001 – 27th Street, built between 1911 and 1914 of Okanagan granite.

Polson Park contains the oldest surviving brick schoolhouse in the B.C. interior, built in 1893. The log cabin of early settler Luc Girouard (circa 1860s) is at the west end of 30th Avenue.

Heritage maps of Vernon show a number of other heritage commercial and residential buildings and landscapes. The Grey Canal, dug to irrigate orchard land, cuts behind Dixon Dam Road. The hills behind Vernon are dotted with historic barns, houses, a bunkhouse, a packing house and other points of interest.

Perhaps the best place to catch a glimpse of turn-of-the-century ranching

is at the O'Keefe Ranch, beside Highway 97 about 12 kilometres northwest of Vernon. Cornelius O'Keefe drove cattle between Oregon and the Big Bend of the Columbia during the Big Bend gold rush in the 1860s. Impressed by the land, he returned the next year and pre-empted it. He and partner Thomas Greenhow then expanded the O'Keefe Ranch to more than 8,000 hectares. In 1967, a hundred years after O'Keefe first saw this land, his son Tierney opened the ranch buildings and machinery displays to the public. The ranch, now a non-profit historic site, contains the ranch buildings, an 1886 church (the first Roman Catholic church in the north valley) and a general store opened in 1872.

The Vernons sold their ranch in 1891 to Lord and Lady Aberdeen, who renamed it Coldstream. They planted orchards and hops; until 1912, when the land was turned to orchards, the ranch produced most of the hops grown in B.C. To find the Coldstream Ranch, follow Highway 6 east from the centre of Vernon to its junction with Kalamalka Road. The Coldstream cemetery is off Kalamalka at the end of Howe Road, by the creek. An irrigation canal runs on the other side of the creek.

Highway 6 leads east from Vernon through the Coldstream to **LUMBY**, first settled by Quebecois loggers and lumber workers in the 1880s. Once into the

Monashees, the highway passes abandoned mining camps that attracted gold seekers in the 1870s and 1880s. A few mouldering logs along Monashee Creek east of **CHERRYVILLE** tell a story of unfounded hope. Storytellers speak of the lost silver lead, a rich vein of silver ore that was found, worked, followed—and lost somewhere in the rocks near Cherryville. Like many another phantom vein, it is supposed to lead to a motherlode, also the origin of placer gold swept down the Monashee creeks.

The Cherryville Museum, financed and built through a huge volunteer effort in this community of 1,000, is at the Goldpanner Campground. You can also try your luck panning in the river here.

North again from Vernon, Highway 97A leads to **ARMSTRONG**. The tracks of the CPR's Shuswap and Okanagan railway run down the main street of this town, which was created around the coming of the rails. Early white settlers took up land north of here but, when the railway followed a different route, merchants created a new community in the cedar swamp where Armstrong now stands. Drained, the land rewarded effort: it is extremely fertile. Vegetable gardens, orchards and dairy farms all prosper. Dutch immigrants who arrived after World War I lent their cheese-making knowledge, and Armstrong became well known for its cheese.

A cattle man shows off his prize bull at Armstrong's fair in the 1940s; the fair is a long-lasting tradition, now running annually for more than 100 years. (BCA C4270)

The blue and white Armstrong Hotel (1892) is at the corner of Pleasant Valley Road and Okanagan Street. Farther along Pleasant Valley Road is Memorial Park, where a cairn commemorates the achievements of Catherine Schubert, the only woman to make the journey with the Overlanders who struggled across the prairies and the mountains in an attempt to reach the Cariboo in 1862–63. The small mountain east of Armstrong is named for Catherine's daughter, Rose, born when the Overlanders reached what is now Kamloops.

The Armstrong-Spallumcheen Museum, at Pleasant Valley Road and Bridge Street, tells the story of the area since 1892. The Old School House, now a restaurant, is said to be mainland B.C.'s oldest standing schoolhouse.

THE SHUSWAP

About two kilometres north of Armstrong, a sign marks the barely noticeable divide that separates the watershed of the Columbia River, including the Okanagan Valley, from that of the Fraser, which drains the Shuswap area. The Shuswap takes its name from the Shuswap First Nations whose territory this is. The area is bounded on the west by the dry country of the Interior plateau and on the east by the Monashee Mountains, and defined by long narrow lakes.

Enderby

Enderby, at the south end of the Shuswap region where Highways 97A and 97B meet, is the Shuswap point closest to the Okanagan—a fact not lost on engineers who wanted to build a canal between the two areas in the 1880s so that steamboats could pass from the Shuswap River system to the Okanagan Valley. But the cost was too high and the land in the area was released for pre-emption instead. First known as Steamboat Landing, Enderby was renamed when—or so they say—a group of women having tea near the river, then in flood, were moved by the recitation of a poem that chronicled the flooding of the English town of Enderby in the 16th century. It's still a pleasant, quiet town, with a number of buildings that date back to circa 1900.

Farmers in this vicinity grew wheat, had it ground at a nearby gristmill and exported it as far as the Orient. Enderby flourished with the building of a sawmill in about 1906 then sagged as timber mill and gristmill closed in the early 1920s.

The Enderby Museum, at *the* traffic light, offers walking-tour brochures. Changing displays at the museum cover such topics as native history, logging, farming, local arts and culture, and transportation. Cliff Avenue, off Highway 97, has some interesting buildings: City Hall at 619 Cliff was built of Enderby bricks in 1909; a clothing and dry-goods store operated at 606 Cliff from 1906; 514 Cliff has been a hardware store since 1911. St. Andrews United Church (1906) is at 1110 Belvedere, and St. George's Anglican is at 602 Knight. The main building of St. George's dates from 1891, the parish hall from 1910 and the manse from 1912. Houses at 806, 800 and 706 Sicamous Street were built by the lumber company for management; those at 709, 713, 715 and 721 Hubert were built for employees.

The Jim Watt heritage walk along the Shuswap River is bordered by signs that depict the history of sites along the river.

The "back Enderby road" (ask locally) passes two fine old farmhouses that date to pioneer days. To reach Lansdowne cemetery, last home of area pioneers, take McLeery Road (off Highway 97A, halfway between Enderby and Armstrong) and bear left.

Shuswap Lake

Highway 97A and the Shuswap Okanagan Railway right-of-way flank the Shuswap River and Mara Lake north to SICAMOUS on Shuswap Lake. Sicamous is at Sicamous Narrows, between Mara and Shuswap lakes. The Eagle Valley Museum is in Finlayson Park. The steel tug MV *Stephanie* and barge are what remains of freight service on the Shuswap; they leave Sicamous three times a week headed for the end of Seymour Arm, first settled in the Big Bend gold-rush era of the late 1860s. Artist Charles Collings arrived at the Seymour Arm townsite in 1910, to build with his family his "Manor in the Wilderness." Now restored as the Seymour Arm Hotel, the house still stands, as do a few old cabins.

Long a junction point for native trails, Sicamous was and is the junction of north-south and east-west roads and railways. The last spike on the Canadian Pacific Railway between eastern Canada and the Pacific coast was driven at

CRAIGELLACHIE, 25.5 kilometres east of Sicamous, in 1885. Follow Highway 1 east to a cairn, plaque and small park.

Also worth seeing is the Malakwa suspension bridge, a block from the railway tracks in **MALAKWA**, built in 1915 and later upgraded so children could cross the river to go to school and farmers could take produce to market.

The four arms of Shuswap Lake—Salmon, Anstey, Shuswap and Seymour—form a wobbly north-south X. Highway 1 leads southwest from Sicamous along the Salmon Arm of Shuswap Lake to the town of **SALMON ARM**, which began as a railway camp and continued as a logging centre, then became a fruit-growing and dairying centre. The Shuswap Centre, also known as Knucwetwecw, includes an interpretive centre and a full-size replica of a traditional winter village. The centre is now under development but is visitable by request.

Four kilometres east of Salmon Arm, just off Highway 1 on Highway 97B, the R. J. Haney Village and Museum features a variety of buildings that were moved here; these include a restored farmhouse (circa 1910), the Mt. Ida church (circa 1911), a Chinese cook's house and a 1918 schoolhouse, as well as several squared-log buildings and old farm machinery. Check out the rhubarb crisp at the tea room (open mid-May to the end September).

South of Salmon Arm, the Deep Creek Tool Museum houses antique tools, engines and equipment. North of town, you'll find the White Post Auto Museum at **TAPPEN**, which houses antique cars.

FALKLAND, southwest of Salmon Arm, is home to the Falkland and District Heritage Park Museum, a one-hectare site with historic buildings and artifacts, including a church, a caboose and a picturesque blacksmith's log cabin built to serve a gypsum mine that operated around 1900. The mine used a kilometre-long aerial conveyor cable system to bring the gypsum from the mine to railway hopper cars.

SORRENTO, northwest of Salmon Arm on Highway 1, dates to 1910, when orchards were planted in the vicinity. Jim's Ford Corral Museum near Sorrento presents an eclectic collection of gas-station memorabilia, farm equipment and scale-model toys. The nearby Notch Hill Historic Site contains various buildings under ongoing restoration, including a small white church built circa 1905, and

A freight train passes Craigellachie, the site where railway executives drove the official last spike on the CPR.

a one-room schoolhouse built in 1915. About eight kilometres west of town, the Squilax bridge crosses the Little River on a road signposted to north Shuswap points. The road continues towards Anglemont and Seymour Arm. At Scotch Creek on this road, check out T & L Reflections, a little museum in a log cabin and another building constructed in 1910 and 1918.

Back on Highway 1, about a kilometre west of the bridge, the Squilax General Store dates from the 1940s. A hostel is housed in three railway cabooses here.

CHASE lies at the end of Little Shuswap Lake and at the western end of the Shuswap region. Whitfield Chase, yet another disgruntled goldrusher, arrived here in 1865. After the CPR was built, Chase was a turnaround point for helper engines powering trains over the hill east of the town, en route to Salmon Arm and Revelstoke. Some old-style wooden-fronted buildings still stand along the main street. A museum is housed in a pioneer church on the way into town. Just west of town, at the Chase Creek Rest Area, a sign details First Nations heritage including, descriptions of *keekwillies*, underground winter homes of the Secwepemc.

West of Chase, Highway 1 leaves the Shuswap and enters the dry rolling hills of the Interior plateau.

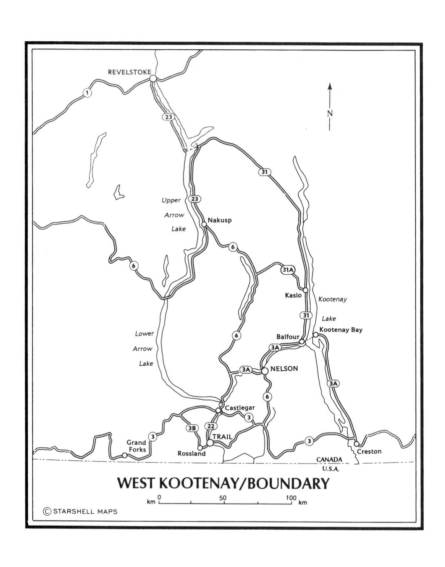

WEST KOOTENAY/BOUNDARY

© STARSHELL MAPS

WEST KOOTENAY/BOUNDARY

The CPR propagandists who eulogized each region the railway ran through had a little trouble with the West Kootenay.

"To those who come from the open or plains region east of the Rocky Mountains," wrote a pamphleteer at the turn of the century, "the absence of large open areas, the timber, and the mountain peaks on the skyline, are at first conducive to a feeling of confinement, but"—the writer finally finding the required optimism—"the cozy home of the valley lands, the absence of high winds and the moderate climate soon induce a feeling of comfort which grows with the years and makes the dweller in the mountain valley the most contented settler the world over."

It was not surprising that a writer more accustomed to the regularity of the prairie landscape or the settled vistas of eastern Canada would be overwhelmed by the sharp peaks and deep wilderness of this region. Eons ago, the shifting and breaching of the earth's crust raised jagged mountains; during the ice ages, moving ice sheared off peaks and scoured deep valleys. The result was the abrupt and beautiful landscape of the West Kootenay. On the map, long blue lines of lake and river score north-south, separated by the deep orange and white that mapmakers reserve for high mountains and glaciers.

It was with an almost audible sigh of relief that the CPR writer passed on to the gentler landscape of the Boundary region next door, praising it as the "great Canadian sanatorium." The Boundary is a pleasant, narrow strip of land, squeezed down upon the American border east of the Okanagan, below the Okanagan Highlands. Unlike the West Kootenay, where clouds forced high above the mountains often drop heavy rain and snow, the Boundary shares a climate with the Okanagan: dry, sunny, mild in winter, hot in summer.

Together, West Kootenay and Boundary make up a region wedged between the Okanagan Valley on the west and the East Kootenay, part of the Mountain Spine region, on the east.

The human history of the area is one of coming to terms with the landscape. The first to do so were the native peoples. The Salmon people arrived perhaps some 9,000 years ago, following spawning fish up the Columbia River. But the climate of the region changed, drought dried the rivers and the salmon disappeared. We do not know the fate of the fishing people. Two thousand years later, when the rivers swelled again, other groups followed the Columbia north and settled along the Arrow Lakes and the lower Kootenay River.

At the same time, the Ktunaxa people were developing their own relationship with the landscape, hunting and gathering in the valleys in winter, on the mountains in summer. As the climate changed once more and game decreased, the Ktunaxa turned to fishing. By 2,000 years ago, a large group had settled at the south end of Kootenay Lake.

David Thompson, on his methodical way through Kootenay and Columbia country in 1808, was the first non-native to map the area. He spared little time for a region difficult to traverse and virtually bereft of fur-bearing animals. Once the Americans claimed the Columbia south of the 49th parallel in 1811, few traders bothered with the West Kootenay-Boundary. Even after road builders cut the Dewdney Trail through from the Okanagan to the Rockies in 1865, few travellers stayed long in the area. No gold had been found here and what potential farmland existed was far from any market.

Then, in 1882, prospectors staked a ledge of rock on the northeast shore of Kootenay Lake. Word of the rich galena (lead-zinc-silver) ore they had found started a mineral rush that eventually reached throughout the region. Over the next 35 years, prospectors staked claims wherever a shiny outcrop or gravel in a gold pan showed promise, across the mountains of the Slocan and along the U.S. border from the Okanagan Highlands to the Purcells.

In the next decade, some 750 claims were staked in the area. Mining camps were born in an instant. Some died almost as quickly, while others throve. The most prosperous towns were almost always those that had more than mines. Kaslo, a key transfer point on Kootenay Lake, where passengers and freight moved from lake boats to trails and then rails to the Slocan mines, had by 1892 a newspaper, five hotels (one run by one of the few women in town), a lawyer, a notary public, an auctioneer, an architect, a "tonsorial artist," the Can Can Chop House, the Noble Five Bath House and Kemp's Therapeutic Mineral Water (from local mineral springs). At Greenwood in the Boundary, a smelter was built. By 1902, that town boasted graded streets, government offices, sawmills, factories, a hospital, schools, a newspaper, a brewery and three chartered banks. And a government report declared that Grand Forks, a Boundary smelter town with a population of 2,000, "is lighted by electricity, has a waterworks and sewage system, and possesses many good business houses supplying local and outside demands, and has four saw and planing mills, foundry, chartered bank and high class hotels."

As ever in boom towns, plummeting prices and diminishing resources spelled an end to prosperity. By the end of World War I, the population of the West Kootenay-Boundary had shrunk from the heady days around the turn of the century. Of all the mining and smelting towns, only Trail, where the smelter processed ore from other parts of B.C. and eventually from around the world, continued as a major metallurgical centre. Though the towns that served the mines often continued on supported by logging and sawmilling, a hundred mining towns were abandoned.

The mining rush, however, had made the country known, and the cutting of trails and building of railroads to serve the mines had made it accessible. Settlers began to take up land and farm the river valleys. Among them were a group of religious refugees from Russia and Georgia, disillusioned by the treatment meted out to them when they immigrated to Saskatchewan in 1898–99. The Doukhobors sent emissaries to seek potential sites in British Columbia; they reported back that the valleys around Grand Forks and along the Columbia near its meeting with the Kootenay seemed fertile and were not yet claimed. In about 1908, some 6,000 Doukhobors moved to the Grand Forks, Castlegar and Slocan area.

The Doukhobors followed a simple, rural, pre-industrial lifestyle, in accordance with their belief in toil and a peaceful life. Their religion dictated that they not smoke, eat meat or drink alcohol, and that they live communally, disdaining all incursions of the state, whether those be military service or state education.

That peaceful life was soon threatened from within and without. A splinter group called the Sons of Freedom burned buildings and marched nude to protest the materialism of the world. Hostile neighbours, financial problems and the indifference of government destroyed communal life and ownership. Doukhobor lands were foreclosed on and eventually taken over by the government. Yet despite their checkered history in this land, the Doukhobor spirit lives on in the West Kootenay-Boundary.

Though many individuals and small groups moved into the region between 1908 and 1942, the next large ethnic group to arrive was made up of less willing migrants. When the Canadian government declared in 1942 that those of Japanese origin living on the west coast were enemy aliens and then confiscated their property and exiled them from the coast, many were transported to camps and all-but-deserted towns in the West Kootenay-Boundary. New Denver, Sandon, Kaslo, Greenwood and half a dozen others housed internment camps. Though they had to wait out government regulations to do so, some of those exiled stayed in the area after the war.

Settlers other than the Doukhobors also saw agricultural potential in the area. At the south end of Kootenay Lake, along the Kootenay River, dykes transformed a flood plain into fertile farm fields. The moderate climate also encouraged orchardists. For several decades, until changing traffic patterns and disease destroyed the industry, boxes of Kootenay apples and cherries were shipped to the mining towns and to the Prairies.

River valleys and lakes had always provided natural transportation routes through the region. From the 1890s on, railway workers laid ties and rails through the West Kootenay-Boundary. Railways took ore from mines to smelters on both sides of the border; lake boats on the Upper and Lower Arrow, Kootenay and Slocan lakes filled in gaps between the ends of steel.

As ore bodies expired and transportation improved, logging and milling largely replaced mining at the centre of the region's economy. Loggers moved out through the region, cutting timber higher and higher on the mountain slopes. Sawmills were built in every small town. Then, here as elsewhere in the province, small mills, considered uneconomic, closed down and milling was concentrated in larger centres. Cities like Castlegar, with an ever-expanding pulp mill, grew larger as villages stagnated or disappeared.

A truth presaged by that CPR writer's words—that the "dweller in the mountain valley [is] the most contented settler the world over"—may in the end prove the strongest historical trend in the West Kootenay-Boundary. Since the time when the Doukhobors arrived, the region has attracted those for whom peace and security are more important than great wealth. Shortly after World War II, Quakers escaping American militarism and materialism established a colony on Kootenay Lake; not far away, an ashram was built by the shore. American draft dodgers and deserters from the Vietnam War chose to live in the West Kootenay. Many of the people who live in Nelson, Grand Forks or the Slocan Valley have chosen their homes because they think it is possible to live a quieter, saner life here than the hectic pace of a city allows.

THE BOUNDARY

Flanking the Okanagan, the Boundary region begins where the Kettle River turns east, to flow south of the Okanagan Highlands.

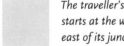

The traveller's guide to the historic West Kootenay-Boundary starts at the western edge of the region, on Highway 3 just east of its junction with Highway 33 at Rock Creek.

The Rock Creek Hotel, still operating, was built in 1893. Midway, 17 kilometres to the east, is the first town along the route and was also the first town founded in the Boundary, in 1893. Some suggest it was named for the Midway Plaisance at the 1893 Chicago World's Fair. Others, more geographically inclined, point

The old train station at Midway, in Boundary country, houses the area museum.

out that Midway is halfway between the coast and the Rockies, halfway between Hope and Fort Steele on the Dewdney Trail and halfway between Penticton and the nearest 1890s railway terminus, Marcus, Washington.

On the western outskirts of Midway, the Kettle Valley Railway station (1900) houses historic railway displays. This was one of the last stations closed when the CPR abandoned the Kettle Valley line from Penticton to Midway in 1978. Ask here about the routes of both Kettle Valley and Great Northern railways; you can walk the railbeds. Next door to the station is the Kettle River Museum, which displays local history, including that of B.C. police forces. A railway bunkhouse and caboose are also on display.

A pair of entwined trees stand off the highway in Midway. One story suggests that the Okanagan First Nations, whose traditional territory knew no national dividing lines, wove two sapling pines together when the Boundary Commission marking the border in 1860 separated American and Canadian bands.

Check out, too, the circa-1905 Kettle River Inn, now a pub, in the village "centre."

A cairn beside the road about six kilometres east of Midway gives information about the building of the Dewdney Trail.

Greenwood

In 1891, prospectors discovered copper-gold ore that was the basis of the Mother Lode mine here, the Phoenix mine to the east, the founding of Greenwood in 1895 and the 15-year mining boom that put Greenwood on the map. In 1897, Greenwood's population stood at 3,000; today, it is around 700, making it the smallest city in British Columbia. Never abandoned, never redeveloped, Greenwood—with its slag heaps, tall smelter chimney and fine turn-of-the-century buildings—guards the Boundary's past glories. Restoration on government buildings, simple miners' cottages and fine Victorian homes make Greenwood well worth a stop.

To reach the old mine and smelter site, turn left (west) from Highway 3 (Copper Street) onto Deadwood. Follow the road across the creek, then up the hill four kilometres to the flooded pits of the Mother Lode, where crushed ore from the mine still lies in drifts. In 1913, dynamiters tried to reach new ore bodies by drilling 5,000 holes and blowing them all at once. As well as breaking windows in the town of Deadwood, where the miners and their families lived, the blast diluted the ore with waste, and the rim of the "glory hole" collapsed into the mine chutes. The Mother Lode and Deadwood were both abandoned.

At the west end of town, in Lotzkar Park, a plaque tells the story of the mining history of Greenwood. To see the 37-metre smelter stack and the oddly attractive slag heaps, turn left (west) from Highway 3 onto Washington Street and follow the signs across Boundary Creek to the smelter and Lotzkar Park. A somewhat quixotic project to reclaim the slag for industrial use seems to have foundered.

The infocentre and Greenwood Museum at the north end of town can supply information on Greenwood's restored buildings and the town's history. Ask for a

The old brick smelter chimney and broken slag bells strewn across the slag heaps are reminders of Greenwood's past as the centre of the Boundary's copper-gold mining industry at the turn of the 19th century.

printed heritage tour and historical fact sheets—or check the museum's website. On Copper Street, look for the Greenwood Inn, once the Windsor Hotel (1899), the most elaborate wood-frame building in town. The brick federal post office building (circa 1913) is at the corner of Greenwood and Government streets; the courthouse (1903) is at Deadwood and Government; the fire hall (circa 1900) is across the street from the courthouse and is less ornate, more utilitarian.

Government Street between Greenwood and Short displays some fine homes; one gingerbreaded example is known as the Red House, but now sports its original green and white colours. Sacred Heart Catholic Church (circa 1900) is at Wood and Church.

By World War II, Greenwood was down on its luck. When the Canadian government issued a request for towns that would take Japanese Canadian internees, Greenwood council was eager; they more than welcomed the newcomers whose arrival might revitalize the town. A thousand came by rail. They were housed in rundown sheds and buildings, among them the Gulley Block (now the McArthur Centre) and the Pacific Hotel (now a café), both on Copper Street. A number of internees stayed on after the war. A Japanese garden flanks the post office building.

The Trans Canada Trail follows the route of the Columbia and Western Railway (later the CPR) in the Greenwood area.

The abandoned town of **PHOENIX** (east up Greenwood Street, then eight kilometres around hairpins and up steep hills) was once the highest elevated city in Canada. Later, open-pit mining obliterated much of the townsite, but the Phoenix cemetery and monument erected for the dead of World War I remain. While the mines operated, Phoenix sprawled across the hillside, encompassing a hospital, tennis courts, churches, hotels where caviar, oysters and green turtle soup were served and 17 saloons where men gambled night and day. In 1918, copper prices plummeted; Phoenix closed down a year later and residents walked away from their houses and the graves of those who died in mining accidents and the 1919 flu epidemic. One of the last things Phoenix residents did was build a cenotaph to commemorate the men of Phoenix who died in the war, using money a Vancouver company paid for the town skating rink. The rink, like some other Phoenix buildings, was dismantled and taken away. The metal phoenix that "flew" at the townsite now surveys Highway 3 in Greenwood.

Grand Forks and Area

You can follow Phoenix Road down yet more switchbacks to Highway 3 farther east—or return to Greenwood and then take Highway 3 to the Grand Forks Valley. That valley is bounded on east and west by inhospitable mountains; today's traveller needs little imagination to understand the elation travellers of a century ago experienced when they came upon this green and sunny place. "We had a famous gallop of about five miles across a corner of the prairie all

Many of the old Doukhobor buildings in the Grand Forks Valley have fallen into disrepair.

level as a bowling green," wrote boundary surveyor Charles Wilson in the 1860s, "and the whole day we travelled along a broad open valley, grass and trees." The earliest white men to spend any length of time in the valley were Hudson's Bay Company traders from the post at Fort Colville, who wintered horses and cattle here, then pastured them on the bunchgrass that clothed the valley bottom. Once the grass was obliterated by over-grazing, the settlers turned to mixed farming.

"Of late," wrote one E. Spraggett in 1902, "there has been a tendency to cut up farms into tracts of 20 or 30 acres each, to be devoted to fruit or vegetable raising." Modern-day evidence of this historical trend can be seen at Rilkoffs produce market at the junction of Highways 3 and 21, near the United States border, where sacks of potatoes and onions, jars of pickles, bags of dried garlic and baskets of apples fill the building. A display of venerable farming equipment parallels the highway.

The Doukhobors who travelled west in 1908 saw the potential of the valley. Many present-day residents are descended from those settlers. Sites throughout the valley convey the essence of the Doukhobor way of life, and you will find Doukhobor specialties being served at Grand Forks restaurants.

South of the highway just west of the town limits beside Cemetery Road is

The Hardy Mountain Doukhobor Village site above Grand Forks is slowly being restored.

the Doukhobor cemetery. The idea that death is simply the natural end of life is part of the Doukhobor philosophy. Mounds of earth and stone, settling gently into the ground, remain from the earliest burials here. Etched on some simple stones are the central Doukhobor symbols: stalks of wheat to represent bread, a pitcher for water, a cellar for salt. Many of the stones bear Cyrillic inscriptions.

Just beyond the cemetery is the Grand Forks Milling Co-operative, where wheat is ground between millstones and sold without additives as it has been since 1915. Check with the Grand Forks infocentre for tour information. Check here, also, for information about the Fructova Doukhobor Heritage Centre, a 1929 Doukhobor community school now restored and viewable on request.

Across the highway and up the hill (follow signs from Highway 3 north on North Fork Road, then west on Hardy Mountain Road) is the Hardy Mountain Doukhobor Village Historic Site. For several decades, Peter Gritchen lovingly tended this 1912 house and its contents, creating the Mountainview Doukhobor Museum and ensuring that it embodied the concept of simplicity that is at the centre of Doukhobor life and beliefs. Worn wooden stairways, whitewashed walls and watermarked ceilings conjure up visions of families sitting by flickering lamplight, eating simple vegetarian meals, carving their wooden implements, spinning and weaving. When Gritchen died, it seemed possible that the museum would die with him, but TLC (The Land Conservancy of British Columbia) and other donors raised funds to buy it, and volunteers are now sifting through the seven-hectare site. Check with TLC to see whether they are scheduling working holidays here.

The city of Grand Forks, at the forks of the Kettle and Granby rivers, is predated by an Okanagan native settlement, here for as many as 9,000 years. Archaeologists have found a large burial site at the forks. In it were human remains, jade adzes, dentalia shell beads traded from the coast, bone jewellery and a variety of bone and stone tools. Some of these can be seen at the Boundary Museum (at Highway 3 and Fifth Street), among other displays of area history.

The modern town of Grand Forks was born of the nearby mines. Ore from a dozen copper mines worked between 1899 and 1919 was shipped to the giant Granby smelter, then the largest copper smelter in the British Empire and the second-largest in the world. The smelter gave Grand Forks, incorporated in 1897, a permanence that mining towns lacked. Wide avenues were laid out by those who expected the town to last; the broad, leafy maple trees that border Central Avenue were planted a century ago. Merchants, senior mine and smelter managers and local professionals built impressive Victorian mansions. The houses that remain include the Candlesnuffer House (1908), at 7376 Bluff Street across the Granby River bridge, so named for the hoods over its dormers and gables; houses at 695, 942 and 981 Central Avenue (circa 1907); and houses on Fifth Street and Market Avenue. Those who know their late Victorian architecture will recognize, as they walk along Grand Forks streets, features from Queen Anne revival, Vernacular revival, Edwardian, Classical revival and other styles.

Also worth a look from Grand Forks boom days are the provincial courthouse (1911) at 524 Central; the old post office (1911–15) at 429 Market, now city hall; and a Selkirk College building (1898) at 486 – 72nd Avenue, which started life as a brewery, something that students probably see as appropriate.

Walking-tour and driving-tour maps of the Grand Forks area are available from the infocentre or from the museum. Ask at the museum for a brochure listing nine historic Doukhobor sites.

To see the slag pile produced by the Granby smelter, head east out of town across the Granby River bridge, then turn north on the North Fork route. Some 10 million tons of slag remained after the copper, gold and silver ores were smelted and the metals shipped out by train. These black hills remained virtually undisturbed from 1919, when the smelter closed, to 1980, when a new company began to convert slag to insulation material and then abrasive material for sandblasting.

CHRISTINA LAKE, 25 kilometres east of Grand Forks at the end of the Boundary, is named for Christina McDonald, the daughter of the Fort Colville chief factor Angus McDonald and an Iroquois/Nez Percé/French woman whom history regrettably neglects to name. One tale suggests that an HBC man travelling with Christina and her husband named the creek and lake for the lady fair; another says that Christina plunged into the water to rescue her father's papers, which were rapidly disappearing downstream. Whichever is correct, Christina retained her affinity for water. Her father wrote that, after she and her husband started a ranch in the Shuswap, she often spent an hour swimming in the chilly Thompson River.

Pictographs, signs of an earlier native heritage, are painted on the rocks on the east side of the lake. The Kettle native people, who lived and traded along the Kettle Valley for thousands of years before white settlers arrived, speared salmon at Cascade Falls south of Christina Lake, chipped stone for tools along the Granby and lived in pit houses and villages along the Kettle River.

The red brick Cascade Power House that stood for decades near the junction of Highways 3 and 395 has been torn down, but its story is part of the larger tale of Nikola Tesla, the man who was, you could say, right at the wrong time. The Columbia and Western Railway reached Cascade in 1898 during the Boundary mining rush, and the CPR made plans to build a smelter near the falls here. The rock-filled dam was 1,200 metres across and 16 metres high; the powerhouse produced power for the area. The project was one of the proving grounds for engineer Nikola Tesla, who argued with Thomas Edison that alternating current, not direct current as Edison favoured, was the way of the future. Time proved Tesla right, but Edison garnered the fame and money that eluded Tesla, who was often dismissed as an eccentric and difficult crank. Later called the father of the 20th century and the true inventor of radio, Tesla died alone and destitute in 1943 at the age of 86. His precise date of death is not known; last seen on January 5, he was found dead in his hotel room on January 8.

The Dewdney Trail—cut through to the gold diggings at Wild Horse Creek in the Rocky Mountain Trench in 1865—is accessible to hikers from a variety of points off Santa Rosa Road: inquire locally, then look for green and white access-point signs or check the Christina Lake website. The trail from Christina Lake through to Paterson south of Rossland on the U.S. border has been designated part of the Trans Canada Trail.

Northeast of Christina Lake at FARRON, on the Columbia and Western railway grade between Castlegar and Midway, is a memorial to Peter "The Lord-ly" Verigin. He was the spiritual leader of the Doukhobors, who was killed on the train in 1924 when a bomb exploded. His assassination is one of the great unsolved mysteries of Canadian history. Check locally about cycling or hiking the railway grade.

WEST KOOTENAY: CASTLEGAR, ROSSLAND/ TRAIL AND THE SLOCAN

East of the Boundary and Christina Lake, Highway 3 climbs the Monashees through Blueberry Pass, then drops down into one of those long narrow river-and-lake valleys that characterize the West Kootenay. Where the highway meets the Columbia River, it resembles a five-legged spider. Highway 3 forms one leg, Highway 22/Columbia Avenue though Castlegar the second, Highway 22 south to Trail and Rossland the third, Highway 3 to Salmo the fourth and Highway 3A towards Nelson and the Slocan the fifth leg. The confusion of roads and bridges in the area makes it advisable to get a map from the tourist infocentre before exploring further; follow signs on Highway 22 to the infocentre.

Castlegar

One of the spider legs, Highway 22 north, follows the west bank of the Columbia into the town of Castlegar, where it becomes Columbia Avenue. Castlegar, at the junction of the Kootenay and Columbia rivers, is a city-come-lately in the Kootenay settlement stakes. Though mining prospects brought some settlers to the area in the 1890s, Castlegar came into its own as a transportation crossroads, where rivers join and east-west valleys and mountain passes link.

In 1891, the CPR completed a railway from Nelson to Robson, across the river from present-day Castlegar. Paddlewheelers carried goods along the Arrow Lakes between rail ends at Robson and Revelstoke. It proved time-consuming to barge mine ore across the Columbia River to reload it onto railcars destined for the Trail smelter, so the CPR bridged the river at Castlegar in 1902. Once the bridge was built, neighbouring Robson declined and Castlegar grew, as a meeting point and as a lumbering and milling centre. Ask about riding or hiking the Columbia and Western Railway grade from Castlegar to Midway.

The CPR railway station in downtown Castlegar replaced a 1902 station that burned in 1906. Moved a short distance from its original location, it now houses the Castlegar CPR museum.

Somewhat priggish but greatly influential explorer and map-maker David Thompson camped near Castlegar in 1811, on one of his journeys to divine the many twists and turns of the Columbia and its tributaries; a plaque on the east bank of the river overlooking Castlegar marks his sojourn.

Zuckerberg Island, on the Columbia, is a repository of both native and later settlement history. To reach the island, park at the lot by the river on Seventh Avenue and walk across the bridge. On the border between Ktunaxa and Interior Salish territory, the Castlegar area was the land of both groups, who came to the junction of the Kootenay and Columbia rivers to fish for salmon that surged up the river to spawn. A beach on the southeast side of Zuckerberg Island was used for salmon drying. Also on the island is a reconstructed version of the pit houses used as winter dwellings by the native people, plus the remains of some original pit houses.

Zuckerberg Island takes its name from Alexander and Alicia Zuckerberg, Russian immigrants and followers of Leo Tolstoy (Tolstoy had campaigned on behalf of the Doukhobors), who came to this area in 1931 to teach Doukhobor children. The Zuckerbergs settled on the island, which is now a park. Among its historic attractions: the Chapel House, built after the onion-domed Russian Orthodox country chapel style; the graves of Alicia and Alexander; and the site of Zuckerberg's waterwheel.

With the opening of the Celgar Pulp Mill in 1959, Castlegar cemented its position as the dominant town of the area: the village of Kinnaird, the original settlement, and Castlegar joined together in the city of Castlegar in 1974. Though there is some doubt about the origin of the name, it is probably a combination of the Gaelic word *gar*—meaning "rock"—and *castle*, a fanciful description of the large rock above the Columbia not far from the city. Eight panels detailing the city's and region's history are to be erected at Spirit Square, at city hall.

Highway 22/Columbia Avenue continues north. Eight kilometres upstream is the Hugh Keenleyside Dam, completed in 1965 to provide power to the provincial network and the Castlegar mill. The rising waters of the Keenleyside reservoir drowned a number of pioneer communities where settlers—among them Mennonites from the Prairies—farmed or tended orchards on the flats beside the lake. By the time the bottomlands along the river were flooded by the dam reservoir, the fruit industry had been all but eliminated by little cherry disease, endemic in the area between the 1930s and the 1950s. Some twisted trees bearing the stunted fruit that is characteristic of the disease may still be seen along Arrow and Kootenay lakes. A plaque in the cemetery at Robson, across the lake from Castlegar, commemorates the community of Renata "and its 58 former residents who now lie beneath the waters of the Arrow Reservoir"—those Renatans whose graves lay in the flooded cemetery.

Along the 1.5-kilometre Waldie Island Trail, on the north bank of the Columbia across from North Castlegar and between the CPR bridge and Brilliant, are panels that explain the historical significance of points on the trail. The panels include information on explorers, steamships, sawmilling, pioneers and environmental change.

Cross the Columbia on Highway 3A north, then follow signs from the road to the Castlegar airport to the Doukhobor Discovery Centre. At one time, many colonies of Doukhobors lived along the east bank of the Columbia River near the Kootenay, and many Doukhobors still live near Castlegar, though they have left behind the communal lifestyle and are more likely to be real estate agents or mill workers than farmers. The historical village re-creates the communal life of the 1908–1939 era, in traditional two-storey brick houses and a single-storey row. The Kootenay Gallery of Art, History and Science is next door.

From Castlegar, continue on Highway 3A across the Kootenay River, then turn west on Broadwater Road to reach **BRILLIANT**, another Doukhobor community and the location of the Union of Spiritual Communities of Christ Cultural Centre. The Brilliant Suspension Bridge, a National Historic Site which can be seen from Highway 3A at the bottom of Airport Hill, was hand-built in 1913 by Doukhobor workers according to plans sent from Vancouver—a difficult task, since the workers could not read English. The Doukhobors wanted a bridge to connect them to the road to Nelson; though the government refused to build a bridge, it did supply $20,000 of the $70,000 required. A sign on the bridge prohibited smoking or carrying firearms over the bridge.

Not far from here is the tomb of Doukhobor leader Peter Verigin, who, as mentioned, was killed by an explosion on the train he was riding in the 1920s. (Continue on Broadwater Road, turn right on Terrace Road and watch for the sign.) Behind this memorial to Peter the Lordly lies the tomb of his sister, Anna Markova. On a weekday, visitors are assured of silence. Sometimes on a Sunday, Doukhobors dressed in traditional clothing hold memorial services in the glade. Visitors who behave as they would at any other sacred place are welcome.

One leg of the Castlegar spider stretches south with Highway 22 to Trail, then Highway 3B to Rossland.

Highway 22 South: Rossland/Trail

ROSSLAND was the first of these cities, founded to house miners and their families working the ores of Red Mountain, staked in 1890. The two prospectors who staked five claims on the mountainside were, according to mining law, allowed to register only two claims each. So they offered the fifth claim to mining registrar Eugene Topping if he would pay the filing fees on the other four. These stories always seem to turn out the same way: Topping's claim was the site of the fabulous LeRoi Mine—the king of the mines, source of half the gold mined in British Columbia between 1900 and 1916, a pile valued at more than $25 million. Topping wasn't made a rich man by his bargain, however; he sold out for $30,000 and the new owners in turn sold for $3 million.

By the 1920s, most of the ore bodies in the area were played out and Rossland declined, becoming a bedroom community for the city of Trail next door. Red Mountain became better known for skiing than for gold.

A number of Rossland buildings hearken back to golden days. On Columbia Avenue are the old courthouse (1901) and the restored Miners' Union Hall (1898). Local 38 of the Western Federation of Miners, an American union, was organized at Rossland in 1895 and began campaigning for an eight-hour day. The government passed eight-hour legislation; the companies, however, stipulated that if their employees worked eight hours instead of ten, they would get paid only four-fifths of their former pay. In 1899, 14 union locals met at Rossland to promote their common cause. In May 1901, the union struck the LeRoi and other Rossland area mines to seek support for fellow miners at American mines just across the border, to increase the pay of muckers from $2.50 to $3.00 a day and to end discrimination against union members.

The company brought in strikebreakers. The strike collapsed. Two companies sued the union for damages, won and seized any union assets, including this Rossland miners' hall. But the company did not register a change of ownership and allowed the union to continue using the hall. When the mines closed, the unions moved to Trail. They bought the hall back in 1962 and have now restored it to its turn-of-the-century appearance.

Outside Red Mountain's mining museum at Rossland.

Also worth a look in town is the BC Firefighters' Museum, in the fire hall (circa 1900) on Queen Street.

At the Flying Steamshovel on Second Avenue at Washington Street, in an 1897 building originally housing the Orwell Hotel, you can debate the question of whether a steam helicopter can fly. Locals insist one can—and did. Enthusiasts say the two-engine, steam-powered machine made its one flight successfully, if in ungainly fashion, buggy-wheel rotor whirling. Skeptics say the machine never got into the air, if it existed at all. Assess the company you're in before you declare your position.

A walking-tour map that points out 30 historic Rossland buildings is available at the Rossland Museum, at the junction of Highways 3B and 22; an info-centre shares the building. The museum fronts what is left of the magnificent LeRoi. Some 250 metres of the 135 kilometres of mine tunnels that burrow through the mountainside are open to the public, with displays of an underground hoist room, an exploration drift, miners' tools and other mining-related artifacts. The tunnel that houses the displays leads some 100 metres down to the LeRoi shaft.

Rossland's growing importance as a ski centre is noted in the Western Canada Ski Hall of Fame, also at the museum site. Among the displays are the trophies and wooden skis of the first Dominion ski champion, Olaus Jeldness, who introduced skiing to Rossland in 1896, and the trophies and memorabilia of 1960s ski champion Nancy Greene.

In almost every area of B.C. where mining dominated the economy, the location of rich ore bodies determined where the first towns were built, but transportation patterns largely determined which towns survived and grew. Though Trail was second to Rossland a century ago, it now dominates the economy of the region.

Founded after Rossland by a prospector who had no luck around the LeRoi, TRAIL was at first little more than the stopping place where the Dewdney Trail crossed the Columbia River. Ore from LeRoi was shipped to Trail Creek Landing, to be loaded on steamboats for shipment to American smelters. Prospectors, gamblers and respectable settlers disembarked from the boats here and set off for the excitement at Rossland.

Eugene Topping had a townsite by the river surveyed in 1891, but little happened until American capitalist Franz Augustus Heinze built a smelter in 1896. At first, it limped along well below capacity; ore was still shipped south. In 1898, the CPR bought the smelter. In 1906, having bought, among others, the LeRoi at Rossland and the Sullivan mines at Kimberley to assure ore supplies for the smelter, the CPR formed a conglomerate known as the Consolidated Mining and Smelting Company—Cominco—that has operated the smelter ever since. The Trail smelter was at the time the largest lead-zinc smelter in the world.

It continued to prosper long after LeRoi closed and is now fed by ores from around the world. Trail is dominated by its smelter stacks and deforested hills, a stark contrast to the mountain beauty of Rossland.

By 1895, two Italians had come to Trail. They encouraged other Italian immigration, and, by 1905, Italian was Trail's second language. Today, close to a third of Trail's people trace their origins back to Italy. Early Italian immigrants settled along The Gulch, a cut along the mountainside above downtown Trail, beside Trail Creek. Cribbing, concrete walls, stonework and terraced vegetable patches still testify to the hard work of early Italian immigrants. The Cristoforo Colombo Lodge (at 584 Rossland Avenue), established in Trail in 1905, keeps Italian traditions alive, housing the only Italian archives in North America. Trail's Silver City Days in May include a grape stomp, a spaghetti-eating contest and a block-long Italian sidewalk café.

One legacy left by an Italian immigrant now bears little trace of its history. Giovanni Vendramini came to Trail in 1923 as a bricklayer. His family came to join him but his wife, Antonia, soon returned to Italy, worn down by Trail winters, a sick child and language difficulties. Vendramini turned to a dream: using rocks and sand from a lot he bought, he built a stone castle against the day

Historic downtown Rossland in the snow.

when Antonia would return to him. Since adding the roof would raise the taxes, he left it open to all weathers. Antonia did come back, and they lived in a cabin he had built. He never finished his castle. After his death, a fellow Italian immigrant converted it to an apartment building, with stucco over its stone walls. Vendramini's castle is now an anonymous structure in East Trail.

The City of Trail Museum, at Trail Memorial Centre (1051 Victoria Street) contains exhibits of native and mining history, including the history of mining unions in the region.

With the economic benefits of the smelter came a downside. Though the smelter no longer belches fumes into Trail's air, close to a hundred years of lead smelting in the town left dead areas, leafless trees and a residue of heavy metals in the soil.

For many years, smelter officials insisted that the smelter smoke did no harm. Columbia Gardens, southeast of Trail, was planted with fruit trees to demonstrate that an orchard could thrive just a few kilometres from the smelter.

 The guide returns to Castlegar and follows Highway 3 to Salmo.

Highway 3: Salmo

Salmo is the Latin word for "salmon," and, one supposes, a more refined name than the original "Salmon Siding," founded and named during the building of the Nelson and Fort Sheppard Railway, and before dams prevented salmon from ascending the river this far. On building walls throughout the town, stone mosaic murals created by the students at a school of stone masonry depict the history of the area. The Salmo Museum, at Railway Avenue and Fourth Street, has displays on local history. Ask there about what remains of the Sheep Creek mines—Kootenay Bell, Reno, Goldbelt, Queens—that operated from 1896 to the 1950s. They are along Sheep Creek Road, which heads east off Highway 3/6 about eight kilometres south of Salmo. Active logging may close or place restrictions on this road. Salmo residents have cleared out and marked sections of the old Dewdney Trail.

North of Salmo on Highway 6 is **YMIR** (pronounced *why-mer*), named for the father of the giants in Norse legend, a town with attractive buildings from the mining era at the turn of the century and a 1936 schoolhouse.

 The guide returns to Castlegar and follows Highway 3A across the Columbia and Kootenay rivers, then Highway 6 north into the Slocan.

Highway 3A Northeast

Perhaps the best way to feel a sense of what Doukhobor life used to be like is to walk the road or sit by the river in old Doukhobor territory and imagine the peaceful, simple, non-material lifestyle. A good place to do this is **GLADE**. Follow Highway 3A north about 14 kilometres to Glade Road, and get on a tiny ferry that crosses the Kootenay River to reach the site of what were, many years ago, 14 Doukhobor villages. Though the colonies are gone, it is not difficult to imagine the farm fields, the simple rhythms and the peace of Doukhobor life 90 years ago.

The Slocan

To enter the Slocan, turn north on Highway 6, 20 kilometres northeast of Castlegar. The Slocan Valley lies along Slocan River and Lake, between the Valhalla and Slocan ranges of the Selkirk Mountains. The word *slocan* derives from an Okanagan word that means "pierce" or "strike on the head," referring to the Okanagan practice of spearing the salmon that once spawned in the rivers and lakes here. But the works of man put a decided end to that practice; after the Americans built the Grand Coulee and other dams on the Columbia, salmon could no longer swim upstream. The only salmon you'll now find in the Slocan is that on your plate.

At the south end of the Slocan, names on mailboxes and the communities of **KRESTOVA** and **CRESCENT VALLEY** testify to long-lived Doukhobor settlements. Krestova was one centre of Sons of Freedom agitation in the 1950s, but few signs remain of those violent times.

The pattern of settlement the Doukhobors established has been maintained by the settlers who followed them. Though the map shows many small towns, most are little more than a post office and tiny store, with perhaps a community hall tucked into the woods. Most people who moved here—from the Doukhobors to 1960s hippies who established communal farms—did so to get away from urban centres and mainstream expectations. People here live on small farms or rural acreages along the river or in the woods.

At Passmore, Winlaw and Slocan, gravel roads lead west towards Valhalla Provincial Park. George Dawson, the government surveyor and geologist who trod these valleys and passes in the 1880s, was deeply impressed by the soaring mountains and named them the Valhallas, for the legendary home where Norse warriors went after their earthly death. Among the peaks are Freya, Gimli, Woden and the Devil's Range.

The 1890s silver rush sent prospectors into the valley, scouring forest and mountainside for telltale signs of mineral-bearing ore. Most of the region's towns and villages were founded in this decade: Slocan, Silverton and New Denver remain today.

SLOCAN, at the south end of Slocan Lake, was once but is no longer the end of the line for railway travellers into the Slocan and a freight and passenger depot for sternwheelers headed up the valley. **SILVERTON**, to the north, still guards false-fronted commercial buildings from its mining-camp days. The local historical society has compiled a walking-tour brochure of this village and cleared old mining trails in the area. Among the town's features are various private residences along the highway (Lake Avenue) that at the turn of the century housed a restaurant, a butcher shop and an ice-cream parlour with a gaming room upstairs. At the corner of Fifth Street and the alley between Lake and Alpha streets is the last of Silverton's log cabins, built in 1897. The Silverton School, built in 1919, is now a gallery and historical interpretive centre. Outside is the Frank Mills Outdoor Mining Exhibit, with displays of hoists, pulleys, pumps, drills and cages.

At **NEW DENVER** (first called Eldorado, then renamed for the successful mining town in the United States), the tourist infocentre and Silvery Slocan Museum are in the circa 1900 bank building, said to be B.C.'s oldest existing wood-frame bank building. Take a look at the restored lake boat in the courtyard.

The narrow-gauge Kaslo and Slocan Railway was cantilevered out over Payne Bluff, near Sandon, with a sheer cliff above and a drop of 330 metres below. (BCA A2592)

Half a dozen other buildings, including a church built in 1892, still stand beside quiet streets.

The Nikkei Internment Memorial Centre is on Josephine Street. The centre is on the site of one of five camps that housed about 8,500 Japanese Canadians after they were banished from the coast in 1942. The camp has been restored by the Kyowakai Society (the Association for Working Peacefully), which was formed during the war. It includes the Japanese United Church, a community hall, a six-seat outhouse and two shacks that were home to Japanese Canadian families.

The first steamer on Slocan Lake was built at New Denver, from lumber cut and milled locally, and furnished with a boiler and propellers brought by

A visitor tests out a rusty and backless safe on the ground at Sandon, the almost-ghost town deep in Slocan mining country.

pack horse from Nakusp. The *William Hunter* was not particularly stable; on one occasion, she rolled over when passengers crowded to one side to wave to friends on the shore.

Ghost towns and ruins hidden in the underbrush along creeks and on mountain slopes evoke the dear dead days of silver strikes in the Slocan. To reach **SANDON**, the best known and most accessible of the ghost towns, go east about six kilometres from New Denver along Highway 31A, then south five kilometres from the sign to Sandon. Though its population of 2,000 in 1898, when it was known as Silver City, has dwindled to a handful of year-round diehards and many of its buildings have been dismantled or carried away by Carpenter Creek, Sandon is still more than just a ghost town.

The surrounding mountains shelve sharply to Carpenter Creek. Since there was nowhere else to put it, the main street of the town was built over the creek. If you stand on the bridge across the creek late on an autumn morning, the valley half in shadow, the creek careering over the smashed and weathered boards of long-ago buildings, you can re-create in your own mind a time when Sandon served half a dozen operating mines and half a hundred unproved claims, when 23 hotels and saloons lined the short streets, when engines from two different railways chuffed into town.

A CPR steam locomotive stands on rails on the original track bed; other pieces of rolling stock are intended to re-create a 1900s freight train. A replica of the Kaslo and Slocan railway station that burned down in 1980 is being developed as an interpretive centre at the start of a five-kilometre hiking and biking trail that follows the narrow-gauge railbed. The trail ends at Payne Bluff, immortalized in photographs of the time, where the railbed seems to hang out in space, cantilevered above a 330-metre drop (see page 163). Two railway companies battled to be first into Sandon: the Kaslo and Slocan, with 51 kilometres of narrow-gauge track from Kaslo on Kootenay Lake, and the CPR branch line from Nakusp, on Arrow Lake. The route of the CPR line can also be walked.

Only a few buildings remain of Sandon's best days, among them a former brothel and a former fire hall. A visitors' centre and mining museum is located in the restored 1900 Mercantile Building. The Silversmith hydroelectric generating station, the only one of eight power stations that remains, has been restored. Tours take visitors through the station June through September. A walking-tour booklet of Sandon is available.

In 1942, Japanese Canadians were sent from the coast to live in the disintegrating buildings at Sandon. Moving from the open coast to this all-but-deserted and isolated town must have disheartened the internees. Little trace remains of the gardens they planted along the creek, and no internee was tempted after the war to stay in the shadows that lie over one side or the other of town most days of the year.

The remains of some of the old mines and the towns that supported them still exist in the Slocan, but each year snow, rain and time destroy more of these relics. Some you will find, unmarked, in the forest. Others are still named: Cody, beyond Sandon on the east side of Carpenter Creek; Alamo, about 1.5 kilometres across Carpenter Creek, 100 metres south of the turnoff to Sandon; Three Forks, just east of the Sandon turnoff; Zincton, another six kilometres along Highway 31A; and Retallack, another five kilometres east. Look for listing buildings and foundations along the road and in the forest.

Arrow Lakes

From New Denver, Highway 6 follows Slocan Lake north, then runs along mountain creeks to Upper Arrow Lake. The Arrow Lakes both reveal and hide history. Until the summer of 1969, they were separate bodies of water, joined by 32 kilometres of river. The Keenleyside Dam at Castlegar backed up water into a reservoir that flooded the valley, overwhelming farm fields, communities and houses. The wide stretches of sand travellers may see along the lakeshore are evidence of varying lake levels created by human control over water in the reservoir; debris on the lake may have been deposited on the shore and refloated many times.

The town of **NAKUSP**, where Highway 6 meets Upper Arrow Lake, was born of the Slocan mining rush. The pack trail from the Slocan mines ended at the lake here, as did the CPR line. Sternwheelers plied between the main CPR line at Revelstoke and the branch line from Nakusp. Nakusp survived when the Slocan mines were worked out because it was a port and an important point on the overland transportation systems. Sawmills built here from the 1890s on continued to operate—giving Nakusp the nickname "the sawdust town." Stroll along the waterfront walk and contemplate the bygone era when lake boats carried people and goods between communities, and prospectors thronged the rails, eager for their first glimpse of Eldorado.

A number of Chinese settlers arrived in mining days, and sawmilling attracted Sikh immigrants. Nakusp's historian notes of the early days, "We were a town of many nations . . . [China], Poland, Holland, Germany, India, Czechoslovakia, Scotland, England, the U.S.A. were established here along with a few Canadians."

Mired in a depression in 1913 and 1914, Nakusp and the Arrow Lakes region sent some 130 men and officers overseas in the Kootenay Battalion, 54th Overseas Regiment, in World War I. Those who returned organized a branch of the Great War Veterans' Association and combined with townsfolk in Nakusp to build a $2,200 war memorial and "drinking fountain for both man and beast." Erected in the centre of town, the memorial has since been moved to the Nakusp Recreation Grounds.

Property at the eastern end of Bay Street was owned by Chinese settler Sam Henry and farmed in the 1890s and 1900s by 20 Chinese immigrants. Henry's grave is in the Nakusp cemetery.

The Nakusp Museum, in a 1912 schoolhouse, chronicles steamboat, logging, mining and native history.

That the small communities on the lakeshore north and south of Nakusp look new is not surprising; the long-established communities of Fauquier and Burton were drowned by the rising reservoir and rebuilt higher up. Halcyon Hot Springs, Leon and Arrowhead all but disappeared, not to be reborn.

The hot springs were probably known to the native peoples of the region, but the first commercial exploitation began in 1890 when a hotel was opened on the site. Within a few years, the hotel became better known for the carousing that went on there than for the springs. This changed when a doctor bought the property in 1924 and opened a health spa, relying on the healing properties of the water—its high lithium content is supposed to have a cheering and relaxing effect. The doctor died in a 1955 fire that destroyed the hotel; anything left standing was drowned by the rising waters of the lake. Only a small cemetery remains (ask locally for directions); a new spa and resort was built at Halcyon in the late 1990s.

From **GALENA BAY**, named for the lead-silver ore of the region, a ferry takes traffic towards Revelstoke. North and east, Highway 31 leads across the mountains to Lardeau River and Kootenay Lake. The highway is paved partway but turns to gravel, then sometimes to one-lane dirt above Trout Lake. Beyond Trout Lake City, it is not for the faint of heart, especially in wet weather.

Pioneer photographer Ida Madeline (Mattie) Gunterman recorded life in the mining town of **BEATON**. Prints from 200 of her glass-plate negatives, rescued almost by chance, are in the collection of the Vancouver Public Library. The Guntermans came to the West Kootenay in 1898 from Seattle, seeking a drier climate that would be better for Mattie's health. The couple farmed and worked in mining and lumbering, and Mattie photographed the life and times of the backwoods mining town, developing her negatives in a woodshed attic.

TROUT LAKE CITY, about 12 kilometres beyond the end of pavement, was founded after mineral strikes drew prospectors to the region in 1893, its grandiose name conveying the hopes of its founders. Still gracing the main street is the Windsor Hotel, built in the 1890s and long the domain of Alice Elizabeth Jowett. Jowett, a widow with children, arrived in Vancouver from England in 1889. For seven years she ran a bakery but she craved a more exciting life and moved to Trout Lake City. There she opened a log-cabin hotel, then bought the Windsor. The doyenne of the town, Jowett insisted on white tablecloths and silver. She went prospecting, riding and hiking through the mountains for more than 50 years, until she was well into her eighties. The Windsor has seen up days and down days since Jowett left, as successive owners seek a way to make the old hotel prosperous once more. Have a coffee or stop for the night, and listen to the stories of the old gold days. Have a look, too, at the vintage gas pumps nearby.

Of the mining towns in the area, only Trout Lake City survived for long after the short-lived silver rush. Brief excitement hit that town in the 1980s, when a consortium proposed a molybdenum mine nearby. The town's excellent telecommunications date from that time, but the project itself was shelved.

A few kilometres northeast of Trout Lake City lie the remains of the town of **FERGUSON**. As late as the 1970s, some of the weather-beaten buildings that once lined the main street still stood, but even those have now disintegrated into piles of boards on the long flat that's not far from the creek.

The guide now returns to Highway 3A, at the junction with Highway 6 east of Castlegar. Highway 3A curves east from the Slocan, following the Kootenay River to Nelson, then heading north along the shores of Kootenay Lake.

West Kootenay: Kootenay River and Kootenay Lake

In the 41 kilometres from Nelson to Castlegar, the Kootenay River drops a total of 110 metres, over rapids, cascades and waterfalls. Though rough water made the route miserable for natives and early explorers in canoes—14 portages in one 22-kilometre stretch—the falling water provided an ideal power source for the Rossland mines. In a 30-kilometre distance, five dams hold back water that has provided power since 1898.

Two kilometres east of the Highway 6 junction, turn right (south) across the Kootenay River on the road to see the Kootenay Canal Generating Plant and a view of Lower Bonnington Dam. Over the next five kilometres along Highway 3A, signs point out parts of the power-generating system. A stop-of-interest sign fronts the turbine runner from the original Lower Bonnington power plant, first power generator for the Rossland mines. The longest (over 50 kilometres) and highest-voltage transmission line then known delivered 23,000 volts to Rossland. In succeeding years, hydro engineers built more dams and power plants to power Cominco operations at Trail and Kimberley. A display at a viewpoint shows the dams and canals to which the river waters were diverted. The power system still provides power for the West Kootenay Power and Light Company and for the City of Nelson. The area is one of the few in the province not served by giant BC Hydro. The province's first hydroelectric plant was built just south of Nelson, on Cottonwood Creek, in 1897.

Nelson

Situated where the west arm of Kootenay Lake narrows into Kootenay River, Nelson is a bonanza for the lover of heritage buildings. Born of the 1890s mining rush, the Queen City quickly grew to a population of 7,000, the largest city between Vancouver and Winnipeg. A service and government centre for the surrounding mining camps, Nelson was built with more care—and more money. As a result, its buildings survived while others disintegrated. Until recently, however, growth was very slow, so heritage buildings were not torn down for redevelopment. A 1977 government study identified some 350 heritage buildings. Four

A historic streetscape in downtown Nelson. (Vivien Bowers photo)

years later, restoration began on some of the most impressive. Nelson today is one of the province's best heritage towns.

Brochures on that heritage, outlining walking and driving tours of the city and area, are available from the museum (at the corner of Nelson Avenue and Anderson Street), the infocentre (follow signs to 225 Hall Street) or online at the City of Nelson website.

Nelson's historic sights include the late-Victorian stone Nelson courthouse at 310 Ward Street, designed by high-flying Victoria architect Francis Mawson Rattenbury and built in 1909; City Hall, at 502 Vernon Street, kitty-corner to the courthouse, in chateau-style Spokane pink brick and Kaslo marble; and the McDonald jam factory, with granite walls 60 centimetres thick that also serve as a retaining wall on Vernon Street. The jam factory won the first Heritage Building of the Year award in 1980. Owner James Albert McDonald made jam "absolutely pure and free of false colouring, glucose and other cheap substitutes."

The 200-, 300- and 400-block of Baker Street form a turn-of-the-century commercial landscape. Clapboard, cedar shingles, Kootenay marble, granite and locally fired brick in High Victorian, Italianate, Romanesque and Queen Anne styles create a highly individual and attractive line of buildings with cornices, arches, inlays, bay windows and parapets. Also worth looking at are a 1911 apartment building at 514 Victoria Street, built from granite quarried on-site, and the restored Capital Theatre at 421 Victoria Street, which brought talking pictures to town in 1927 and is now once more open for live theatre. Drop in at the beautifully renovated 1898 Heritage Inn (422 Vernon Street) for lunch or a drink.

Streetcar No. 23, built in 1906 and brought to Nelson in the mid-1920s, runs on a line built in 1899. The car carries passengers along the lakeshore, avoiding the precipitous route up and down Nelson's hills that often resulted in derailments.

Two museums are worth visiting: the Nelson Museum (recently rebranded as Touchstones Nelson: Museum of Art and History) in the 1902 former post office/city hall at Nelson Avenue and Anderson Street, with displays of area history and local art; and the Chamber of Mines of Eastern BC Museum at 215 Hall Street, with displays and information on mining in the eastern part of the province.

Miners headed for the rich silver strikes of the Slocan followed trails or boarded sternwheelers headed up Kootenay Lake. Modern travellers take Highway 3A northeast across Kootenay River and along the west arm of Kootenay Lake.

Three kilometres from the bridge across Kootenay River is the Tudor-style mansion built by Selwyn Gwillym Blaylock in the 1930s. Blaylock, a metallurgist who became president of Cominco at Trail, built this massive summer home of granite quarried on-site, with doors from England, Asia, Europe and the United

States, and a bronze sundial and elephant sculpture. The elephant later became the Cominco symbol. The renovated mansion is now a luxury inn.

At **BALFOUR**, Highway 3A is linked to the east shore of Kootenay Lake by means of a free ferry.

The guide continues north along the lake's west shore, following Highway 31.

AINSWORTH HOT SPRINGS, the first town founded in the Kootenay Lake/Slocan area in 1882, lies about 15 kilometres north of Balfour on Highway 31. Named for an Oregonian mining promoter, Ainsworth began as a mining camp and continued as a spa, attracting weary travellers to its natural hot springs, where the water is said to have the highest mineral content of any hot springs in Canada. Though much of the original town burned in 1896, the Silver Ledge Hotel and the J. B. Fletcher store survived. The store has been restored to circa 1898; on display are original fixtures, artifacts and mineral samples. The U-shaped cave that bathers follow from the hot pool was once a mining tunnel.

The Woodbury Mining Museum, four kilometres north of Ainsworth, has displays on the history of area mining and a blacksmith shop.

Kaslo

Twenty kilometres north of Ainsworth is Kaslo, which was the main supply centre for the Slocan mines to the west. In the 1890s, wood-burning tugs, sternwheel steamers and would-be miners in rowboats made their way up the lake from trail end at Bonner's Ferry in Idaho. Few stayed in town long. In the early days, most followed a rough trail, supplanted by a wagon road in 1892, over the mountains. In 1895, the 40-kilometre narrow-gauge Kaslo and Slocan Railway was completed between Kaslo and Sandon, and Kaslo grew ever larger, with 20 hotels, a Front Street lined with stores and saloons, and vaudeville entertainment on the revolving stage of the Comique Theatre—until the first town council closed down that affront to respectable citizens.

Fire and flood in 1894 didn't destroy the town's optimism, but bank failures

▼ This steam donkey is one of the machines displayed beside Ladysmith streets and roads.

▲ The replica totem poles at Victoria's Thunderbird Park are reminders of a much older past than the Empress Hotel that stands behind them.

The buildings of Market Square form a historic streetscape in downtown Victoria.

▼ *The Coquihalla tunnels near Hope exemplify a railway engineer's triumph over rock and canyon. (photo by Alena Vackova)*

▲ *A guide tells of First Nations history and culture at the Squamish Lil'Wat Cultural Centre, newly opened at Whistler in 2008.*

Domestic ducks waddle past the buildings of the Kilby Historic Site near the Harrison River east of Mission.

◀ *The McIver House and xeriscaped gardens are beside Kelowna's Benvoulin Church, which dates from 1892.*

▼ *The grist mill at Keremeos is one of the most interesting restored historic sites in the province.*

The last of the Haynes Ranch buildings near Osoyoos recall an era when ranching dominated the Okanagan Valley.

▼ Carpenter Creek rushes through the old mining town of Sandon, in the Slocan; in years past, it carried away many of Sandon's historic buildings.

▲ Modern advertisements vie with much older ones on this brick wall on Greenwood's main street.

An abandoned house speaks of failed dreams in mining country near Trout Lake.

▼ This old wagon is on display at the Windermere Valley Museum in Invermere.

▲ The general store in Sirdar dates to 1913.

Valemount's museum is housed in this classic railway station.

▼ The Quilchena Hotel near Merritt was built for travellers in the days of horseback and stagecoaches.

▲ Murray United Church, in Nicola (east of Merritt), is a fine example of the simple country churches so common in small-town British Columbia.

Hat Creek House, north of Cache Creek, welcomed many a traveller en route to the Cariboo goldfields. (photo by Alena Vackova)

The old docks of Ocean Falls, with their fading pier-side buildings, see little traffic since the Ocean Falls mill was closed. (Gary Green Photography)

◀ Totem poles at Kispiox testify to the power of First Nations heritage and art. (Gary Green Photography)

▼ The Huble homestead north of Prince George lies close to the divide between Pacific and Arctic waters.

Wonowon, at Mile 101 of the Alaska Highway, once the site of a major highway construction camp, is now a hamlet with a few houses, store and gas station.

and falling silver prices did. Kaslo, like many another Slocan town, all but succumbed: the population dropped from 7,000 to a few hundred. Now it stands at about 1,000—but that 1,000, with government grants, private contributions and fierce energy, have restored historic buildings and rescued and restored the last sternwheeler to ply Kootenay Lake.

The SS *Moyie*, launched in 1898 and retired in 1957, is displayed on the waterfront. Designated a National Historic Site, the *Moyie* is also a monument to the determination of Kaslo residents and interested outsiders who raised the money, and to the craftspeople who brought her back to her former glory. The *Moyie* is the oldest surviving vessel of her type in Canada.

The Langham Cultural Centre, on A Avenue, was restored in the 1970s. Originally the Langham Hotel (1893), the building was left to decay. Like other decrepit buildings in town, it was home to Japanese Canadians interned here after 1942. The Langham contains an archival display on the internment years.

Also in Kaslo are the restored municipal hall, built in 1898 and the oldest remaining municipal hall on the B.C. mainland; St. Andrew's United Church (circa 1896) on Fourth Street; the Kootenay Lake Farmers' Institute building (the area was known for fruit farming until disease and fading markets destroyed

Firemen in 1890s Kaslo test the water pressure in this town built mostly of wood. An 1894 fire destroyed much of the downtown. (BCA F1294)

the industry); a mining museum in the old fire hall at 402 Front Street; and a display on K&S Railway history at the *Moyie* visitor centre.

West of Kaslo, Highway 31A follows the old K&S Railway grade across the mountains to Sandon. Several score of old mines (and more claims than you could list) were—and some still are—located along this road, and some tattered buildings still stand. Forays up rough logging roads will disclose weather-beaten piles of rough-sawn boards, old mine workings or the brightly coloured surveyor's tape that marks active claims—testament to the ever-present optimism of the prospector.

The Lardeau

Highway 31 leads from Kaslo into the Lardeau, north of the end of Kootenay Lake and the site of another 1890s prospecting boom. Names like Argenta and Copper Creek are all that remain of this rush: the Lardeau did not long reward those who sought riches. The Lardeau Valley Historical Society museum is in Meadow Creek. Of interest is the nearby Copper Creek placer gold-mining site. The historical society sometimes offers conducted tours through the Lardeau country.

At the north end of the lake a road crosses the Kootenay River and leads on to **ARGENTA** and Johnson's Landing. Though its name suggests the silver rush, Argenta was never much of a mining town. This settlement and Johnson's Landing grew as would-be farmers planted orchards and market gardens to produce fruit and vegetables for the mining towns down the lake and in the hills. Wharves at the two tiny communities remain from the days when sternwheelers picked up apples and other produce and carried passengers on the only route into and out of the lakehead. Argenta, peaceful and remote, attracted a Quaker group in the early 1950s. Some of the Quakers, who wanted to escape militarism and materialism in the United States, still live at Argenta and meet in the Quaker Meeting House up the hill.

Some of the mining settlements farther north in the Lardeau were drowned when power engineers built the Duncan Dam on the Duncan River in the mid-1960s, backing up river waters over what were villages and pioneer ranches and apple orchards. **HOWSER**, where the Lardeau River flows into the Duncan, was once known as Duncan City, on the route of both Canadian Pacific and the stillborn Great Northern Railway lines; the original townsite is now beneath reservoir waters. The Hall Creek Pack Trail is by the Duncan River north of Duncan Lake. Farther along the highway, which turns into a narrow gravel road, are the jumbled and scarcely identifiable remains of one-time mining camps such as Gerrard and Poplar.

The guide now returns to Highway 3A at Balfour.

Kootenay Lake: East Shore

Those who cross Kootenay Lake by ferry from Balfour to Kootenay Bay approach what was the richest ore body of the Kootenay Lake/Slocan mineral strikes. **KOOTENAY BAY** itself was never a mining camp; it has been a small resort town since the 1920s. The road that runs north from Highway 3A just east of the ferry dock leads to **RIONDEL**, site of the famed Blue Bell mine. A stop-of-interest sign at Riondel Road gives information on the mine.

The Ktunaxa native people spoke of the "big ledge" ore outcrop here. In 1882, prospectors began to explore the region. American Robert Sproule first laid claim to the ore; Thomas Hammill staked claims next to Sproule's Blue Bell. The two then apparently jumped each other's claims. A court case gave the Blue Bell to Sproule, who sold the claim but worked it under contract. Bad feelings continued between the two men, and, on June 1, 1885, Hammill was found shot in the back. He died soon after.

The local provincial police constable and a Ktunaxa assistant chased down Sproule. He was tried, sentenced to hang, given a temporary reprieve, had his hanging date set once more, given a few more days' grace, another month's grace, then another month's grace, until finally he was given six months' delay as newspapers from Victoria to New York pleaded his case—to no avail, for he was finally hanged in October 1886.

Meanwhile, work at the Blue Bell went on and a smelter was built down the lake, south of Kootenay Bay; some brick remains can still be seen from the ferry.

The general store in Sirdar dates to 1913.

In 1905, a French company headed by Count Edouard Riondel bought the mine and operated it for 16 years. In 1931, Cominco bought the property. From 1951 to 1971, some 200,000 tons of lead-zinc ore were taken from the mine each year and the company town of Riondel grew to 600 residents.

When the mine closed, the community should have died. Instead, retired people bought the houses, turned the school into a curling rink and recreation centre and kept Riondel alive. A waterfront trail takes visitors past some of the concentrator foundations and rail tracks. The Riondel museum is in the recreation centre.

A number of small communities, born of the mining boom or settled later by orchardists, dot Highway 31 between Kootenay Bay and Creston. At **CRAWFORD BAY**, look for the Crawford Bay cemetery, with headstones dating back to the 19th century. Here also is a blacksmith's shop, where the blacksmithing techniques date back to the 19th century as well.

At **GRAY CREEK**, once a steamboat landing and home to English settlers lured by the promise of good orchard lands, are the Gray Creek Community Hall (1911), with hand-hewn cedar logs and mitred corners, and the Gray Creek Store. The store, in business since 1913, operated as a supply depot as long as boats churned the lake but is now a general store. The *City of Ainsworth* paddlewheel steamer lies below the waters near Gray Creek, well explored by underwater adventurers.

SIRDAR was named for Lord Kitchener, a *sirdar* (or commander-in-chief) of the Egyptian army at the height of imperial feelings. The town prospered when the BC Southern Railway built its roundhouse and rail yard here in 1898. The CPR still operates the railway. From Sirdar, you can follow the railway tracks around the curve of the lake to the site of the original Kootenay Landing, which was, from 1898 to 1930, one of the most important places in the region. In 1898, the CPR built its rail line to the landing. Paddlewheelers carried passengers and freight thence to the tracks at Nelson, while railway barges moved the rail cars. When the CPR joined Creston to Nelson by rail in 1930, the landing died. A few pilings still stand at the site, but you'll search in vain on modern maps for Kootenay Landing, and locals are likely to refer you to another place altogether, farther south, where a ferry once took vehicles across the river.

Also in Sirdar are the terraces built and fruit trees planted by Italian immigrants, and the 1913 general store.

Creston

Highways 3 and 3A rejoin near Creston, on the Kootenay River south of Kootenay Lake. Although land near here was staked in the 1890s, little of value was found; the Creston Valley was more important as a transportation corridor. But the real story of the Creston area is one of land reclamation.

The traveller who passed this way any spring over a hundred years ago would see what the Ktunaxa had long seen and what explorer David Thompson commented on ruefully when he tried to cross the Creston flats: flooded land with little to encourage settlement. Yet some saw the potential under the perennial floodwaters of the Kootenay River. The first to publicly declare this potential was adventurer/entrepreneur William Adolph Baillie Grohman (see Canal Flats in the Columbia Valley section of Chapter Five, The Mountain Spine). He wanted to divert the waters of the Kootenay River into the Columbia near the sources of the two rivers, thus controlling the floods. He would then be only too happy to sell the resulting rich land to would-be farmers.

Baillie Grohman's scheme foundered, but his vision was acute: a 1902 agricultural report suggested "the accumulated silt and vegetable deposit of centuries ... [made] an inexhaustible depth of the most magnificently fertile soil." Between the 1890s and the 1930s, government and private enterprise built dykes along the riverbanks and created more than 10,000 hectares of fertile farmland.

Creston's history is solidly linked to this land. The only grain elevators in southern British Columbia, the only substantial grain fields outside the Peace River country, an alfalfa-processing plant, fruit orchards, a brewery and even a mural on the town's main street are evidence of the soil's productivity.

The valley is on the flyway used by thousands of migrating birds every year. Ask at the interpretation centre at the Creston Valley Wildlife Management Area west of town for a map that shows you the dykes that you can walk. Dykes and gates are used for flood and control here, both providing stability for agriculture in the valley and establishing wetland habitat for birds, animals and plants.

Creston's museum, at 219 Devon Street, is housed in the Stone House, built over a period of 15 years by stonemason Rudy Schulze. Displays include a replica of a Ktunaxa canoe—a sturgeon-nosed boat that points down at each end—and agricultural implements.

Some five kilometres south of Creston on Highway 21 is the Yaqan Nuki Heritage Centre, housed for the moment in the Legend Logos buildings on the Ktunaxa reserve. The centre displays some of the truly unique culture of the area Ktunaxa, including a model of a *tulle tipi*, a teepee made from cattail-stalk mats that are themselves creative use of what was once an abundant resource in the wetlands; and a model of a sturgeon-nosed canoe, used by the Ktunaxa to cut through the waters of the wetlands. The Yaqan Nuki Heritage Society is working towards a freestanding heritage centre where they can display artifacts and present videos and photographs that detail their culture. The Yaqan Nuki are also taking steps to preserve their language, considered endangered since now fewer than 10 people speak it fluently; the language incorporates both spoken words and hand signs.

Some signs of the old Dewdney Trail built in 1865 are also still visible near Creston. From the Summit Creek picnic area on Highway 3 about 10 kilometres west of Creston, walk across the suspension bridge over the river and follow the path that in turn follows an old trail to Williams Creek. The remains of log cabins can be seen here.

From Creston, Highway 3 continues east into the East Kootenay, part of the Mountain Spine region that parallels the Rocky Mountains from the American border to the Robson Valley.

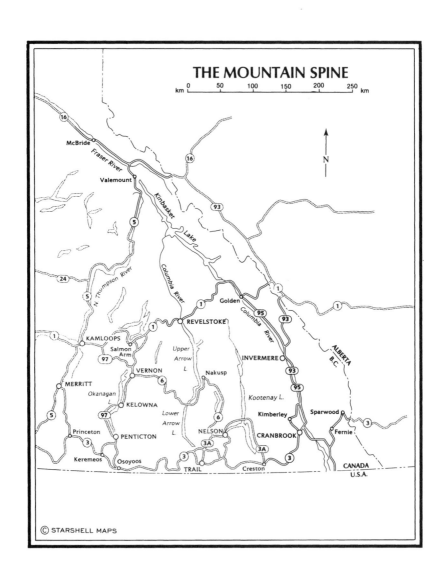

THE MOUNTAIN SPINE

km | 0 | 50 | 100 | 150 | 200 | 250 km

N

McBride
Fraser River
Valemount
Kinbasket Lake
Columbia River
N. Thompson River
Golden
Columbia River
REVELSTOKE
KAMLOOPS
Salmon Arm
Upper Arrow L.
Nakusp
INVERMERE
VERNON
MERRITT
Okanagan L.
KELOWNA
Lower Arrow L.
Kootenay L.
Kimberley
Sparwood
Princeton
PENTICTON
NELSON
CRANBROOK
Fernie
Keremeos
Osoyoos
TRAIL
Creston
ALBERTA B.C.
CANADA
U.S.A.

© STARSHELL MAPS

THE MOUNTAIN SPINE

Canadians who live "back east" sometimes seem to think that the Rocky Mountains are the only mountain chain in British Columbia. They are wont to declare that you can see the Rockies from Vancouver, somehow subsuming the intervening half-dozen mountain ranges into this one set.

They have good reason. The Rockies are the quintessential North American mountain chain, known around the world for their beauty and their splendour. A traveller heading west sees them from a distance, the foothills abruptly breaking the flat plains of prairie Canada. For thousands of kilometres to the east, from these foothills to the Atlantic Ocean, no point rises more than 1,700 metres above sea level—some 2,300 metres lower than the highest peak in the Rocky Mountains. For all the grandeur of British Columbia's other mountain chains, the Rockies are truly Canada's mountain spine. This line of peaks rising above the plain has always marked the beginning of something completely other: a climate, topography and lifestyle different from that in the rest of Canada.

Four of the province's great rivers rise from the mountain spine: the Columbia and Kootenay in the south, the Thompson and the Fraser farther north. The Columbia and Kootenay run along the Rocky Mountain Trench, a 1,400-kilometre-long depression that extends along the western edge of the Rockies from the Yukon to Montana. Born in the Rockies, the Fraser soon angles westward across half the province. The North Thompson quickly leaves the trench to flow southwest into the province's Interior plateau. Throughout early prehistory and history, though the mountains barred the way to the traveller, these rivers beckoned.

The human history of the mountain spine, then, is one of dealing with the barriers presented by the mountains and taking advantage of the rivers and their valleys. The Rockies mark a division for native people: the Cree and Piegan range the plains and forests east of the mountains; the Ktunaxa live in the river valleys to the west. Though the groups were not allies in pre-contact times, and, indeed, were often enemies, they did cross the mountains by way of the high passes, the easterners seeking salmon and game, the westerners hunting buffalo on the plains.

The early explorers and fur traders saw the Rockies mainly as a barrier between them and the Pacific Ocean. David Thompson, travelling for the North West Company in the early 1800s, made repeated forays into the eastern foothills of the Rockies before he found Howse Pass, which led him to the Columbia River. He was the first to record meeting natives on both east and west sides of the Rockies. The Piegan he feared: they wanted to control any trade between white and native in the region and tried to keep Thompson from establishing posts west of the Rockies. The Ktunaxa Thompson trusted and relied on: they showed him the best places to build his posts and guided him through the region.

First Nations and white explorers alike used the rivers as transportation routes. But the Columbia and the Kootenay confused Thompson. The two rivers rise close to each other, then flow in opposite directions until they reunite near present-day Castlegar. Thompson descended the Columbia (which he did not recognize as such, and misnamed the *Kootenae*), to establish the first fur-trading post in the area near Windermere Lake. Thompson did eventually trace the Columbia to its mouth, but too late to claim it for the British: Americans had established a post at the river mouth a short time earlier.

The fur trade along the Columbia did not amount to much. The route through the mountain passes was difficult and demanding, eastern posts were far from the Pacific coast, and transport through the region was not a simple matter. When the establishment of the 49th parallel as the border between the United States and British territory made it impossible to use the Columbia as a trade route, the southeast corner slipped from the fur-trade map. Life continued much as it had for several thousand years along the mountain spine until, in the 1860s, gold was discovered at Wild Horse Creek, a tiny tributary of the Kootenay. The Dewdney Trail was extended from Hope to the southwest corner of the region, and prospectors flocked to the diggings on the creek.

The discovery was followed by others over the next 40 years: lead and silver at Moyie and Kimberley, coal at Fernie and in the Elk River Valley. Between the 1860s and 1900, prospectors and miners poured into the southeast corner of British Columbia. Many were American. Few came overland from the east: distance and the solid barrier of the Rockies made the trip most uninviting. Half of the towns in this area derive directly from the mines, most of the rest indirectly. Of this latter group, some were on water routes used to take ore to American smelters or bring people and goods in. Some were on the routes of railways built north from the United States or east from the rest of British Columbia or, eventually, west from Alberta.

In the northern part of the mountain spine region, north of present-day Revelstoke, there were very few mineral discoveries to encourage settlement. Here, the building of railways between east and west brought people in to found new towns and establish farms.

In 1871, British Columbia joined Canadian Confederation on the promise that a railway would be built to the coast within 10 years. The Rockies and the parallel ranges to the west—the Selkirk and Monashees—were a major barrier to the fulfillment of that promise. Finally, after several years of seeking suitable passes through the mountains, the Canadian Pacific Railway chose a route through the Kicking Horse Pass in the Rockies, the Rogers Pass in the Selkirks and on through the Monashees. In 1884, workmen pushed the rails across the Great Divide.

As the head of steel moved west, workers built construction camps and the railway company established division points. Field, Golden, Donald, Revelstoke—all owed their existence to the railway. The building of the railway also established images of the Rockies in the minds of Canadians and Europeans. In 1885, inspired by the mountains' beauty, the Canadian government set aside small park reserves near Banff and west of the Kicking Horse Pass. These reserves would become the basis of the Rocky Mountain national parks. The parks, subsequently expanded, became the epitome of wild beauty for travellers from around the world. Quick to realize their potential, the CPR established hotels along the railway route from Banff to the western flank of the Monashees and imported Swiss guides to take tourists into the mountains.

For a number of years, CPR riverboats and trails linked the CPR to the Windermere Lake area and the mining towns and railways farther south. Transportation brought the same kind of land speculation that occurred across the southern Interior in the decade after 1900. The Columbia Valley between Windermere Lake and Golden is generally broad and pleasant. The area was heavily promoted as yet another Garden of Eden in British Columbia, suited to English families of a certain class who wished to make a prosperous life in a new land. These promotions, however, were misleading: the climate, the soil and the promised amenities were not as described. Nor were many of the city-bred English settlers well suited to a pioneer life. Many of the settlers left, some to fight and die for Britain in World War I. But some stayed; the towns and farms they founded were the basis for later settlement in the valley.

In the 1860s, a gold rush to the Big Bend of the Columbia engendered some excitement on the great curve the river makes before flowing south. But the rush died quickly, and the area here and to the north remained almost unknown until the economic boom B.C. and the rest of Canada experienced circa 1912 encouraged entrepreneurs to attempt new transcontinental railways. The Grand Trunk Pacific chose to route its line through the northern part of the mountain spine, across the Yellowhead Pass and past Mount Robson, the highest peak in the Canadian Rockies; along the Fraser from its source through the Robson Valley to Prince George; then on to Prince Rupert.

When the GTP came through in 1912, it seemed at first as if the Robson Valley would become as busy as Banff to the south. The mountain peaks were glorious, the valley was broad and inviting and now the railway could bring settlers and tourists. Mountaineers hastened to climb Mount Robson, railway division points became towns and some farmers came to raise crops and cattle on the benches above the Fraser. But despite all this, the timing was bad. The boom collapsed, World War I began and the area remained quiet. Only after

World War II did many tourists begin to visit the area—and most of these were drawn to Jasper, on the Alberta side of the Rockies. Even today, Highway 16 from Prince George to the Robson Valley and the Rockies, built only in the 1960s, attracts little traffic. The only direct land link between the Robson Valley and the rest of the mountain spine in British Columbia was cut in the 1970s when the Mica Dam at Revelstoke backed up the waters of the Columbia River into a long reservoir that drowned the connecting road. Yet the valley remains a part, in history and geography, of the long mountain spine.

---•---

The mountain spine region parallels the Rocky Mountains from the United States border north to Mount Robson and the Robson Valley. Within it lie the Rockies and the Rocky Mountain Trench from the Alberta border west to the Purcell, Columbia and Cariboo mountains. The region also takes in the mountainous area from the Rockies through the Monashees along the Trans-Canada Highway and the historic route of the Canadian Pacific Railway.

This section of the guide begins at the south end of the region, where Highway 95 coming north from Idaho joins Crowsnest Highway 3.

HIGHWAY 3: YAHK TO THE ALBERTA BORDER

Highways 3 and 95 follow the Moyie River northeast through the village of Curzon, named, as were Kitchener and Sirdar to the west, for a man who helped run the British Empire: the Marquess of Curzon was viceroy of India.

YAHK, about four kilometres from the Highway 95 junction, is an old lumber town. Its name possibly means "arrow," but more probably "female caribou" or even possibly "bow in the river." From about the turn of the century to the late 1920s, loggers cut a wide swath through the region from here to Cranbrook. Mills at Kitchener, Yahk and now-abandoned towns such as Lumberton, Wycliffe and Bull River produced railway ties and building lumber, but by the late 1920s accessible timber in the area had been logged off and the mills closed. The town

186

of Yahk, on the railway, survived, though its population dropped from 450 to 100. With its proximity to the American border, it is said to have a rum-running history from the days of Prohibition in the United States. Across the tracks from the highway are the last historic buildings in the town, two 1920s buildings that no longer function as hotels. The auto camps—forerunners of modern motels—down by the river that dated back to the 1930s are either gone or no longer in public use. They originate from the early days of rubber-tire traffic, when intrepid holiday travellers ventured forth over rough roads.

In 1808, explorer David Thompson tried to return to his post near Windermere Lake by following the Moyie River. The river was in flood, windfalls made passage extremely difficult and sharp stones cut the horses' feet. Game had fled the land and the group might well have starved had Ktunaxa not given them year-old dried carp and bread made from black tree lichen. Though Thompson had named the river for his clerk, Finan McDonald, the name that stuck was a French name given by later traders: *mouillé* is the French word for "wet," a common fate for travellers who tried to follow the river at flood time.

Thompson's travels are commemorated in a stop-of-interest sign at the highwayside community of **MOYIE**, on Moyie Lake. A religious, upright, stubborn

St. Peter's Catholic Church (1904) at Moyie.

and multi-talented man who did more to map western Canada than any other, Thompson was perhaps the most complex personality of the trading-company explorers who ventured into British Columbia between 1776 and 1843.

Moyie's story centres on the friendship between Pierre Nicklehead, a Ktunaxa, and Father Nicolas Coccola, a Corsican missionary and priest who ran the St. Eugene Mission near present-day Cranbrook. Urged by Coccola to keep an eye out for mineral deposits, Nicklehead brought in rock samples from the hills near Moyie Lake. He led Coccola and James Cronin, a mining promoter, to the spot, and the three filed claims where the galena—lead-silver ore—looked most promising.

Coccola and Nicklehead quickly sold out their claims. Most of the $12,000 they received went to build a church near the St. Eugene Mission and another at Moyie. Nicklehead retained $300 and had a house built. He adopted the last name of Cronin; his grave is in the St. Eugene cemetery.

The St. Eugene mine near Moyie operated from 1893 to 1911. Some mine buildings, a slag heap, the 1907 fire hall, the blue and white St. Peter's Catholic Church (1904) and the cemetery west of town remain from those years. The Moyie High House museum contains memorabilia from the town's past. Tailings dumped into the lake during the mine's glory days were later recovered and re-milled, and other claims in the area were staked and worked. Pioneer newspaper editor Fred Smythe recorded that a shortage of women in the town didn't keep the people from forming up for a quadrille: the seven Moyie women were joined by a man with a handkerchief tied around his arm, to make up two sets.

Cranbrook

The site of present-day **CRANBROOK** was for centuries camp and pasture land for the Ktunaxa. Early settler James Baker bought the land from the original pre-emptors and promptly fenced it, shutting out the Ktunaxa and their horses. Chief Isadore refused to give up the land. He and his band also freed two Ktunaxa held without evidence in the slaying of two white miners and ordered a police constable and land surveyor to leave Ktunaxa land. When it heard of Ktunaxa actions, the Dominion government sent a troop of North West Mounted Police under Sam Steele to the area. The dispute was resolved, though not perhaps as the Ktunaxa might have preferred: Chief Isadore and the band were forced to cede the land and retreat to the St. Eugene lands on the St. Mary River north of Cranbrook.

Baker farmed what was now his land, built a house in 1888 and, in some way not documented, persuaded the CPR to route their Crowsnest line through that land, bypassing Fort Steele. The new town of Cranbrook became the railway division point; Fort Steele dwindled and Cranbrook throve after the first train came through in 1898.

As befits a city made by the railway, Cranbrook is home to one of the province's best railway museums. The Canadian Museum of Rail Travel is in new quarters at 57 Van Horne Street South, on Highway 3 at Baker Street. (Note that William Van Horne was the head of the CPR when the first transcontinental line was conceived and completed.) The museum contains what is considered the best collection of vintage passenger equipment in Canada. Of interest is a luxurious restored 1929 CPR train, the Trans-Canada Limited, which includes a dining car, a solarium car, deluxe sleeper cars and a day parlour car. Quite probably the only set of its kind in the world, the train was designed as a travelling hotel: it's an example from the days when first-class rail across Canada was the epitome of fine travel. A new feature at the museum is the Royal Alexandra Hall, the café from the Royal Alexandra Hotel in Winnipeg painstakingly rebuilt piece by numbered piece. The museum is near the rail yards, still crowded with operating rail stock. Interestingly, a CPR subsidiary now offers amazingly expensive luxury passenger tours of the Rockies, using Cranbrook as one of its bases.

A heritage walking-and-driving tour of Cranbrook is available from the infocentre or museum. Among the 40 heritage buildings are those in the Baker Hill residential area, with a variety of opulent homes built between 1900 and 1914; Colonel Baker's 1888 home, on First Street South between 13th and 14th; various downtown business buildings, especially those on the east side of the 100-block of 12th Avenue; and churches built between 1898 and 1927.

Northeast of Cranbrook (turn east off Highway 95A two kilometres north of Cranbrook) is Aqam, the St. Mary's Ktunaxa reserve. Two buildings here illuminate the history of the Ktunaxa since the 1800s. The St. Eugene Mission Church was built in 1897 with funds from the mine claims filed jointly by Pierre Nicklehead and priest Coccola (see the Moyie section in this chapter). This fine Gothic-style mission church has Italian stained and leaded glass, louvres, pinnacles and buttresses. It has been restored to its original splendour. Close by is the stone St. Eugene Mission residential school built in 1912. Many Ktunaxa still bear bitter memories of their time at this school, when they were forbidden to speak their own language or follow their own traditions. The school—with other buildings to surround it—is the site of the Ktunaxa Interpretive Centre, with displays that explore the past and present of the five bands that make up the Ktunaxa Kinbaskit nation. The centre is part of a resort that contains a casino, golf course and hotel.

When the resort development was being contemplated, one of the elders noted that it was within the SEM school that the Ktunaxa culture was taken away, so it was only fitting that it is within that building that the culture should be restored.

Highway 95A follows the St. Mary River northwest, then veers north to **KIMBERLEY**. In 1893, the North Star Mine began production of lead, silver and zinc here; shortly thereafter, the Sullivan Mine went into operation. The North Star shut down some years ago. With the closure of the Sullivan at the end of 2001, the city lost its last operating mine. Though Kimberley has tried to attract more tourists by assuming a Bavarian theme, it retains strong links to a rougher past. The Kimberley Underground Mining Train—once used in underground mining—chugs 12 kilometres over switchbacks and through narrow valleys from downtown Kimberley to the site of the Sullivan. An interpretive centre houses a variety of exhibits on the mine and the surrounding area. Cominco—owner of the Sullivan—has published a number of brochures and pamphlets on mining history and processes, available at the centre.

In town, history is on display at the Kimberley Heritage Museum, at 105 Spokane Street. The North Star schoolhouse (1903) has been brought down from the mountain and reassembled about two kilometres from downtown on the road to the North Star ski hill. And the energetic can follow parts of the McGinty Trail, the route used by the horse-drawn wagons that carried ore from the Sullivan to the Kootenay River, where it was loaded onto riverboats and taken to the smelter at Great Falls, Montana. Ask at the museum or infocentre for access points to the trail.

The guide returns to Cranbrook and follows Highway 3 east towards the Alberta border.

Highway 3, now joined with Highway 93, goes across the Kootenay River at **WARDNER**, then veers away from the river, which broadens into Lake Koocanusa (an abbreviation of Kootenay, Canada and U.S.A.), the reservoir created when the American Corps of Engineers dammed the Kootenay at Libby, Montana, in 1973. Travellers can see the reservoir from the Jaffray side road or from roads that branch from Highway 93 south of Elko.

The dam and reservoir are in an area that has had a long history of cross-border transactions: north-south is often easier than east-west when mountain chains bar the east-west routes. Gold miners came north from Montana and ore went south to American smelters. As for the Ktunaxa, they were not constrained by artificial boundaries.

Highway 93 coming north from the United States joins Highway 3 near Elko. Continue east on Highway 3.

Fernie and Area

William Fernie was prospecting for gold in 1887 when he discovered outcroppings of coal on Michel Creek, north of present-day **FERNIE**. He and brother Peter prospected the Elk River Valley and realized the great size of the coal deposits. From that time on, coal mining dominated the life of the southeast corner. Fernie was founded in 1898, with the coal mines and the coming of the CPR. Trains on the Great Northern Railway from Montana rolled into town a few years later.

It's said that William Fernie persuaded a young Ktunaxa woman to tell him where the coal deposits were by promising to marry her; when he reneged, her mother called upon the spirits to curse the town. Legend or bad luck, coal and fire brought Fernie more than its share of misery. An explosion at the Coal Creek mines in 1902 killed 128 of the 150 men on shift. A fire in 1904 destroyed much of the wooden business section of the town. Unsuccessful strikes in 1906 and 1907 threw hundreds of men out of work. But Fernie had recovered and rebuilt by 1908. Then, on August 1, just as rescuers were digging out 20 men trapped in a minor cave-in, wildfire from slash burning raced down the Elk River Valley and destroyed everything in its path. Residents fled the city in special trains that barely outran the flames. Nine people were killed.

Almost everyone returned to the smoking ruins and rebuilt the city with aid that poured in on trains from east and west. This time, they built in brick and stone; many of these buildings still stand—aided, perhaps, by the fact that Ktunaxa chiefs lifted the curse in a special ceremony in 1964.

The town infocentre and the Fernie and District Historical Museum sell a heritage walking-tour brochure that describes historic buildings. Among them are the only chateau-style courthouse in British Columbia, complete with stained-glass windows; the few houses that escaped the fires, on Riverside (4A) Avenue and on First and Second streets; the Elks Hall (491 First Avenue), at various times a Chinese laundry, a restaurant and a shoemaker's; the City Hall, built in 1905, survivor of the 1908 fire, protector of the people who crowded in to escape the flames; and the 1908 railway station, now relocated as an arts centre. The museum is moving from its cramped quarters in the infocentre to the 1910 Renaissance Revival brick Home Bank Building at the corner of Second Avenue and Fifth Street.

Outside of town, beside the provincial infocentre on the highway is a reconstruction of an oil-drilling derrick, plus oil-drilling equipment, some dating from just after World War I when drillers found oil in the Flathead Valley southeast of Fernie. The Coal Creek Heritage Trail leads to the old townsite of Coal Creek. The pioneer cemetery, with tombstones that reflect Fernie's accident-filled past, is on a hill south of town.

Many of the dots on the map between Cranbrook and the Alberta border are truly whistle stops, named more in hope than in fact when the CPR came through. Historian Fred Smythe commented that "townsites were plotted and real estate agents flocked in like yellow jackets at a picnic." In 1899, the coal company built **MICHEL**, with 60 duplexes, 60 houses and three boarding houses for its employees. Rents were set by union agreement. For more than 70 years, miners and their families lived in this town and neighbouring **NATAL**, named in the spirit of the times for a South African town in the news during the Boer War. Though passersby commented how dirtied by coal dust the buildings and streets were, a civic pride still existed. When the federal and provincial governments built **SPARWOOD**, northeast of Fernie, in the 1960s and people moved from the old to the new town, the Crowsnest Pass Coal Company began tearing down the old houses of Natal and Michel, and some tears were shed. By 1971, most traces of these towns were gone, the buildings flattened and a huge open-pit coal mine operating where they used to stand. Now, only the increasingly derelict Michel Hotel remains. Murals on the side of Sparwood buildings re-create the old life of Natal and Michel.

Beyond Michel, Highway 3 runs through the Rockies by way of the **CROWS-NEST PASS**, probably so named because a band of Crow natives was killed here by Blackfoot who found them in their camp or "nest." From the time of the first railway camps, bootleggers thrived in the little town of Crowsnest on the B.C.–Alberta border. Once Prohibition began in Alberta in 1915 and in the United States in 1920, Crowsnest and Fernie welcomed thirsty neighbours—a traffic that local police forces seemed oddly unable to halt.

The guide now returns to the junction of Highways 3, 93 and 95, northeast of Cranbrook. Follow Highway 93/95 north to Fort Steele.

The Columbia Valley: Fort Steele to Golden

John and James Galbraith founded the first settlement at Fort Steele in 1863, with a cable ferry that took eager prospectors across the Kootenay River on their way to a gold strike on Wild Horse Creek. The town was renamed after Superintendent Sam Steele, and a troop of North West Mounted Police rode in to mediate in a dispute between white and native (see the Cranbrook section in this chapter). Though Steele stayed less than a year, his name remained. The town prospered when the North Star mine opened at Kimberley and ore was transferred from wagon train to riverboat here. It virtually died in 1898 when the CPR bypassed the site and went instead to the new townsite of Cranbrook. In 1961, the B.C. government began reconstruction of Fort Steele as a heritage site, rebuilding original buildings, moving in turn-of-the-century buildings from nearby sites and constructing some replicas. Today, Fort Steele is one of the province's most popular historic sites. The grounds are open year-round; summer visitors see re-created period activities, ride a passenger wagon behind Clydesdale horses or hop aboard a steam train. Though summer is the most popular time, romantics may prefer a visit off-season, when they can imagine their own turn-of-the-century dramas.

To reach **WILD HORSE CREEK** and see the remains from the 1860s Wild Horse gold rush, turn right (north) from the fort onto Highway 93/95, drive about 300 metres, then turn right onto the Fort Steele/Bull River Road. Turn left at the top of the hill onto Wild Horse Creek Road, which follows the last mile of the Dewdney Trail, extended from the Okanagan to the East Kootenay in 1865 because of the gold rush. A few kilometres along this road, you can see what remains of the placer mining camps, including the remains of the Victoria Ditch, the Chinese and Caucasian gold-miners' cemeteries and piles of rock moved by hand, as well as the remains of a later hydraulic mining effort.

Once called Stud Horse, renamed in what may have been the only example of propriety in the history of 19th-century gold rushes, Wild Horse saw more than 5,000 fortune hunters between 1863 and 1865, some of them after gold from the ground and some of them after gold from the miners. Fisherville, with its 50 makeshift buildings, lasted just a few seasons. In 1865, miners tore the buildings down, seeking gold beneath them. Most miners then left, but 500 Chinese stayed, patiently working the gold sands; by 1902, most of these had gone as well. Visitors must look hard for rubble in the underbrush to discover the remains of shacks and other buildings. Wild Horse provides a fascinating contrast with Fort Steele and its buildings and grounds, the natural decay of a boom town differing from the well kept, preserved and restored.

North of Fort Steele, the highway follows the Rocky Mountain Trench and the Kootenay River towards its source. It passes through **WASA**, named by a Finnish settler for his native town of Vasa, and **SKOOKUMCHUCK**, its name the Chinook jargon for "turbulent water." At **CANAL FLATS**, the road bridges the Kootenay River, then crosses the low divide between the Kootenay and Columbia rivers.

Both rivers rise in the trench. The Columbia has its source in Columbia Lake, the Kootenay in a number of small mountain streams to the northeast. The two rivers run parallel, the Kootenay south, the Columbia north, for about a hundred kilometres. At Canal Flats, they are separated by less than two kilometres of fairly flat land. That narrow neck of land prompted one of the more ambitious schemes ever promoted in B.C.: the diversion of the waters of the Kootenay into the Columbia. By so doing, sportsman and promoter William Adolf Baillie Grohman planned to eliminate yearly flooding of the flats near Creston, create fertile farmland, sell it to investors and, not incidentally, make himself rich.

By his own account, Baillie Grohman was an aristocrat, born of a castle-owning Austrian father and a country-house English mother. In 1882, looking for opportunities sporting and economic, he was hunting mountain goats in the Rockies with Teddy Roosevelt—or so he said—when he devised his great scheme, a canal between the Kootenay and the Columbia. At high water in the spring, the flooding waters of the Kootenay would be diverted northwards. Baillie Grohman floated a land company to achieve his aims. He had built part of his canal when the federal government, alerted by the CPR, riverboat operators and outraged settlers along the Columbia, politely informed the provincial government that it had no right to authorize the diversion.

Grohman was disappointed but not destroyed; terming himself and other entrepreneurs "busted Britishers," he continued with a scaled-down project, but only two boats and no water ever passed from one river system to the other.

The name Canal Flats remains. BC Hydro tried to revive the diversion scheme in the 1970s but was stymied by local opposition. If you stand at water's edge in Canal Flats Provincial Park (go northeast through town and follow the signs), you can look to the north and sing praises or sigh, depending on your opinion of megaprojects that rearrange the landscape.

After it crosses the divide, the highway follows the shore of Columbia Lake, then parallels the infant Columbia. **FAIRMONT HOT SPRINGS,** just to the north, was a favourite stopping place for Ktunaxa, Secwepemc and Blackfoot travellers, who valued its warm, odourless, curative waters. At the turn of the 19th century, white settlers saw the potential for tourist development. A bungalow camp opened early in the 1900s, charging rates from a dollar to $2.50 a day, $3.50 with meals—somewhat less than the rates at today's resort, expanded in the 1960s and expanding ever since. The 1887 house of homesteader George Geary still stands at the southern end of the mountainside golf course.

Windermere/Invermere

Though Windermere, Invermere and Athalmer derive their names from a common source, they were named by three different people, none of whom could have been looking at the nearby Rockies when they noted the area's resemblance to English lakes country. Surveyor G. M. Sproat named Windermere in 1883; an aristocratic civil engineer–turned-settler changed "Salmon Beds" to Athalmer; Copper City was changed to Canterbury, then finally to Invermere when the Columbia Valley Irrigated Fruit Lands Company took over the land at the head of the lake from the CPR in 1908.

Company principal Robert Randolph Bruce, mining engineer and former CPR land agent, promoted the area as the usual Eden. He advertised in England, attracting the "right kind" of vaguely upper class, slightly down-on-their-luck English who believed his specious promises of irrigated benchlands where apples would grow below the beauteous mountains. East of the mountains, he proclaimed, prairie dwellers stood, money in hand, begging for such fine produce.

Those who came found not the promised railway nor the irrigation canals nor the markets—not even a climate suitable for fruit growing. Few stayed long; most returned to England, where many of the men served in World War I.

Perhaps **WINDERMERE**'s most famous building, its story often retold, is the Stolen Church. Originally St. Peter's Anglican, the church began life in 1887 in Donald, on the CPR main line. When the CPR transferred its divisional point from Donald to Revelstoke, it moved houses and buildings to the new site. But when Donald residents Cecilia and Rufus Kimpton moved to Windermere with their two sons, Cecilia missed her old church. Rufus and friends went back to Donald, dismantled the church and shipped it by train to Golden, then by boat to Windermere. When Revelstoke churchmen arrived to take the church to their city, they were dismayed to find it missing. They complained, synod officials wrote measured letters—but somehow, their letters were misplaced and the church stayed where it was. Finally, all was forgiven and the bishop consented to reconsecrate the stolen church. The 250-kilogram silver-toned bell disappeared while the church was being moved; it now rings from a steeple in Golden.

Windermere Lake has become a favourite resort for Albertans who crowd the valley in summer and in the winter ski season. The earliest traveller to build a temporary home here was David Thompson, fur trader and map-maker. Thompson, travelling for the North West Company in 1807, crossed the Rockies from the North Saskatchewan River through Howse Pass to the Columbia, then ascended the river south to Lake Windermere. Not surprisingly, he mistook the river for the Kootenay. He built first by the lake then moved to a more protected position on Toby Creek, which he named Nelson Rivulet. Salmon from the river sustained him, his wife, their family and the fur-trading party during their first winter, but it could not do so today: American and Canadian dams on the Columbia have made it impossible for salmon to return upstream.

With the help of the Ktunaxa, he explored and mapped the Kootenay and Columbia rivers and established trading posts in what is now American territory. The time Thompson spent exploring the Kootenay and Columbia show him at his methodical best and seeing-the-large-picture worst. Careful and thorough, unhurried when perhaps he should have hurried, he arrived at the mouth of the Columbia some weeks after American traders, who thereby established the American claim to the area. And perhaps he could have been more prudent at times. For example, he sent mountain-goat furs back east and the "ignorant, self-sufficient partners" ridiculed him; he therefore refused to send more even when they changed their minds.

A cairn marks the site of Thompson's Kootenae House. To reach it, take the road towards Invermere from the highway, turn right on Wilmer-Panorama Road, then right on Westside Road. The fort site is a few hundreds metres along this road on the right.

INVERMERE still has something of the look of a pioneer town, though townhouse developments and coffeehouses are making it more 21st than 19th century. The town began to develop in about 1912, spurred by the Kootenay Central

Railway link between Invermere and Golden, and by mines that began operation on Toby Creek. A map of a historical walking tour of the town is available at the Windermere Valley Museum to the right of the road on the way into Invermere. Displays here present, in seven restored buildings, Shuswap and Ktunaxa history and the days of fur traders, explorers, steamboats on the river and lake and other early transportation in the Columbia Valley.

What remains of historic Invermere gives clues to its eclectic history. From Beach Drive south of town, you can look out over the site of the second Invermere golf course, now converted to housing. The first golf course was at Fort Point, beside the lake at the CPR tracks. Dignitaries could ride into town on their private railcars, park on a siding and take part in golf competitions, being particularly meticulous about the sand "greens." The course was replaced when the CPR built a lodge and the David Thompson Memorial Fort, which was a remarkable semi-replica of Kootenae House, with kerosene lamps shaped like teepees. The replica has since burned down.

In 1915, land promoter and later B.C. Lieutenant-Governor Robert Randolph Bruce built a fine log house for himself and his wife, Lady Elizabeth Norton—though she died before the building was finished. The house still stands near the lake; follow signs to the Pynelogs Cultural Centre. Other downtown buildings were erected between 1911 and 1928.

RADIUM HOT SPRINGS attracted Ktunaxa and other First Nations long before whites discovered the mineral hot springs, which bubble out of the ground at about 45.5°C. The springs acquired their present name in 1915, when it was believed that the water was highly radioactive. English investors began building the first pool on the site in 1914. It was still unfinished when the federal government created Kootenay National Park and took over the site in 1920. The hot pool and the Banff-Windermere Highway both opened in 1923.

Kootenay National Park was the last dedicated of the four mountain parks. East of Radium, flanking Highway 93 in the park, is Sinclair Canyon, 10 kilometres of rocky walls. Known to the native people for obvious reasons as Red Rock Gorge, it was renamed when trader James Sinclair led a group of Métis away from increased settlement in southern Manitoba, across the Rockies and

199

through the canyon, to new lands in Oregon. A stop-of-interest sign describing their efforts is located beside Highway 93/5 two kilometres south of Radium.

A monument commemorating the 1841 journey of George Simpson, governor of the Hudson's Bay Company, is 55 kilometres from the west entrance to Kootenay Park. Another eight kilometres east, a visitor centre is on the site of a CPR bungalow camp from the 1920s. And another 20 kilometres east, Paint

Pots marks the site of a source of vermilion used by Ktunaxa and Stoney people for many years.

Back at Radium, Highway 95 continues north towards Golden, through the narrowing Columbia Valley. Residents in this part of the valley still outnumber tourists. The small town of **EDGEWATER**, like so many here laid out before World War I, was to be a model farming community, with flumes, cleared fields and a 24-room hotel with tennis courts and livery stables. However, the war called English settlers away, the company that owned the land went bankrupt and Edgewater dwindled away to a score of residents. A few buildings date from before the war; others date from the community's revival in the late 1920s.

Farther north, in **SPILLAMACHEEN**, is St. Mark's, a small, 1898 log cabin church on a hill.

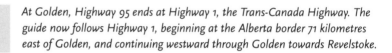

At Golden, Highway 95 ends at Highway 1, the Trans-Canada Highway. The guide now follows Highway 1, beginning at the Alberta border 71 kilometres east of Golden, and continuing westward through Golden towards Revelstoke.

HIGHWAY 1: ALBERTA BORDER TO THREE VALLEY GAP

Highway 1 and the tracks of the Canadian Pacific Railway descend through mountain passes and valleys from the Alberta border to British Columbia's Interior plateau. From the Great Divide, road and rail wind down the western slopes of the Rockies, then through the Selkirks and Monashees, both part of the Columbia Mountain chain.

The Kicking Horse Pass through the Rockies was named when a pack horse kicked James Hector—who was exploring with the Palliser Expedition of 1859—in the chest and knocked him senseless. Long a route for the Plains and Ktunaxa First Nations, Kicking Horse was surveyed by Major A. B. Rogers for the CPR in 1881. Two years later, geologist George Dawson, mapping the country for the Canadian government, explored and named many of the area's geographic features.

The CPR was built through the pass in 1884. Looking for a job working on the railway, English traveller Morley Roberts issued a lament many a subsequent

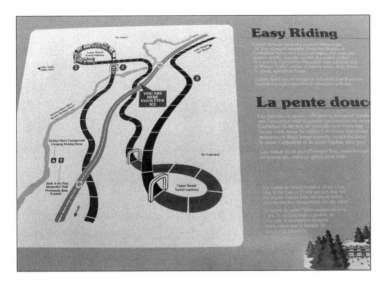

Viewpoints and displays describe the Spiral Tunnels that replaced the Big Hill to the Kicking Horse Pass.

traveller could agree with: "I am fain to confess that my memories of the next two days are so confused that whether Tunnel Mountain came before the Kicking Horse Lake or whether it didn't, whether we crossed one, two or three rivers before we got to Porcupine Creek, whether it was one mountain fire we saw or two or more, I can hardly say with any certainty. All was so new and wonderful to me that one thing drove the other out of my head, and when I think it was so while I was walking slowly, I am lost in astonishment to see so many fluently describe mountain passes they have traversed in the train. I am afraid the guide books must be a great aid to them." Rocks, glaciers, forests, roaring mountain streams: all these would be familiar to later tourists.

The first tracks that the CPR built, in the 1880s, descended from the pass at a grade of 4.5 percent; 2.2 percent is considered the normal maximum railway grade. One of the first trains to attempt the descent derailed, and three men died. Stricter safety rules were enforced, and engineers took their trains down at a crawl. Frequently, four engines were needed to haul trains back up the steep grade.

About nine kilometres west of the Alberta border along the highway is a viewpoint where travellers can see the spiral tunnels that replaced the Big Hill in 1910. The two spiral tunnels curve through the mountains, reducing the grade to the magic 2.2 percent. The entrance to one tunnel, 880 metres of looping track inside Mount Ogden, is visible from the viewpoint; a second, 975 metres long, is hidden inside Cathedral Crags to the south. Excellent displays summarizing the CPR railway building in the area flank a boardwalk that leads to the viewpoint.

Some four kilometres west of the viewpoint, a side road leads to Takakkaw Falls and to displays on the ancient fossil record of the Burgess Shale. About a kilometre along this road, a viewpoint overlooks an old shaft from the Kicking Horse lead-zinc mine on Mount Field, worked from the 1890s to the 1950s. Another 1.5 kilometres up the road, a viewpoint looks across the valley to the Upper Spiral Tunnel.

202

The highway and railway follow the Kicking Horse River down the mountains to the town of FIELD, named for trans-Atlantic cable layer Cyrus Field, who visited here when the CPR was being built. A small and pleasant village now housing some 200 people, most of whom work in Yoho National Park, Field was the hub of the area from the 1880s to the 1950s, home to both extra engines needed to pull trains to the summit and their crews. The CPR built Mount Stephen House here in 1886, one of a number of mountain stops where the CPR fed passengers instead of adding the weight of a dining car to the train. Once the Rockies became a major tourist attraction, the company expanded these restaurants to hotels and Mount Stephen House welcomed guests from around the world. Swiss guides imported to guide visitors through the mountains were housed at Field. When they were moved to Banff, Mount Stephen became a YMCA operation used by Field residents and railway crews as a social centre. It was demolished in 1954. Only a turntable and multiple tracks and sidings remain of the Field railway yard. A disused brick telegraph office still stands near the tracks.

The area is part of Yoho National Park, much larger now than the 25-square-kilometre reserve set aside near Mount Stephen in 1886. Together with a similar reserve near present-day Banff in 1885, it was the basis of Canada's national mountain park system.

Golden

Rail and road follow the Kicking Horse River to Golden and the Columbia River. Golden became Golden in a fit of one-upmanship. Not far away, Silver City lured the credulous with what turned out to be silver samples from somewhere else. Not to be out-hustled, Kicking Horse Flats residents renamed their town Golden City, with equal reason. "Golden City is a beautiful and alluring name, but I scarcely think that its most ardent supporters would allow that it really deserved such an adjective," wrote Morley Roberts in 1884 of the few log huts, blacksmith, bootleggers, tents and handful of stores that were Golden.

The town began as a railway camp. The history of those and later years is visible at the Golden and District Museum, located at 11th Avenue and 13th Street. A classic old railway station sits beside the museum. Also here are a log schoolhouse and a blacksmith's shop. Edelweiss, the name given to a number of homes the CPR built in 1912 for their Swiss guides, is above Golden, on the hillside above Highway 1 just west of the entrance to town.

About ten kilometres west of Golden, a stop-of-interest sign lists the achievements of surveyor Walter Moberley. Twenty-eight kilometres west of

One of the houses of Edelweiss, above Golden, built for Swiss mountain guides imported to the town by the CPR.

Golden is **DONALD**—but if you want to see Donald's oldest buildings, you'll have to continue west to Revelstoke, where they were moved. Donald was CPR construction headquarters for this section of railway, then the divisional point. In 1899, the CPR moved most of its division operations to Revelstoke and offered to move its employees' houses as well. West of Donald, a small sign labels the Big Bend Highway, a route that used to follow the big U-bend of the Columbia River north, then south again to Revelstoke. The road was cut when dam reservoirs flooded the valley.

Road and rail follow the Beaver River into Glacier National Park towards **ROGERS PASS**, a National Historic Site. In 1882, Major A. B. Rogers, the cigar-chewing, mustachioed surveyor for the CPR, found a railway route through the Selkirks along the pass that now bears his name. A sign at a rest stop, just east of the eastern entrance to the pass, points to the pass and describes Rogers's efforts.

A kilometre farther west, a viewpoint with a descriptive tablet looks out over part of the first railway line built through the pass. The stone-arch bridge that carried the line across Cascade Creek is visible across the valley. The bridge was one of a series that crossed mountain streams. They and the line they supported were replaced in 1916 by an eight-kilometre-long tunnel, the Connaught, that cut below the valley. Locals warn against following the avalanche path to the bridge, since grizzly bears also cross this area.

If the terrain hasn't already done so, a sign at the Tractor Sheds viewpoint, another 5.5 kilometres west, explains some of the problems the pass has caused road and rail builders. An average of nine metres—and up to 18 metres—of snow falls on the pass each year. Steep slopes and moderate temperatures make this one of the world's worst avalanche zones. The CPR built snowsheds over the most avalanche-prone parts of the rail line; the remains of one of these original sheds are visible at the back of the Tractor Sheds picnic area. Beside a sign in the picnic area explaining modern methods of avalanche control is one of the gun positions used for the howitzer whose shells trigger intentional avalanches.

The Rogers Pass Discovery Centre, just before the pass summit, was built according to plans for the original snowsheds. The pass is a National Historic

Site. Information on the history of transportation here is available at a small museum at the centre. A re-creation, complete with model train, shows the pass as it was in the 1890s. From the centre, self-guided trails take walkers along an abandoned railbed that follows the original CPR line to two snowsheds, slide paths and the original summit townsite. This tiny settlement, which was the headquarters for the extra engines that pushed and pulled trains to the summit, lasted just a few years. It was destroyed in 1899 by an avalanche that buried eight people—some of the hundred caught in avalanches in the railway's first century.

The trail leads—as does the highway—to a pull-off where a monument commemorates the opening of the Trans-Canada Highway through the Rogers Pass in 1962. Federal and provincial governments were feuding at the time—no surprise, that—so the highway was opened twice. One cairn stands here at the 1,330-metre summit, the other 40 kilometres to the west.

The Illecillewaet Campground, some two kilometres west of the summit, is near the site of Glacier House, a CPR hotel made obsolete by a retreating glacier. The CPR opened Glacier House in 1887 as a travellers' dining room. Tourist demand for accommodation meant great expansion and the arrival of two Swiss mountaineering guides in 1899. At that time, the Illecillewaet Glacier was less than two kilometres away. The glacier receded (the tongue is now about five kilometres from the hotel site), and fewer tourists came after the tunnels bypassed the hotel. The CPR closed the hotel in 1925 and tore it down in 1929. A trail leads to the site; a longer, uphill and somewhat difficult trail leads to Avalanche Crest and views of the original CPR route.

Two kilometres west of this campground, a one-hour trail leads from the Loop Brook campground on an abandoned railbed built to maintain an acceptable grade on the CPR line. Stone pillars from disused bridges and interpretive signs help re-create an older era.

A second CPR tunnel, parallel to but much longer than the Connaught, was completed in 1988. The Mount McDonald Tunnel, the longest in North America, reduced the grade from 2.2 to 1 percent. The western portal to this 15-kilometre tunnel is four kilometres west of Loop Brook.

Twelve kilometres west of the tunnel's west portal are the Laurie Tunnels and snowsheds, first built in 1885 and rebuilt later by stonemasons whom the CPR brought from Italy.

No official pull-off exists to view the tunnels and snowsheds. Here and elsewhere along this route, motorists should take extreme care: this section of highway is known as one of the most dangerous in B.C.

The highway swings down from the Selkirks into Mount Revelstoke National Park. The provincial cairn noting the opening of the road is at the Illecillewaet Rest Area west of the park entrance (accessible to eastbound traffic only). Major Rogers, with 10 native guides and packers, first glimpsed the pass through the Selkirks when following the Illecillewaet River near here.

Until 1973, the Columbia described a mighty U, flowing north from its source in Columbia Lake along the Rocky Mountain Trench, then bending northwest and south again around the Selkirk Mountains. This was the Big Bend, site of a minor gold rush in the 1860s, and of a Depression-era road-building project that linked north and south. In 1973, under the Columbia River Treaty provisions, Canada built the Mica Dam 135 kilometres north of Revelstoke. The reservoirs created by the dam flooded a long northern arm known as Canoe Reach and the southern arm, Columbia Reach. The flooding drowned tiny lakeshore communities, a hot-springs pool and the road that connected Golden to Valemount. Boat Encampment, which was a stopping place for David Thompson and subsequent fur traders, is also underwater. After the flood, Kinbasket Lake was renamed McNaughton Lake for General A. C. McNaughton, who led the Canadian team in Columbia River treaty negotiations. But the name reverted to the original Kinbasket, chosen after Secwepemc chief Kinbasket helped surveyor Walter Moberley. Kinbasket acted as guide and was twice nearly killed, once when Moberley's revolver discharged accidentally and once when mauled by a wounded bear.

The Mica Dam and the Revelstoke Dam, the latter four kilometres north of Revelstoke, vastly changed the Columbia and engendered much controversy. The controversy doesn't die: critics who thought Canada bargained badly still say the country should try for new and better terms when the remaining provisions expire in 2024—or cancel it entirely.

The Columbia Reach of Kinbasket Lake is accessible from side roads east and west of Donald. The Revelstoke Dam, the Mica Dam, Revelstoke Lake and Kinbasket Lake are all accessible from Highway 23 north from Revelstoke. The earth-filled Mica Dam, 200 metres above the riverbed, is the largest of the Columbia Treaty dams.

Revelstoke

REVELSTOKE is relatively young among mainline CPR towns, its development delayed by the usual type of quarrel that accompanied townsite promotion in the 1890s and later. The first small settlement was named Second Crossing because the rail line crossed the Columbia for the second time here. The CPR had to pay A. S. Farrell, who had pre-empted the land, for a right-of-way but declined to pay him for his riverfront land. Instead, they built their shops and laid out their own townsite to the east. Then the federal government decided that the provincial government had been wrong to grant land within the railway belt to Farrell. The ensuing court case dragged on for 10 years. Meanwhile, no land could be sold or property titles registered.

When the dispute was settled in 1897, the CPR moved their divisional point to Revelstoke. Since the town was built in the best of economic times and the

Born of the railway, Revelstoke is still a busy railway centre, with rail yards, sidings and multiple tracks.

THE MOUNTAIN SPINE

Revelstoke's 1912 courthouse features a neoclassical facade, huge granite blocks and a nine-metre-high copper-covered dome topped by a two-metre lantern.

original buildings were not torn down in the worst, the downtown is one of the best preserved turn-of-the-century urban landscapes in the province. A heritage walking and driving tour brochure is available from the infocentre or from the town museum in the 1926 former post office and customs building at 315 West First Street. From time to time the museum holds special events, and walking tours such as cemetery tours. A heritage garden beside the museum incorporates some of the many cultures that combined to create Revelstoke: included are an Italian vegetable garden, a Chinese medicinal herb garden and a native plant garden.

Among the historic sites in the town are Mackenzie Avenue between Victoria Road and Seventh Avenue, with a variety of elegant houses and commercial buildings; First and Second streets on either side of Mackenzie; and the courthouse on Kootenay Street between Second and Third, an imposing 1912 granite building trimmed in red brick and marble and topped with a copper-sheathed dome. Some smaller, less imposing houses on the east end of town came from Donald, transplanted here for CPR employees.

The Revelstoke Railway Museum, impressively large, is alongside the tracks. Though passenger service to Revelstoke ended some years ago, this is still a railway town, with sidings, rail yards and new and old rolling stock. The museum emphasizes the last great era of steam in the 1940s and 1950s and the roles of railway workers. Occasional steam train excursions depart from the town.

West of Revelstoke, the highway and railway cross the Monashee Mountains, passing by Three Valley Gap, a privately owned collection of restored, recreated and reassembled buildings from around the area. Among them are a turn-of-the-century hotel from Sicamous, a general store and a log schoolhouse.

Past Three Valley Gap, Highway 1 leaves the mountains and enters the Shuswap. For information on that area, turn to the Shuswap region in Chapter Three, Similkameen/Okanagan/Shuswap.

———•·———

The flooding that created large reservoirs along the Big Bend of the Columbia River severed the historic land connection between the Revelstoke area and the rest of the mountain spine, along the Columbia and north on the western edge of the Rockies to Valemount and the Robson Valley. Highways built in the 1950s and 1960s linked this northern area to Prince George and to Kamloops. Travellers who wish to trace the Rocky Mountains north must follow Highway 1

Members of the Albert Canyon Ski Club near Revelstoke pose in 1899 with their long wooden Nordic skis and the single, long thick poles that they used to propel themselves. (Revelstoke Museum and Archives)

east into Alberta, then travel north along Highway 93 through Jasper National
Park or make a wide detour with Highway 1 to Kamloops, then turn north on
Yellowhead 5 towards the Rockies.

*This guide to the Mountain Spine picks up
Highway 5 at the Alberta border.*

Valemount and the Robson Valley

The Alberta border marks the eastern limits of Mount Robson Provincial Park. It
isn't known for whom Mount Robson, the highest point in the Canadian Rockies, was named, though the name was probably in use as early as 1927 and may be
a lazy pronunciation of Robertson, for HBC man Colin Robertson. The second
oldest provincial park in B.C., Mount Robson Provincial Park was created in
1913, six years after a group travelled 41 days from Lake Louise in an unsuccessful attempt to climb the peak. Several of the men returned the next year. After
they waited a week for suitable weather, they declined to climb that day—it was
Sunday and they had a minister among them. Then the weather closed in again

and they had to leave. The Reverend Kinney returned again in 1909, determined to beat "a party of foreigners" he had heard were on their way to Robson. He went alone with $2.85 and three pack horses. A second man joined him and they attempted the mountain in July, equipped only with a length of manila rope and a makeshift ice axe. After four days, they reached what they claimed was the mountaintop. But, in fact, they had not reached the summit. The Alpine Club of Canada made the first successful climb in 1913, walking part of the way along the new railway grade.

The Yellowhead Pass to the east and the railway town of **TÊTE JAUNE CACHE** were named for Métis trapper Pierre Bostonais, a blond French/ Iroquois who guided a Hudson's Bay Company group through the pass in 1920. Tête Jaune Cache (pronounced *ti-jon*) was thrown up in 1911 for railway workers at the head of navigation on the Fraser River, which is born near Mount Robson. Flat-bottomed sternwheelers brought railway supplies up the river; the supplies were taken to railway camps in the mountains. For a year or so, Tête Jaune's population topped 3,000, but it quickly died once the railway was completed. The precise location of the old town is hotly debated, but it is known that the townsite was by the river, near where the Tête Jaune road crosses the railway tracks. All that remains from railway days are a few posts from the wharves that once stretched more than a kilometre along the river. The base of an old water tower is visible along this road.

Near Tête Jaune Cache, Highway 5 joins Highway 16. **VALEMOUNT** lies 20 kilometres south on Highway 5. Valemount is near the route of natives and early explorers and fur traders who crossed the Yellowhead Pass, then came south on the Columbia. Many of the creeks and mountains in the vicinity are named for some of those early adventurers but nothing else remains to mark their passing.

The Canadian Northern Pacific Railway—later to become part of Canadian National Railways—extended its tracks through Valemount in 1914. The museum of Valemount and area is housed in the former CN station. Check out the model railway that runs even through the bathroom, plus displays on topics such as Japanese-Canadian internment camps and local war heroes.

South of Valemount is **ALBREDA**, where a pioneer cemetery with a view of Albreda Glacier holds the graves of area pioneers.

To continue west from Tête Jaune on an old road and railway route through the **ROBSON VALLEY**, a broad and pleasant stretch amid the mountains, take Highway 16 west, then turn left on Croydon Station Road to cross the Fraser; turn west immediately across the bridge. A ferry once connected North Croydon to South Croydon but it was replaced by the bridge. Once a village of 200, South Croydon is now all but deserted, though a one-room schoolhouse and old store/post office still remain. The road continues along the river and rail tracks through Dunster, where one of the last remaining original CN stations still stands, then returns to Highway 16 west.

MCBRIDE was also founded because of railway construction but it has survived and, to some degree, thrived. Originally a divisional point and supply town, it is now the government and service centre for the Robson Valley. McBride was laid out according to one of the standard Grand Trunk Pacific townsite plans. The McBride station was built in 1918 on the foundations of a 1914 station that burned down. It has been beautifully renovated using locally milled wood, and contains an infocentre, gallery and café. The small museum is in the library on Dominion Street. The Elks Hall was built in 1915 as the Empress Theatre but is now much changed. Other than that, little remains of the 13 kilometres of rail yards, two water towers, a dam, a roundhouse, engine sheds, a multi-storey bunkhouse and an ice house. Ice was once cut behind the dam at McBride for the trains that carried fish from Prince Rupert to New York.

A 1930s log cabin stands in Koeneman Park, just east of the town by the river.

Surveyors who came through this area found the brush almost impenetrably thick. A fire that blackened the valley not long after destroyed forest on the townsite, valley and mountainside; some residents saved themselves by jumping into a creek. The fire did the work settlers would have had to do, clearing land for farms. The Robson Valley, from Tête Jaune west to Crescent Spur, is still a farming area.

From McBride, the highway angles northwest with the Fraser towards

Prince George. The highway was completed only in 1968. Villages and farms were established decades earlier along the rail line built before World War I. It's hard to draw a dividing line here between history and the present: many valley residents are still pioneering, some of them across the river where a thrice-weekly, whistle-stopping train is the only transportation, electric power is supplied by private generator and phone service is still a thing of the future.

To follow Highway 16 into the province's north, see the Prince George and Area section of Chapter Eight, The North.

213

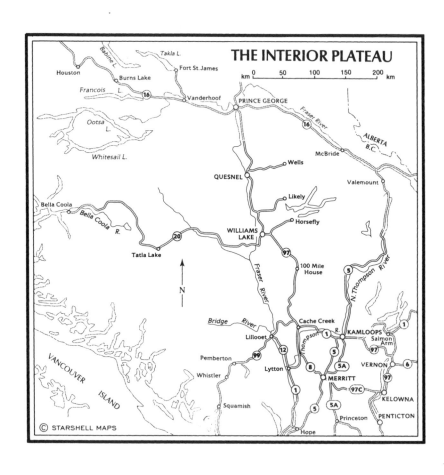

THE INTERIOR PLATEAU

km 0   50   100   150   200 km

THE INTERIOR PLATEAU

It is almost 400 kilometres across the Interior plateau from the steep flanks of the Coast Mountains on the west to the rising slopes of the Cariboo Mountains on the east. North to south, the plateau extends almost 450 kilometres, from the widening V of the Nicola Valley to the spruce and lodgepole pine forests of the north. The plateau takes in the valleys of the Thompson and Nicola rivers, the backcountry west of the Fraser behind Lillooet and the wide reaches of the Cariboo and Chilcotin, east and west of the Fraser River.

Those great distances across hill and valley create a sense of space. And that sense of space encourages a certain independence, a thread that runs through the human history of the plateau. Listen to Alexander Mackenzie, travelling overland to the Pacific in 1793, complain about the Tsilhqot'in native guides who had taken him within sight of the Coast Mountains.

"It was my wish to continue with them whatever way they went; but neither my promises or entreaties would avail: these people were not to be turned from their purpose [to leave Mackenzie on his own]; and when I represented the state of our provisions, one of them answered that if we would stay with them all night, he would boil a kettle of fish roes for us."

Perfectly polite the Tsilhqot'in were, but no more to be shifted in their design than any Cariboo rancher today. Mackenzie was welcome to share in whatever food was on hand, and then he was welcome to fend for himself. The Tsilhqot'in, Dakelh (also known as Carrier) and Secwepemc who shared the plateau before the arrival of the newcomers valued their land and their independence; the Tsilhqot'in in particular fiercely resisted any attempt to intrude upon their land. Their history, which dates back thousands of years, is still visible in their way of life today.

The first outsider to record passing through this region, Mackenzie travelled from the Peace River to the Pacific across the plateau on native routes and trails. Mackenzie was himself independent by nature, a man who took care not to inform his employers of his projected trip lest they tell him to stay home and look to his fur trading. He was followed by other explorers and traders, among them Simon Fraser, himself an enterprising and adventuresome man who followed the Fraser to its mouth despite hardships and setbacks.

The forests to the north were better territory than the plateau for furbearing animals; the traders simply passed through the Interior plateau on their way north or south. For more than 60 years after Mackenzie's cross-country expedition, the Tsilhqot'in, Dakelh and Secwepemc were left more or less in peace. Then the discovery of placer gold on the sandbars of the Fraser River and along the creeks that feed the river brought thousands of gold seekers into the region.

Who, in this age when the word "gold" sends us to our brokers, can gauge the excitement that the lure of gold created then? Men who had flocked too late or too unluckily to the California gold rush after 1849 took heart when rumours of gold on the Thompson and Fraser rivers trickled south in 1857. In 1858 alone, more than 20,000 adventurers took ship from San Francisco for Victoria, magazine correspondents sent home glowing reports to England and the east coast, and some 30,000 men and women entered British territory seeking to make their fortunes from the mines—or from the miners.

They stopped at the Fraser sandbars above Fort Hope or they continued into the Cariboo, following the feeder creeks they hoped would lead to the motherlode. Between 1858 and 1865, several dozen new towns were founded in the Interior, the Cariboo road was built to connect Fort Yale to Quesnel and thence to the hottest strikes at Barkerville in the shadow of the Cariboo Mountains, and millions of dollars in gold dust and lode gold were panned and sluiced from the creeks and dug and dynamited from the rocks.

As in other gold rushes around the world, once the easily obtained gold was gone, companies with capital took over hardrock mining, and thousands of prospectors, the ultimate independent businessmen (and a few women), left.

Merchants, stagecoach drivers, schoolteachers, freight-line owners, clerks, gamblers, danseuses, madams —all had seized the opportunity to profit from the gold rush. Though many left, some stayed, among them Chinese gold panners, who flushed thousands of dollars in gold from bars and riverbeds that less patient hands had abandoned. Along the Cariboo Road, from Lillooet to Clinton, then to 100 Mile House and to Quesnel and through the valleys of the Nicola and Thompson, ranchers assessed the countryside as ideal for cattle raising, preempted land and settled in. Some of these ranchers controlled huge areas of land, the basis for ranches that would become the largest in the world. The Interior in 1868 was much quieter than it had been in 1858, but it was still far busier than it had been in 1848. In those 20 years, it had acquired a road, riverboats, towns, roadhouses, ranches and a vastly expanded population.

The First Nations of the Interior, who had acted as guides for the explorers, took part in both the gold rush and ranching. Early photographs show Secwepemc families at work over rocker boxes and gold pans; they also show Tsilhqot'in and Secwepemc men working on the ranches—Indian cowboys, an anomaly Wild West movies never mention. The Tsilhqot'in nation continued to demonstrate its fierce independence when road surveyors and builders entered their land without permission. Antagonized by the interlopers' behaviour, fearing that they brought dreaded smallpox and determined to defend their territory, the Tsilhqot'in warned the incomers that they must leave, and then, in several separate incidents, killed 19 of them. Five Tsilhqot'in paid for the killings with their own lives.

The Interior saw the next flurry of activity in the 1880s with the building of the Canadian Pacific Railway. Navvies and skilled men laid rails from the Shuswap through the new division point of Kamloops and the new town of Ashcroft on the Thompson, south through the Fraser Canyon and the Fraser Valley. Thousands of Chinese, Canadians, Norwegians, First Nations and others worked on the rails, and not a few of the newcomers stayed behind to ranch or farm or make a living in the new towns. Ashcroft, for example, a roadhouse and ranch before the CPR, became the stop for all of the Cariboo, the point where cattle were loaded and supplies unloaded and sent north on freight wagons.

In the 1890s, coal mines started operations in the Nicola Valley and a CPR spur line was built from Ashcroft to the new town of Merritt. South of Merritt, the stations of the Kettle Valley Railway, built after 1910, brought business and a few settlers to the valley.

Despite the new towns, despite the railways, the mines and new logging and milling that began after the turn of the century, the greater part of the plateau, still sparsely settled, remained the realm of the individual. A would-be rancher who asked the B.C. government in the 1930s about the Chilcotin was told the area was still unmapped.

Nevertheless, by 1921 the Pacific Great Eastern railway developed a route through the area. The PGE was, unintentionally, another example of individuality. While other railways were busy going from somewhere to somewhere, the PGE chugged uncertainly from nowhere to nowhere. Announced in 1912 as the means to open wide stretches of the Interior plateau and the area to the north of it, by 1920 the PGE went only from Squamish, a long boat ride away from Horseshoe Bay, to Clinton at the southern end of the Cariboo. Three years later, the rails were extended to Quesnel, still 130 kilometres from Prince George and the Grand Trunk Pacific line.

The Cariboo and Chilcotin continued to lure the fortune seeker. In the 1930s, when the American government raised the price of gold, new goldrushers flocked back to the Barkerville area, to pan on the creeks; others came to work in the new hardrock gold mine at Wells. Few prospectors stayed but the hardrock mine operated until the 1960s, and every few years, another gambler takes another crack at opening or reopening a gold mine.

The end of World War II brought more change to the region. Roads that had been notorious mudholes each spring were improved. In 1953, Chilcotin and Bella Coola Valley people, who refused to believe the government that a road couldn't be built, raised their own money and rented their own heavy equipment to cut a road through the Coast Mountains to Bella Coola. The PGE was extended to Prince George in 1952. The BC Power Commission was established to bring power to rural regions. The economy of the Interior shifted from a reliance on ranching to a greater reliance on logging and sawmilling.

In recent years, the mountain pine beetle has attacked the forests of the Cariboo and Chilcotin. Thousands of hectares of forest have been killed, and the beetle-killed timber harvested. Probably caused by a combination of warmer winters brought by climate change, by reforestation that has resulted in large stands of trees identical in age and type and by modern fire-suppression techniques, this massive and historic change to the landscape is evident throughout the region.

Malls and stoplights have made their appearance, and Kamloops grows so rapidly that it's difficult to find something that you knew was there just last year. But the essence of the Interior plateau doesn't change. Little more than a decade ago, the Tsilhqot'in and non-native allies battled successfully to see a vast reach of their traditional territory preserved within a provincial park. The rolling hills that fade off into the distance are the same as they were when Mackenzie passed this way. People are as willing as ever to yarn over a coffee or a beer. And a visitor who asks for advice is as likely as not to be told to go ahead with his plans and "make a fool of yourself any damn way you please."

The Interior plateau can be roughly divided into five sections: along the Fraser and into Bridge River country; the dry country along the Thompson River; the Nicola Valley; the Cariboo; and the Chilcotin. Each has a distinctive past, but all are linked by the hills that characterize the plateau, the rivers that cut through these hills and the small lakes that lie in the high valleys.

ALONG THE FRASER: BOSTON BAR TO LILLOOET

North of Boston Bar, the traveller emerges from the coastal rainforest and mountains, through the narrow rocky canyon of the Fraser and into the sunshine and dry hills of the Interior plateau. Highway 1 follows the Fraser north to its junction with the Thompson, then jogs east with the Thompson.

The guide to the Interior plateau begins at Boston Bar and follows Highway 1 north to Lytton, then continues with the Fraser to Lillooet and into Bridge River country behind Lillooet.

BOSTON BAR, 40 kilometres north of Yale, grew up on the site of a Nlaka'pamux village named *Koia'um*, meaning "to pick berries." The bar got its new name from a group of American men, known as Boston men who panned and rocked for gold on the sandbars revealed as the river dropped in summer. Boston Bar Alex kept one of the roadhouses en route to the Cariboo here; his food was reputed to be good and his beds more than adequate.

Today's Boston Bar has little left of gold-rush heritage. But transportation history is on display: the old aerial ferry car, which used to be the only way across the river to the CPR's divisional point at North Bend, is at the community hall. (A bridge has now replaced the ferry.) From the east or west bank of the Fraser here, you can see the tracks of both Canadian National and Canadian Pacific railways, running on either side of the river. In the mid-1920s, CN silk trains rushed silk in sealed baggage cars—lined with special paper to protect the fabric from dust and dampness—from Vancouver to the silk exchange in New York, and changed engines in Boston Bar.

Little is left of old NORTH BEND, across the river; look for a First Nations cemetery, plus several circa-1900 houses.

Like many another point along this route, JACKASS MOUNTAIN, 25 kilometres north of Boston Bar, was named during the gold rush. Before Cariboo Road replaced the rough and narrow miners' trail that squirrelled around the mountain, a loaded mule toppled over the edge here. Another three kilometres north is KANAKA BAR, named for the Hawaiians who were brought to British Columbia by the Hudson's Bay Company and who left the company to work as placer miners. A historic Anglican church is in the Kanaka Bar First Nations community, on a side road that leads west one kilometre north of the village.

About 30 kilometres north of Boston Bar and 11 kilometres south of Lytton, located on Siska First Nations land, is the Siska Museum, featuring examples of traditional art, basket weaving and fishing. Five kilometres farther north,

Canadian Pacific and Canadian National rail tracks trade sides of the Fraser across the twin Siska Creek bridges. The CPR, the first railway built, crossed to follow what its engineers considered the superior route along the west bank. By the time the CNR (then the Canadian Northern Pacific) arrived, new technology allowed engineers to follow the technically better route along the east bank.

Lytton

The brown muddy Fraser and the green-blue Thompson rivers meet at Lytton; you can see their dramatic joining of colours from the main bridge in town. Long before traders and explorers followed the Fraser south, the First Nations used the rivers and the trails along them as trade routes. Where the Fraser and Thompson meet, the Lytton First Nation sited their village, Kumsheen—or *Lkamtci'n*, "the confluence." The Lytton reaction ferry—which runs on cables and is driven by the river current—takes travellers across the Fraser; 4.5 kilometres north is the beginning of the Stein Valley Nlaka'pamux Heritage Park. Another two kilometres up the trail are a cairn and pictographs. Archaeologists have discovered a wealth of sites dating back to A.D. 200 in this area.

The Lytton Museum, in a 1942 CNR house, features pioneer, gold-panning and railway displays. Across the street in Caboose Park is a 1918 rail caboose. A walking tour takes you past historical buildings, including St. Ann's Catholic Church (1913), several houses circa 1912–13 and a memorial to Thompson Chief David Spintlum, the man who ensured peace between his people and the incoming whites. He died in 1887.

Highway 12 to Lillooet

At Lytton, Highway 1 veers off with the Thompson River. The guide continues along the older, gold-rush route along Highway 12 and the Fraser River.

About eight kilometres up Highway 12 from Lytton is Lytton Heritage Park. You can walk through the trees to the river to see a Nlaka'pamux pit house and what remains of rock piles and walls left behind by Chinese miners.

222

From Lytton to Lillooet is 64 kilometres. For about the middle one-third of that route, you can stop at almost any pull-off (be cautious: the route is narrow and winding) and look out across the Fraser River to the benchlands to see abandoned homesteads, sections of the old Lytton-Lillooet stage road and the occasional old cemetery or evidence of placer mining (washed piles of sand and gravel along the riverbank). Not far from Lillooet, an open area shows the landscape changes that wildfire can create: 1,277 hectares burned in the summer of 1931.

Across the Fraser from Highway 12 is **LILLOOET**, originally a village site for the St'at'imc people, who found this to be a highly productive fishing area. Simon Fraser stopped here in 1806 and was impressed by their hospitality. The

St'at'imc people still fish for salmon here; their drying racks are visible along the riverbanks. When the whites arrived, the First Nations people moved to a higher bench above the river; unfortunately a 1971 fire destroyed all but three of the oldest houses. Cultural tours are available from Lillooet; St'at'imc guides take visitors to see traditional salmon fishing and drying, as well as to archaeological sites and a reconstructed pit house.

The first government-sponsored trail to the Cariboo began here, at the head of a land-and-water route from the Fraser Valley via Harrison River and Lake, Lillooet River and Lake, and Anderson and Seton lakes. Lillooet was designated Mile Zero on this original Cariboo Road. When the new Cariboo Road was built along the Fraser Canyon and north, Lillooet went back to sleep. Mile Zero is marked by a cairn on Main Street; Cariboo mile houses (for example, 83 Mile House, 100 Mile House) still number from Lillooet.

The river flats and long sunny days attracted farmers—and still do. Chinese miners and road builders who passed this way 140 years ago might have been delighted if they could have seen a future that included the growing of many hectares of ginseng.

During World War II, Lillooet, along with many other small towns in the B.C. interior, housed Japanese Canadians exiled from the coast. A Japanese Canadian internment camp was located near the mouth of Cayoosh Creek. The Miyazaki Heritage House, a house built in the 1890s, was the residence of Dr. Masajiro Miyazaki, a Japanese Canadian interned here who stayed on to provide medical care in the area.

A walking-tour brochure of historic Lillooet is available at the museum or infocentre, both in the Anglican church on Main Street. Main Street, said to point due north, is itself a historic attraction, wide enough to turn a double freight wagon pulled by 20 oxen.

The Hangman's Tree, claimed as the site where gold-rush-era judge Matthew Baillie Begbie sentenced someone to die, is on benchland above Main Street. Since Begbie rarely found it necessary to impose a death penalty, this may well be just a frontier legend.

Lillooet attracted many Chinese miners, who washed the gravel of river bars long after more impatient miners had left. Tailings left behind by these miners are visible below Hangman Tree Park (moved from their previous riverside location) as well as near the old suspension bridge across the river.

Lillooet's Bridge of the 23 Camels was named to commemorate the animals that were a dismal failure as beasts of burden on the Cariboo Road. Brought to the Douglas Trail by freight entrepreneur Frank Laumeister in 1862, they were far from popular. Their tender feet were cut by the rough and rocky trails and their smell terrified the other pack animals, causing a number of accidents. Other packers on the Cariboo Road warned Laumeister to get rid of his beasts. He did so: the last camel was said to be still roaming the area around Lillooet at the turn of the century.

Just outside Lillooet, about five kilometres south along Highway 99, a BC Hydro pull-off overlooks SETON LAKE. Here are depressions and other evidence of two St'at'imc pit houses. In summer, a number of signs give information about the steamboats that used to ply the lake, and about a flour mill that operated on Cayoosh Creek.

Bridge River Country

Lillooet was the jumping-off place for another gold rush, when prospectors headed to the Bridge River region in the 1920s and 1930s. The area around Lillooet abounds in historical evidence: ghost towns, railways, old mines, old trails, flooded valleys. To explore the most accessible of these, follow the gravel Bridge River Road north, then west, out of Lillooet, as it winds its precipitous way around hairpins and across the plateau towards the Coast Mountains. You can pick up information for this route at the Lillooet infocentre/museum. Check out souvenir shops in Lillooet for gold nuggets and trinkets.

At Xwisten, 11 kilometres from Lillooet, a path leads through 2,000 years of St'at'imc history, with an extensive archaeological site that has revealed the sites of pit houses and food cache pits. About 30 kilometres from Lillooet, a kilometre or two east of where the Yalakom River flows into the Bridge, at the end of four switchbacks that snake down the mountainside, the results of a hydraulic mining operation show in a horseshoe-shaped bank of the river. Here, miners tried and failed to remove gravel and reach bedrock in 1932. All along this river are the remains of old and still-worked claims. Up to 200 miners worked the banks of the river in 1859–60, and men and women have panned and sluiced for gold here ever since.

Approximately 48 kilometres out of Lillooet, a side road forks across the Bridge River to Shalalth and to **SETON PORTAGE**. The hairpins and descents on this road can be dangerous; some locals prefer to take the train from Seton Portage to Lillooet. The Terzhagi Dam completed here in 1958 was one of British Columbia's earlier hydro-power projects, intended to bring power to the city of Vancouver. The dam was named for Austrian-born Karl Terzhagi, who supervised construction. When writer Lukin Johnston, passing through in the 1920s, saw the beginnings of this project, he spoke with awe of men moving mountains in this scheme to tunnel through Mission Mountain and harness the Bridge River, channelling its waters to a power station on Seton Lake. Carpenter Lake, created by the dam at its head, flooded out many old mine diggings and tiny communities. It also flooded, with little warning, traditional native hunting and fishing sites; the effect on First Nations communities as the dam and the power lines cut across their lands was not considered. Downton Lake, beyond Carpenter Lake, is named for the surveyor who conceived this scheme in 1911.

Beyond the dam is **SHALALTH**, from the St'at'imc word for "lake," the site of the hydro powerhouse. BC Rail—formerly the Pacific Great Eastern (PGE)—still stops at this tiny community, once a jumping-off point for the Bridge River goldfields. Shalalth Lodge, an inn for passers-through in the heady gold-rush days, is today a private home. The St'at'imc here offer various cultural tours.

Nothing is left now of what may have been the first railway in Canada: a five-kilometre, narrow-gauge run between Seton Portage (the settlement) and Anderson Lake. Built in 1861 and used by horse-drawn rolling stock, the rails conveyed prospectors and their baggage between the lakes.

From Seton Lake, a BC Hydro access road known as Highline Road parallels the lakeshore south to **D'ARCY**, but the road is narrow, winding, steep and poorly marked. It is not recommended without a four-wheel-drive vehicle and a good sense of direction—and it's impassable in winter. The BC Rail line along the shore provides a better way to see what the goldrushers saw as they made their way by boat between D'Arcy and Lillooet.

Return to Bridge River Road, which now follows the 53-kilometre shoreline of Carpenter Lake to Gold Bridge. Prospectors first found Bridge River gold in 1859 but the rush was short-lived. Interest peaked again in 1897 and in 1915. The real Bridge River gold rush began in 1928 and carried on for 20 years.

Less than a kilometre east of the Gun Creek Recreation Site, towards the western end of Carpenter Lake, is the site of the former town of Minto, a company mining town that in the 1930s boasted streets, houses, stores and mine buildings. In the 1940s, it became a Japanese Canadian internment camp; in 1958, it was drowned when Carpenter Lake rose. At low water in summer, some of the streets and foundations are still visible.

GOLD BRIDGE was the un-company town of the 1930s gold rush. Down the road at Bralorne, mining company officials forbade shady ladies, whisky and probably song. So the miffed miners built their own shanty town at Gold Bridge. Little historic evidence is left of this raucous monument to independence.

Beyond Gold Bridge are Bralorne, Bradian and Pioneer, which lived and all but died with the Pioneer, Lorne, Coronation and Ida May mines that started up between 1897 and 1911. Occasional efforts to reopen one mine or another begin with brave predictions and usually end in failure—though not before investors have put their money into mining stocks. In 2008, hopeful press releases yet again announced "significant new mineralization" and the expected reopening of the Bralorne, King and Pioneer mines. If this comes to pass, access may be limited.

These towns and mines are among the most fascinating reminders of British Columbia's mining history. To reach them from Gold Bridge, follow Bralorne Road along the east side of the Hurley River. Where the road forks, bear right for the mines, left for the town of Bralorne. The remains of the Pioneer mine by Cadwallader Creek, listing and broken, are well worth a visit.

The company town of **BRALORNE** draws dreamers and planners who are lured by its beauty and its remarkably cheap houses but are often defeated by the town's remoteness and difficulty of access. For years, Bralorne has been the preserve of only a few dozen residents. The classic white wooden Bralorne Community Church has recently been restored and reopened, and a small but vibrant museum maintained by volunteers, open in summer, displays relics, photos and clippings from the 1930s, including the story of the strike that saw 55 miners occupy the mine, with other miners assigned to hunt, and wives preparing food to feed the strikers. A 1970s plan to grow mushrooms in the warm, dark and humid conditions of the mine shaft in the main Bralorne shaft died aborning.

BRADIAN, not far away, was abandoned for many years, but a number of its 22 neat green- and red-roofed houses lined up beside gravel streets are being restored, with hopes the town will be revived as a recreational hub.

You can return to Lillooet the way you came, or you can take a two- to three-hour trip to the Pemberton Valley by taking the gravel Hurley Road, rebuilt recently but still switchbacked in places. Note that it is usually closed in winter.

From Lillooet, Highway 99 continues north and east to Highway 97 north of Cache Creek.

About five kilometres past Pavilion Lake, the road from the town of **PAVILION** leads up over Pavilion Mountain, following the route of the original Cariboo Road. Only the brick chimney remains of the Pavilion General Store at this turnoff; it was, until it burned down in 2000, the oldest operating general store in the province. Check locally for conditions on the Pavilion road: the first few kilometres here and the last narrow twisting ones down to **KELLY LAKE** can be treacherous. This pretty and lonely unpaved ranchland road leads through the old Carson Ranch, one of the first ranches to be established in British Columbia's Cariboo country.

ALONG THE THOMPSON: LYTTON TO KAMLOOPS

Highway 1 follows the softer contours of the Thompson River north, away from the incised hills and banks of the Fraser. The town of **SPENCES BRIDGE**, 37 kilometres northeast of Lytton, was known between 1862 and 1865 as Cook's

Ferry, because Mortimer Cook owned the ferry that ran across the Thompson River here. When Thomas Spence built a bridge in 1865, under government contract, the settlement logically became Spences Bridge. A historic packing house and pioneer cemetery remain from earlier days. The Inn at Spences Bridge lays claim to being the oldest continuously operating hostelry in the province. Locust trees planted in 1904 by a pioneer rancher arch over an old road below the present highway. Just southwest of town, you can see across the river to where, in 1905, part of a hillside slid into a small First Nations village, burying several people, drowning 13 more and damming the river.

Highway 8 leaves Highway 1 here, crossing the river on the one-lane bridge, then continuing through town and on along the Nicola River into the Nicola Valley. For information, see the Nicola Valley section later on in this chapter.

Twenty kilometres north of Spences Bridge, a plaque marks the 1915 driving of the last spike on the Canadian Northern Pacific Railway, the third transcontinental railway, now a part of CN.

Ashcroft

ASHCROFT, about 40 kilometres north of Spences Bridge, dates from one of those quintessentially colonial efforts that enliven the history of British Columbia. Cambridge graduates and brothers Clement Francis and Henry Pennant Cornwall arrived in B.C. in 1862 to establish a ranch—though one could ask why barrister Clement wished to exchange London temple life for the western wilds. In true going-to-the-colonies tradition, they named their ranch Ashcroft, for the family home in England. They raised wheat, milled flour and became well-known hosts and eccentrics. They held annual races on Cornwall Flats (horses courtesy of the Arabian stud they imported). Lacking the requisite fox, the hunters pursued the noble coyote in the Ashcroft Hunt. When the CPR—never up on the social niceties—used the name Ashcroft for its railway station nearby, the Cornwalls renamed their home Ashcroft Manor. The manor, restored, is now a tea house and gift shop, and is located just south of the southern road turnoff to the town. The elms in front of the manor were shipped as seedlings from England.

Ashcroft was the rail point closest to the Cariboo and thus became a supply and freighting centre for the region. It dwindled in importance when the Pacific Great Eastern Railway built north from Vancouver to the Cariboo in the 1920s. Farming then increased in importance. Ashcroft Choice tomatoes, packed as an Aylmer brand, issued from Ashcroft's cannery, located in a converted livery stable rendered obsolete by automobile and rail. To commemorate the modest fame of Ashcroft tomatoes and potatoes, the hotel pub, once called Spuds, displays photos of the farming era. For, as one writer declared, the Ashcroft spud "gladdens the heart of the epicure. It is white as snow and, when broken, glistens salt crystals. It is mealy and dry. Its proportions are a thing of beauty and its flavour a joy. The Ashcroft potato is the King of All Spuds."

The Ashcroft Museum is housed in the 1917 post office at Fourth and Brink streets. Its displays of First Nations, commercial, railway, telegraph, farming, ranching and mining history are well presented. The museum also portrays Ashcroft's Chinese community, now almost gone but up to 600 strong at the height of the agricultural boom.

The Heritage Stage Coach Depot at Sixth and Railway was built in 1911 for the BC Express, the major transportation company in the area. The 1889 Opera House has recently been restored. Also worth a look is the bell from the old fire hall, destroyed by fire in 1916 when much of the town burned; the bell hangs in a tower beside Railway Street. And two old churches still stand: Zion United (originally Presbyterian, built in 1892); and St. Alban's Anglican (built in 1891). A walking-tour guide is available from many town businesses.

CACHE CREEK, at the junction of Highways 97 and 1, was an overnight stop on the way to the Cariboo. Little remains of historic significance.

The guide continues east towards Kamloops on Highway 1. It runs through dry ridged hillsides, above irrigated fields that now flank the river and past the failed settlement of Walhachin about 16 kilometres east of Cache Creek.

The potential in these benchlands, at the turn of the century as dry as the surrounding hillsides, attracted the attention of American real-estate promoter Charles Barnes in 1908. Barnes formed British Columbia Horticultural Estates

Irrigated fields occupy the benches above the Thompson River now, but lack of water was one of the many drawbacks that doomed the colony of Walhachin.

Limited and advertised for the "right kind" of people for his planned settlement at Walhachin: upper-class young English families who would thrive by planting fruit trees and taking tea on the banks of the river.

Like many another agricultural dream of the era, this one fell apart—though not before Barnes made his profits. It's hard to say why Walhachin has become the best-known of the many failures, a cautionary yet somehow romantic tale of hope denied. Lacking the technology to raise water the few hundred metres from the river, the settlers hired Chinese and native labourers to build wooden flumes from the Deadman River to their orchards. The remains of the flumes can still be seen snaking across the hillsides north of the highway east of Walhachin. The families duly planted trees, rode to hounds at the annual Walhachin hunt and danced to the grand piano at the hotel, where proper dress was expected. But the colony demanded hard and rarely rewarding work, and it was probably with some relief that the young men returned to England to fight in World War I. Without their efforts, the orchards dwindled and the flumes collapsed. As did Walhachin. Now only a stop-of-interest sign along with a few twisted apple trees and the weathered flumes on nearby hillsides mark its former site.

A few kilometres east of Walhachin, the Deadman-Vidette Road branches north. "Don't sweat the small stuff" might be the lesson learned from this valley's name. Fur trader Pierre Chivrette (or, possibly, Charette) was killed here in 1817 when he and his native companion argued over where they would camp for the night. Remains of the Walhachin flumes can be seen along this road. About 40 kilometres up the valley is what remains of the dam Walhachin settlers built on Snohoosh Lake so they could store water for their orchards. Also beside the Deadman road, in the Secwepemc village of Skeetchestn, is St. Mary's Church (circa 1909), with attractive stained-glass windows. The valley is an ancient gathering place for the Secwepemc.

As early as 1859, Corsican Francis Savona (sometimes called Francois Saveneux) was in residence at the west end of Kamloops Lake. Trader Donald McLean wrote that Savona spoke French, Spanish and Italian and would work as a translator if required. The government apparently did not require his services, for Savona stayed put, installing a cable ferry across the river, which he ran until his death in 1862. His name persists in the community of **SAVONA**, between the Deadman River and Kamloops.

Kamloops and Area

The town of **KAMLOOPS** was established as a fur-trading post in 1812. After the gold rush, miners-turned-ranchers occupied land in the area. The usual land speculation schemes at the turn of the century saw promoters promise that Kamloops could rival the Okanagan as a fruit-growing centre. But it was railways—the CPR in the 1880s and the Canadian Northern Pacific around World War I—that made Kamloops a division point and a transportation crossroads.

Rapid growth in the Kamloops area has meant that much evidence of Kamloops history has disappeared beneath housing developments. However, something remains of the turn-of-the-century town in the downtown area. Some 20 sites, including a Chinese cemetery, a cattle car and a courthouse, are on the city's heritage registry. The Kamloops Heritage Railway runs steam-train excursions from downtown along the rail lines east of town. The Kamloops Museum, at Seymour and Second Avenue, incorporates Kamloops's oldest building, a fur-trade cabin that dates to mid-19th century. Other museum displays portray more fur-trade history, Secwepemc culture, pioneer and Victorian life, transportation and local industry.

The site of Kamloops, where north and south branches of the Thompson River come together and flow into Kamloops Lake, has been inhabited for some 8,000 years. The Secwepemc Museum and Heritage Park, at 355 Yellowhead Highway (take the Jasper exit north off Highway 1, cross the river on Highway 5 north and follow the signs), incorporates the oral history and legends of the Secwepemc. Trails lead through the five hectares of the heritage park, which contains the archaeological remains of a 2,000-year-old Shuswap winter village site together with four reconstructed winter pit houses and a summer village. Here are a summer mat lodge, a hunting lean-to, a fish-drying rack, a fish trap, a smokehouse and traditional food plants in an ethnobotanical garden.

The Chief Louis Centre on the grounds is in the buildings of the former Kamloops Indian Residential School. Chief Louis was one of the delegates who sought recognition of the Secwepemc government with a petition to Sir Wilfred Laurier that told the events of the past from the Secwepemc point of view. These buildings, which date from the 1920s, now house First Nations government and cultural and business organizations. The Powwow Stadium nearby welcomes dancers, drummers and singers from across North America for events each year.

Highway 5 (Yellowhead North) continues north towards Tête Jaune Cache in the Rocky Mountains. This area is still sparsely settled; the occasional abandoned homestead or boarded-up mining tunnel suggests its past. About 54 kilometres north of Kamloops, a stop-of-interest sign commemorates the Overlanders, men and women mainly from Ontario who set off overland for the Cariboo in 1862, choosing the North Thompson as their route from the Rockies to the Interior. Most of the Overlanders completed the journey but very few turned to mining; most found other pursuits such as ranching or farming.

BARRIERE, 62 kilometres north of Kamloops, dates from fur-trade days and is named for rocks in the river nearby or for Simpcw fish weirs. The North Thompson Museum is located here in a 1930s forestry building.

At **LITTLE FORT**, Highway 24 heads west into the Cariboo. Little Fort was briefly (from 1850–52) a Hudson's Bay post. North again is **CLEARWATER**,

233

where an infocentre for Wells Grey Park displays information on the Simpcw, the Overlanders and other area history.

VAVENBY has a name that comes oddly off the tongue. It is, in fact, a mistake. Early settler Daubney Pridgeon, himself equipped with a fine name, wanted the place named for his birthplace in Lincolnshire, England; postal authorities misread his writing, and Navenby became Vavenby.

WIRE CACHE, marked now only by a picnic area, once concealed rolls of telegraph wire, left behind when an early contract for a telegraph line from Kamloops to Edmonton was broken. At **AVOLA**, an old log schoolhouse houses the library—but the meaning of "old" here, as in many other places, is relative, for the village dates only to 1913.

Beyond Avola, the road leaves the plateau and rises to the mountain spine. (See the Valemount and Robson Valley section of Chapter Six, The Mountain Spine.)

THE NICOLA VALLEY

The Nicola Valley is a dry, sun-warmed stretch of hills and small lakes between the Thompson River, the Okanagan Valley and the Cascade Mountains. A number of highways cross the valley, modern equivalents of First Nations trade routes and of the Hudson's Bay Company brigade trail between the Okanagan and Fort Kamloops. Highway 5A and the Coquihalla Highway 5 run north-south between Kamloops and Princeton and Hope; highways connect Merritt to Ashcroft and Spences Bridge in the west and to Kelowna in the east.

The guide begins in Merritt, in the centre of the valley, where the Coldwater River joins the Nicola River.

Merritt

Modern settlement in the Nicola Valley began as ranchers moved in to pasture their cattle on the bunchgrass hills, and increased as coal mining, logging and sawmilling developed. **MERRITT**, first known as The Forks, was founded when promoters decided that coal deposits in the area were worth exploiting. When the CPR laid tracks east from Spences Bridge in 1906 to serve the coal mines, The Forks was renamed Merritt to honour a mining and railway promoter, and the growing settlement became the main community in the valley.

Several buildings remain from this era, the most impressive the Coldwater Hotel (1908), once considered the best hotel in interior B.C. Note the four-storey turret with copper dome; the exterior beige-coral colour is as close a match to the original as possible. The Adelphi Hotel, also downtown, dates to 1911; a close look at today's hotel compared to old photos reveals little structural change, though the exterior has been stuccoed and bricked over.

The Nicola Valley Museum, at 2201 Coldwater Avenue, displays local First Nations, ranching and mining history and features exterior murals.

The Baillie Property at 2202–2250 Voight Street contains a house, a barn and other buildings and a heritage garden. Around 1913, Cosom Bigney built the farmhouse here as a home for his fiancée, who would be coming from England to marry him. However, on the trip over she found someone she liked better and never arrived in Merritt.

Evidence of the Nicola's history is visible along several of the highways that cross at Merritt. Highway 5A follows Nicola Lake east. The lake was the focus of early settlement, both First Nations and white. **NICOLA**, the town at the western

Murray United Church was built at Nicola in 1876.

end of the lake, was the main settlement in the valley before Merritt vaulted ahead. Turn-of-the-century pictures show a well-developed town with neat streets and two-storey buildings. Murray United Church (1876) and its cemetery are among the most picturesque in the province; well-tended graves date back to the 1880s. Also at Nicola are St. John the Baptist Anglican Church (1899) and a few houses from the turn of the century.

Just to the east, at **QUILCHENA**, is the Quilchena Hotel, built in 1907 by rancher Joseph Guichon, who was convinced guests would hasten by coach and carriage to his fine hostelry. He was right—until the railway and cars took over from horses. The hotel survived from bar profits for a time. There were no stools at the bar, or so the story goes; if a man could not stand up, he had obviously had enough. The Quilchena was closed from 1919 to 1958, when a descendant of Guichon reopened the almost untouched building. Nicely restored, its polo grounds converted to a golf course, it welcomes guests today.

Some 27 kilometres east of Merritt, where Highway 5A curves north along the lake towards Kamloops, a secondary road leads east into the Okanagan at Westwold. Along this road, at the west end of Douglas Lake, is the First Nations

A log and shake house sits abandoned in the fields north of the Douglas Lake Road.

The Douglas Lake Ranch maintains the memories of its storied past in trim white and red buildings and in other relics like this wooden wagon.

community of **SPAXOMIN**, where a wooden church dates to 1889. Confounding the stereotype, cowboys are Indians here: Spaxomin cowboys have long managed herds on this rangeland. Beyond Spaxomin, the pastures of the Douglas Lake Cattle Company, once the largest ranch in the world, stretch to north and south. A melding of half a dozen pioneer ranches, the Douglas Lake dates from the days when bunchgrass grew thickly on the surrounding hills. The general store building at Douglas Lake was built around 1900, though its stock today is more likely to include rental videos than horseshoes.

Located 11 kilometres south of Merritt off Highway 5A, the Laurie Guichon Memorial Interpretive Grasslands Site presents information on the grasslands, as well as on First Nations and ranching history.

The guide returns to Merritt and Highway 5 (the Coquihalla), which follows the Coldwater and Coquihalla rivers towards Hope.

Take Exit 356, or follow the Coldwater Road from Merritt, then continue under the highway to reach **BROOKMERE**, about 15 kilometres along the road. A sign just east of the highway on Brookmere Road encapsulates the history of the Kettle Valley Railway. Brookmere was a two-railway town, served both by the KVR and by the Vancouver, Victoria and Eastern branch of the American Great Northern Railway; the two used joint trackage between Princeton and Hope. The water tower that still stands at Brookmere (though moved from its original site) has two spouts; some say that each served the engines of one railway, but railway historians suggest that one spout served engines on the main line, the other, those being serviced on a spur line. The Brookmere station is now a private house; railway-crossing signs still guard the trackless railway bed, which is now part of the Trans Canada Trail, and foundations of the roundhouse and turntable are still in evidence.

The Coquihalla Lakes Exit 228, two kilometres north of the Coquihalla toll booth, leads (if you turn right from the rest area, rather than left into the rest area) to a pipeline maintenance side road, usually accessible except in winter, that parallels the Coquihalla River and either parallels or is built on the old railway grade of the KVR. In the narrow canyon, the old grade runs above the highway; look up to the tunnels along the railbed. Farther south, just past where the road crosses the river, the Bridal Veil Falls trestle stands above the creek. From here south, sharp eyes can spot remains of trestles and tracks collapsed over time by the heavy snowfalls of the Coquihalla. The gate at the south end of the pipeline road is locked; travellers must return to Coquihalla Lakes. Two signs at the rest area outline the history of transportation in the Coquihalla Valley and of the Hope-Nicola Cattle Trail, used in the 1870s.

South of the toll booth along the Coquihalla are signs marking stations along the KVR line, among them Falstaff, Iago, Portia and Shylock.

Highway 8 leads west from Merritt to Spences Bridge. Though the rails have been removed, the railbed of the old CPR line is clearly visible.

The guide now returns to the junction of Highways 1 and 97, at Cache Creek, and follows Highway 97 north through the historic Cariboo.

East of the Fraser: The Cariboo

Because many areas that were at the centre of the gold rush of the 1850s and 1860s were little touched once gold-rush frenzy died, the Cariboo probably contains more evidence of 19th-century history than anywhere else in British Columbia outside Vancouver Island and the Lower Mainland. Buildings and other evidence remain along Cariboo Road and east of Quesnel and Williams Lake, some mouldering, some restored, to shed light on this era.

Though Hat Creek Ranch (11 kilometres north from Cache Creek, then

Horses were— and still are— the centre of life at Hat Creek House, a stopping place on the famed Cariboo Road.

west on Highway 99 (formerly Highway 12), then left at the sign for Hat Creek Ranch) was well known as a roadhouse in the 1860s, its owner, Donald McLean, was probably better known, both for his own exploits and those of his sons. Before he bought the roadhouse, he was a chief trader with the Hudson's Bay Company. Turned Cariboo rancher, he led a band of volunteers to find the Tsilhqot'in who killed road surveyors in their territory (read about the Chilcotin War in the Chilcotin section later in this chapter). A reckless leader, he was killed one morning when, it is said, he forgot to put on his protective coat of mail under his jacket. Three of McLean's sons were notorious as the McLean Boys, who robbed, stole cattle and sometimes beat their victims. They were hanged in 1881 for the killing of a policeman.

Hat Creek House passed from owner to owner, and each added or expanded. The ranch is now a B.C. Heritage Trust site, with roadhouse, barns, freight horse barn, blacksmith's shop, mower shed, pig barn and chicken coop restored to 19th-century appearance. The site includes a heritage apple orchard. Wagon, stagecoach and trail rides are offered.

A short walk along Hat Creek, you will find a Shuswap native heritage village that has been reconstructed, with displays on different types of housing, hunting, trapping and food preparation. An August powwow brings hundreds of people, with drumming, dancing and other events.

Clinton

At CLINTON, the real Cariboo begins. Clinton dates to gold-rush days, when it was known as 47 Mile House or Cut-off Valley. Once the Cariboo Road was completed, the town was renamed for British Colonial Secretary Henry Pelham Clinton, the fifth Duke of Newcastle—who, of course, never visited his namesake, and would probably have been dismayed by its Wild West air if he had dropped by. The original Cariboo Road from Lillooet joined the second road, from Yale, at Clinton.

The South Cariboo Historical Museum, housed in an 1892 schoolhouse built from locally fired brick, contains a wealth of information on First Nations, Chinese and other gold-rush and pioneer history. The Clinton cemetery, off

Highway 97 just north of town, contains interesting headstones from as far back as 1861. The main street presents some ersatz history, but also some turn-of-the-century buildings.

Just past the railway crossing north of Clinton, a side road jogs west towards Big Bar Lake Provincial Park. Between 1920 and the 1940s, washing soda (sodium carbonate) was recovered from some of the lakes along this road. The large log "boats" where the ice was left to melt and the soda recovered can be seen along some of the lakeshores.

JESMOND, a kilometre along Jesmond Road, was the site of a ranch first homesteaded in 1871. The original house, no longer a store or post office as it was for years, is now a private residence.

At **BIG BAR**, 19 kilometres down Jesmond Road, where a reaction ferry crosses the Fraser, you can see rock piles on the riverbank where Chinese miners worked the gravel for gold.

The road from Clinton through the backcountry, much of it dirt and gravel, abounds in steep hills and switchbacks. It leads north through ranching country, past deserted homesteads and thriving ranches to the Gang Ranch, another of those one-time claimants to the "largest in" titles. The Gang is across the Fraser—follow the signs 46 kilometres past Big Bar Provincial Park, then cross the historic suspension bridge over the river and bear right up the hill. The hairpins that lead down from the benches to the bridge are so tight that the cattle trucks from the Gang cannot negotiate them and must go north to the Chilcotin Highway. The Gang is so-named because founders Thaddeus and Jerome Harper were the first in the area to use the gang plough; the Gang's cattle are still branded with the JH of Jerome Harper.

Most of the communities along the road are First Nations communities. **DOG CREEK** gets its white name from a dog encounter, its Secwepemc name, *Xqet'em*, from its location—the word means "deep canyon" and refers to the canyon the creek carves to reach the Fraser. **ALKALI LAKE**, named for the distinctive lake nearby, was founded by German immigrant Henry Otto Bowe in 1859. He drove 500 head of cattle up from Oregon and prepared to feed the goldrushers who followed old trade-trails through the region.

The road continues past Alkali Lake to Highway 20 just west of Williams Lake.

The guide returns to Highway 97 north of Clinton, and continues north through the Cariboo.

About 32 kilometres north of Clinton, turn east on Green Lake Road for a pleasant trip along the lakes and through birch woods to **LONE BUTTE**. (You can also reach Lone Butte by turning east on Highway 24.) Sadly, now that the pine beetle scourge has turned whole swatches of forest a reddish brown, the trip is not as pleasant as it once was.

Named, logically, for the lonely flat-topped hill near town, Lone Butte contains the last remaining water tower built to service the steam locomotives of the Pacific Great Eastern Railway, circa 1920. It is one of just three original PGE structures still standing. A replica of the Horse Lake schoolhouse is nearby, as are interpretive signs about the era of railway steam. Regrettably, the log Lone Butte Hotel has burned down.

100 Mile House

Return to Highway 97 and continue north. Stop in at the 83 Mile House Farm Equipment Museum, which is along the way to 100 Mile. Though **100 MILE** carries a name from gold-rush days, little remains from that era except the restored 1860s Barnard Express stagecoach beside the Red Coach Inn. The town's later history is perhaps more interesting than its earlier. In 1912, the Marquis of Exeter bought 4,800-hectare Bridge Creek Ranch. In 1930, his son, Lord Martin Cecil, came to B.C. to operate the ranch. He founded the Emissaries of the Divine Light, a religious order that was New Age before New Age existed. Though Lord Martin died in 1988, the Emissaries are still strong in 100 Mile and a number of local businesses are run by the group. Look for religious literature at these businesses. Exeter, the BC Rail station west of 100 Mile, is named for the Marquis.

North of 100 Mile, at the 108 Heritage Site (take the north entrance to the 108 resort, on the west side of the highway), ranch buildings from the 105

These classic Cariboo log buildings are at the 108 Mile Heritage Site beside the Cariboo Highway.

Mile Ranch and elsewhere in the area have been restored or rebuilt by the 100 Mile and District Historical Society. They include the Watson Clydesdale barn (1908), one of the largest log barns in Canada; the 105 Mile roadhouse; the 108 Mile telegraph office and store, built in 1867, rebuilt in 1885; the 108 Mile Hotel, built in 1867 and moved to its present site in 1892; and a number of outbuildings.

LAC LA HACHE, farther north along the highway, is probably so-named because a mule loaded with axes fell into the lake, although another story suggests that a French Canadian fur trader dropped an axe through a hole in the ice.

Some 45 kilometres north of Lac La Hache, Mission Road leads to the west and the one-time site of St. Joseph's Mission, an Oblate mission established in 1866 for the First Nations people of the region. A few farm buildings and a small cemetery remain.

The roadhouse at **150 MILE HOUSE** benefited from a quarrel between road contractors and Williams Lake settler Tom Manifee. The contractors asked Manifee for a loan so they could continue their work; Manifee turned them down. The contractors then approached ranchers at 150 Mile who were happy to help, and the road was built past these ranches rather than past Manifee's ranch and roadhouse.

The 150 Mile schoolhouse beside the highway dates from 1890.

Horsefly/Likely

The Horsefly-Likely Road, trending northeast out of 150 Mile, leads into Cariboo history. Some of the earliest strikes in the gold rush were made along this route.

The Horsefly-Likely Road splits just beyond 153 Mile. The right—east—fork leads to **HORSEFLY**, a name of obvious derivation. Visit the Jack Lynn Memorial Museum on Campbell Avenue to see evidence of mining, trapping and logging in days gone by. Horsefly, as befits the name, is a place of eclectic distinction. It was probably the site of the first—though not particularly profitable—gold find in the Cariboo; a historic cookbook compiled here celebrates the many uses of rhubarb; and John Gruhs, at six foot nine the tallest man in the Canadian forces in World War I, hailed from Horsefly.

You can get to **LIKELY** by following the road out of Horsefly along Quesnel Lake, but this road may be deep in mud. A better route is to return to the road fork mentioned above and take the left, or north, fork.

This road passes Bullion Pit, also known as Hydraulic, billed as the world's largest pit left by gold mining, a three-kilometre-long, 90-metre-deep canyon washed out by hydraulic mining. To reach Bullion Pit, turn north off the Likely Road five kilometres west of Likely. If, as is entirely possible, you note on your way in that the sign has disappeared, ask in Likely for directions. Hydraulic miners worked Bullion from 1892 to 1942; in 1938, the mine used more water every day than the entire city of Vancouver.

"Plato John" Likely held court in a philosopher's grove of cedars by Quesnel Lake when he wasn't panning and sluicing for gold in nearby creeks. Sometimes, he took his listeners on retreat to a small island in the lake. But philosophy did not impede his mining efforts: he was one of the most successful miners here in the 1920s. Try the Likely Deacon Hotel pub for modern philosophy dispensed below displays of 19th-century mining equipment. In recent years, Likely has been in the news more for Acapulco gold than placer gold: a huge marijuana bust with accompanying property confiscations took place in 2008.

From Likely, cross the bridge over the Quesnel River, then turn northeast on Quesnelle Forks Road 200 metres beyond the bridge. **QUESNELLE FORKS**, eight kilometres along the road that may be hard and dry or wet and gluey, was for some brief moments in 1861 the largest city on the B.C. mainland, but is now a ghost town. It is near one of the original gold finds in the Cariboo. Long after the opportunists left, hard-working Chinese miners remained, sluicing tiny flakes of gold from the river gravel as they worked from rafts anchored in the stream; the remains of the oldest known Chinese tong house in Canada are at Quesnelle Forks. The remaining log buildings of Quesnelle Forks, ever more covered with undergrowth and sliding into oblivion (though some are under renovation/preservation), do what re-created Barkerville cannot: allow the visitor to imagine in the subsiding buildings and fast-rushing river the quickly born, quickly dying excitement and drudgery of a gold rush. Some of these log buildings are being stabilized; the cemetery, too, has been restored. (See page 251 later on in the chapter for more on Barkerville.)

Intrepid travellers can try the back road that follows part of the original trail to Barkerville, on Williams Creek. Check locally to see whether Yanks Peak Road is open or whether, as often happens, a bridge is out. Obtain a Forest Service or other local map of the area, since the road forks frequently and the wrong fork inevitably leads, after much twisting and turning, to a dead end. But, if you can make it (four-wheel drive and high clearance necessary), it's a trip well worthwhile, since it gives a much better indication than the main roads of the kind of terrain that faced the original goldrushers—though they fought through forest and swamp, not clear-cuts.

Along some switchbacks on the road are the remains of the buildings of SNARLSBURG—a one-winter village constructed by stranded miners, who gave it its name because of the attitude prevalent in the absence of females.

Just south of Cariboo Lake, a left fork leads up to the old mining community on KEITHLEY CREEK, one of the tent towns set up in 1860 when gold was found where the creek runs into the lake. Not much remains of the short-lived town, though you can visit, by appointment, the ranch and townsite that supplied some of the food for the Barkerville area.

Less adventuresome travellers can return to Highway 97, then proceed north to Williams Lake.

Williams Lake

Bypassed by the Cariboo Road, **WILLIAMS LAKE** was just a small collection of ranches and stores until the Pacific Great Eastern Railway came through in 1920. The oldest building remaining in Williams Lake is the BC Rail station (1920) at the foot of Oliver Street, which also houses an art and artisan gallery. Also in town is a 1947 pumper truck on display at the fire hall, at Fourth Avenue and Borland. The Museum of the Cariboo Chilcotin, at 113 North Fourth Avenue, is dedicated to preserving the ranching history of the region, focusing on ranching and rodeo as well as on the native presence in the area. It also houses the BC Cowboy Hall of Fame.

Highway 20 leads west from the south end of Williams Lake into the Chilcotin. This route is detailed in the Chilcotin section at the end of the chapter. The guide continues north on Highway 97 through the Cariboo.

Some 35 kilometres north of Williams Lake along Highway 97, take McAllister Road west, then turn onto Indian Reserve Road to visit a traditional-style pithouse village of the Xats'ull people, on a site where archaeologists are discovering evidence of life going back more than 2,000 years. The band here presents programs on the history and tradition of the Xats'ull; visitors can stay overnight in the teepees on-site.

The Soda Creek Townsite Road veers west towards Soda Creek half a kilometre beyond Roberts Road. About five kilometres along this road across the railway tracks, turn left, then take a hard right about two kilometres farther on where the road banks down between some older houses towards the river. In 1863, Cariboo Road builders finished their task here at the head of a canyon on the Fraser. The Fraser is navigable from here for 650 kilometres north. At **SODA CREEK**, sternwheelers took over the task of taking goldrushers up the Fraser and bringing gold and people down until the road was extended to Quesnel in 1865. Sternwheelers continued to operate on this section of the Fraser until 1921, when the railway took over. The *Enterprise* was the first ship built in the area, constructed of local lumber, its machinery and a boiler brought in on mule-back.

It's fitting that this steamboat captain who died young should be buried at Soda Creek, where steamboats for many years braved the vagaries of the Fraser River.

Little is left of old Soda Creek now, but what remains is well worth seeing, as much for the atmosphere of silence and sunshine on the riverbank as for the actual relics. A cairn and a straggling row of buildings face the river, accompanied by some pilings and silvered boards. The cemetery is farther up the hill, with tombstones for steamboat captains and area pioneers.

Four kilometres north of the hamlet of **MARGUERITE**, a cairn beside the road marks what may have been the site of Fort Alexandria, built by the North

West Company in 1821. It was named for Alexander Mackenzie, who turned back at about this point in 1793 when he decided that the Fraser could not provide a workable fur-trade route to the Pacific. The fort, more likely located closer to the river, was the northern terminus of the Hudson's Bay Company brigade trail after the two companies merged in 1821.

AUSTRALIAN, upriver from Alexandria, guards no relics of its origin: it was named for Andrew Olsen and Stephen Downes, Australians who chose ranching here over gold mining farther north. It is said that the two invented the trundle barrow, a one-wheeled barrow that could carry 180 kilograms of goods over the humps and bumps of the Cariboo Road.

KERSLEY, too, bears the name of an early rancher attracted by the broad bottomlands along the river here. A stagecoach robbery may or may not have occurred near here in gold-rush days. Money disappeared from the coach, tenanted only by the driver, but the driver retired shortly thereafter. And **DRAGON LAKE**, just to the north, is regrettably not named for a fire-breathing monster, but for early settler Dick Dragon.

Quesnel and Area

Jules Maurice Quesnel was a 22-year-old clerk travelling with Simon Fraser in 1808. Though he left for Quebec soon after, his name remains on a city, a river and a lake. The city of Quesnel, where the Quesnel River enters the Fraser, was born when sternwheelers brought gold seekers north. They left the Fraser here and headed overland to the gold creeks to the east. Mining declined but Quesnel grew, a supply centre for the north Cariboo and a lumber and pulp town.

A number of downtown landmarks recall key events in Quesnel's history. Of special interest is a cluster of buildings and artifacts at Ceal Tingley Memorial Park–Heritage Corner, to the left from Carson Avenue (Highway 97) along Front Street. The Hudson's Bay Building, at Carson and Front, was built in 1867 and continued as an HBC outlet until 1919. Across Front Street are a Cornish wheel of the type used to power mining equipment, sawmills and gristmills during the mining and pioneer eras, and a cairn commemorating the building of the B.C. portion of the Russian-American Telegraph, a grandiose venture designed to link Europe and America via the Bering Strait. The line was never completed, but hundreds of kilometres of cable were strung through the British Columbia wilderness, and the telegraph connected Quesnel to New Westminster, in 1865. Also nearby are some of the remains of the sternwheeler *Enterprise*, and a steam shovel (circa 1887) used at Bullion, near Likely. The Riverfront Trail here features various historic points of interest. In West Fraser Timber Park, a heritage garden is being developed.

Flanking the infocentre and the Quesnel Museum, at the south end of town where Highway 97 becomes Carson Avenue, are a statue of gold-rush pioneer Billy Barker, an old fire bell and a 1914 PGE caboose/wooden boxcar. The museum features First Nations, pioneer and gold-rush history, and runs heritage walking tours in summer. Across the street is the 1920 railway station, with two later additions. The pioneer cemetery is behind the infocentre and museum. For an energetic and possibly profitable reminder of gold-rush days, try gold panning—the area where the Quesnel spills into the Fraser is open for public panning.

The 450-kilometre historic route taken by Alexander Mackenzie and his Dakelh and Tsilhqot'in guides on his way to the Pacific has been mapped, marked and described for those who want to hike part or all of the trail. The names Nuxalk-Carrier Grease Trail/Alexander Mackenzie Heritage Trail take account of both the coastal and plateau peoples who used it for hundreds of years to transport eulachon grease and other goods between regions, and of the man who made it famous by following it to the coast and back. Obtain information about the trail from infocentres, museums or local bookstores, where you can buy a trail guide. Before you decide to take a stroll to Bella Coola, you might note that this is at least an 18-day trip. Day-trip brochures are available from area infocentres.

The telegraph trail first cut for the Russian-American line, later followed by the Yukon Telegraph built in 1899, has been traced for part of its length between Quesnel and Fraser Lake. To take a walk on the trail, cross the Fraser on the Moffat Bridge for West Quesnel, then turn right immediately, bear left at the Y onto North Fraser Drive, then turn right 10 kilometres on at Quesnel-Blackwater Road. Drive about 10 kilometres, then turn right about a kilometre past the end of the pavement. Park in the area provided and follow the signs to

This mining water wheel at Quesnel's riverfront dates from mining rush days in the Cariboo.

the trail. Note that the society that was working to preserve the trail has now been disbanded, so access may vary.

Highway 26 to Barkerville

Much remains or has been restored in the area east of Quesnel where gold-rush activity and later gold mining flourished. Five kilometres north of Quesnel, Highway 26 heads east towards the Cariboo Mountains and gold-rush country, ending at Barkerville. Cottonwood House, a restored provincial heritage site 24.5 kilometres east of the Highway 26 turnoff, was a roadhouse built in 1865 to cater to gold-rush traffic. One of the oldest buildings still standing in interior B.C., it was a hostelry until 1951. John and/or Janet Boyd ran Cottonwood House from 1874 until Janet's death in the 1930s.

Cottonwood House Historic Park contains the roadhouse, barns, implements and other historic artifacts. From May to mid-September, visitors can tour the property with guides in period costumes or ride a replica stagecoach. The property is open year-round.

Mexican Hill (30.5 kilometres from Highway 97) was one of the steepest grades on the wagon road that led from Quesnel to Barkerville. A pull-off at the top of the hill gives great views of the hill.

Throughout most of this area, visitors will see mine remains. Some date from the 1860s; most come from later attempts at placer or hardrock mining. At Wingdam (about 38 kilometres from Highway 97), the highway parallels Lightning Creek, one of the richest in the gold-producing area. Almost nothing remains of the town or of the mining shafts.

Some 41 kilometres along Highway 26 is the grave of Charles Morgan Blessing, an Ohioan who left Quesnel with gambler James Barry; only Barry arrived in Barkerville. Blessing's body was found later, shot through the head. Barry was hanged for the crime, one of just two men ever hanged at Williams Creek (the other a native man convicted of a Soda Creek murder)—an interesting comment on what is often considered one of the rowdiest periods in B.C. history. Black settler Delaney Moses, who had started out on the fateful trip with Barry and Blessing, took up a collection to put a headstone on Blessing's grave.

About 60 kilometres along the road, a side road veers to the ghost town of STANLEY. Less than a kilometre along the road is the Stanley cemetery, where headstones hark back to the 1860s and 1870s and the depressions remain from temporary Chinese graves. Chinese who died in the Cariboo were buried here until their bones could be shipped to eternal rest in China. Half a kilometre up the road is what remains of Stanley. The two-storey log building, the Lightning Hotel, may have been built before 1900, but other buildings date from the gold excitement of the 1930s. Several companies have tried in the past few decades to revive the diggings near Stanley. Here, as elsewhere, mining companies may be active in the area, so respect No Trespassing signs. A short trail leads along the creek to the ghost town of Van Winkle.

Maybe he was Italian; perhaps he was from Missouri. He was certainly a gambler. The Jack of Clubs Lake south of the highway at Wells (70 kilometres from Highway 97) was named for someone with that nickname—either because of some card-playing incident or because he cut his beard in the shape of the trefoil on the jack of clubs (if true, a feat well worth commemorating). Mine pilings remain beside the road before Wells; mining continued here until 1967.

WELLS was a creation of the 1930s, when the United States raised the price of gold and men left unemployed by the Depression came to the Cariboo Gold

Quartz Mine and the model town built to support it. Though its population is much reduced from the glory days, Wells refuses to die. A walk through old Wells, north of the highway, reveals small miners' cottages beyond the hill, more upscale houses on Nob Hill for mine managers and businessmen, and false-fronted buildings on the main street. Sadly, fire and neglect have swept away some of Wells's most interesting buildings. No more are the Jack of Clubs Hotel and the pool hall, but the Good Eats café still stands and the Sunset Theatre has reopened as a live performance venue. Plaques have been placed on the historic buildings and a walking-tour brochure is available from the info-centre and most businesses.

Check out the museum in the 1930s Island Mountain Mine office near the west entrance to town. The restored bright-yellow community hall features carpenter gothic detailing with interior finishes of fine edge-grain Douglas fir. Various other restoration projects are also under way. For those with time and imagination, this is one of the more interesting historic towns in the Interior—especially during the summer arts school in August.

South of the highway (follow the cross-country ski-trail markers; if the creek is high, you may have to build your own bridge) lies what remains of the afore-mentioned Cariboo Gold Quartz Mine. Efforts are still under way to reopen the mine, so access may not be possible. A few decades ago, this was one of the most atmospheric ruins in the province—metal roofs rattling in the wind, brush poking through boards—but a mine caretaker who feared accidents burned down most of the buildings. Mine tailings and rusted machinery remain. Please be responsible: take nothing from the site.

BARKERVILLE is a further seven kilometres along Highway 20. The re-stored, reconstructed gold-rush town is British Columbia's best-known historic site. Forty restored buildings, displays, several restaurants, gold-sluicing operations, theatre performances, a bakery and a newspaper are highlights of the town. Barkerville was the largest, longest-lived of the gold-rush towns, sliding into ghost-town status only as the gold dwindled. In tourist season costumed actors re-create for you the town's heyday, but an off-season visit, when leaves sweep down the all-but-deserted streets or snow piles up to the eaves, may give an

The muddy
main street of
Barkerville was
flanked by
rough wooden
business buildings
and houses in
the 1860s.
(BCA G801)

252

even better idea of what life was like when this was billed as the largest west-coast town north of San Francisco. Take a walk up the hill to Richfield to see the courthouse where various magistrates kept the local gamblers, madams and miners in line.

The guide returns to Highway 97, which leads from Quesnel out of the Cariboo, towards Prince George and the province's north.

Travellers usually speed along this part of the highway, wearied by almost too much history. But one or two places are worth a stop. Little remains now of old **CINEMA**, just north of the Cottonwood Creek bridge. The hamlet got its name from early settler Lloyd Champlain. "*Cinema*," he said, "means action . . . and that's what we are: action." In 1919, after he and his housekeeper sold supplies to railway builders, the two set out for Hollywood, returning only several years later and founding the town. Not much action here these days.

The fourth Duke of Sutherland travelled by train to Ashcroft in 1911, loaded himself and his followers into three cars and his liquor into a fourth and headed north. He bought 1,600 hectares of land north of Quesnel, named the river

Naver and the estate Strathnaver for one of his alternate titles, then sent home for Scottish settlers. Unfortunately, the duke died in 1913. Only the whistle stop of **STRATHNAVER** remains of his grand scheme.

 To continue on this route to Prince George, see Chapter Eight, The North. The guide now returns to Highway 20, which leads west from Williams Lake into the Chilcotin.

WEST OF THE FRASER: THE CHILCOTIN

Yesterday still lives vividly in the minds and conversation of many a Chilcotin resident. In other parts of the province, pioneers are part of a dim and distant past. In the Chilcotin, they are your next-door neighbours—although next door may be 50 kilometres away. Though paved highways and satellite dishes have undoubtedly changed the pioneer Chilcotin way of life, it's still difficult sometimes to draw the line between history and the present.

Most travellers approach the Chilcotin from Williams Lake, driving Highway 20 west and entering the Chilcotin—loosely defined as the plateau between the Fraser River and the Coast Mountains—across the Sheep Creek bridge 24 kilometres west of Williams Lake. This bridge was built in 1961; it replaced a 1924 bridge that replaced a 1904 wooden suspension bridge that replaced a ferry/ford/ice bridge combination. Remnants of the older bridges can be seen downstream from the present bridge.

Almost all of Highway 20 is now paved, with just some 60 kilometres remaining of the old teeth-rattling gravel. About 25 kilometres farther on, the Farwell Canyon Road takes a mighty loop south of the highway. The canyon is on the ice-blue Chilcotin River. In summer and fall, when salmon are running upstream to spawn, travellers can see a sight that dates far back in Chilcotin history: Tsilhqot'in natives dip-netting for fish from the riverbanks, then splitting the salmon and spreading them on racks to dry in the sun. Rock paintings are inscribed on the rock overhang south of the road bridge. The original inhabitants of this site were Secwepemc, but the smallpox epidemic that devastated B.C. native peoples in 1862 wiped out this group. The Tsilhqot'in moved in later.

First Nations people—mostly the Tsilhqot'in and Dakelh (Carrier)—make up about half the population. Chilcotin place names are as likely to commemorate native leaders or denote native gathering places as they are to refer to later arrivals.

RISKE CREEK, just west of the Farwell Canyon turnoff from Highway 20, isn't risky: it's *riskie,* for L. W. Riskie, a Polish pioneer here.

Some 35 kilometres farther west, a plaque at a viewpoint overlooking rolling Chilcotin hills describes the ill-fated Yukon cattle drive. In 1898, rancher Norman Lee, who started a ranch here in 1886, decided to drive cattle from his Chilcotin spread to the Yukon, where hungry Klondike prospectors would surely pay a premium price for fresh beef. But it's a long and difficult way from Chilcotin to Yukon; by the time the drive reached Teslin Lake, the cattle were so emaciated and weak that Lee had to butcher them on the lakeshore and load their sorry carcasses onto scows for the last part of the journey. The scows overturned, the beef was ruined and Lee returned to his ranch with neither cattle nor money.

A few kilometres farther on are **LEE'S CORNER** and **HANCEVILLE,** named for Lee and pioneer trader Tom Hance. The two settlements, little more than a store, gas station and motel, are located where gravel back roads swing south to Big Creek, Nemiah Valley and Chilko Lake. The Lee's Corner general store is the fourth here since 1893. Though the building is fairly new, the store's role is traditional: a supply centre for the region and a place to drink coffee and catch up on the activities of your far-flung neighbours.

A gravel road leads south from Hanceville to Ts'il?os Provincial Park, established in 1994 and administered by the Xeni Gwet'in people. In 2008, the Xeni Gwet'in Traditional Village Site opened in the park. The area contains archaeological and burial sites; traditional hunting, trapping and food and medicine gathering still take place in the area.

West from Hanceville is **ALEXIS CREEK,** named for Chief Alexis of the Tsilhqot'in. Bull Canyon and Battle Rock, just beyond Alexis Creek, were the sites of various battles between the Tsilhqot'in and the Secwepemc and the Bella Coola. **TATLA LAKE** is halfway between the Cariboo and the coast. That the road west from here exists at all is a tribute to the people of the Chilcotin and the

Bella Coola Valley. Until 1953, Bella Coolans who wanted to "go out" could do so only on their own feet, on the back of a horse or aboard one of the coastal ships that called at Bella Coola. Chilcotin residents travelled on a crude wagon track reputed to swallow vehicles whole in the spring mudholes. The 60-kilometre gap on what became known as the Freedom Road was bridged when people from both sides of the Coast Mountains—informed by the government that building such a road was too difficult and too expensive—financed and built a road themselves. The gap was closed in 1953; one of the first cars to use the road bore the provincial highways minister and his aides.

The Graham Inn at Tatla Lake is the old Graham ranch house. Bob Graham founded his ranch in 1901, and though the ranch was later sold to German interests, the inn remains independent and the social centre of this part of the Chilcotin.

The waterways that drain east to the Fraser and those that drain southwest to saltwater inlets are separated only by narrow ridges of land south of Tatla. In 1862, surveyor Alfred Waddington noted the valleys that almost connected the coast and the interior and planned a road much shorter than the Cariboo Road

The provincial government didn't offer much help to residents of the Chilcotin and coast when they built a road through the mountains to Bella Coola. (BCA H04466)

via the Fraser. In 1864, surveyors and road builders bushwhacked their way into the Chilcotin.

They had not counted on the fierce pride of the Tsilhqot'in people, who regarded intruders onto their land with deep and well-founded distrust. A brief war broke out after the Tsilhqot'in killed two of the surveyors who refused them food. Resenting the road builders, who behaved rudely and used Tsilhqot'in land without permission, and fearing that they brought the smallpox that had killed many Interior natives, other Tsilhqot'in then killed a further 17 members of the road-building party.

When he heard of the deaths, Governor James Douglas sent a force up from the coast; they were met by a second party coming overland. Five Tsilhqot'in deemed responsible for the deaths were arrested, tried and hanged. Ironically, Alfred Waddington died in 1872 of smallpox. A historic site marker describing the Chilcotin War—from a non-native point of view—is located beside the highway five kilometres west of Nimpo Lake.

ANAHIM LAKE is the site of a long-time Tsilhqot'in settlement, named for Chief Anaham. It engenders some confusion since the Anaham reserve is located near Redstone farther east. Chief Anaham had moved east from Anahim Lake to found a new settlement when he decided the winters in the shadow of the Coast Mountains were too cold and the growing season too short. The settlement at Anahim Lake is much expanded over former days: in the 1940s, the Ulkatcho people of the Dakelh nation moved here from remote villages to be closer to services.

Lessard Lake Road leads north from Anahim Lake (check locally for road conditions) to some of these abandoned Ulkatcho villages, marked now only by cemeteries and dwindling buildings.

Also near Lessard Lake Road is the Home Ranch, founded after World War II by Americans Pan Philips and Richard Hobson, and celebrated by Hobson in his books *Grass Beyond the Mountains* and *The Rancher Takes a Wife*, both of which are strong on the kind of story-telling that takes place on long Chilcotin nights.

Tweedsmuir Provincial Park, the largest park in British Columbia, was established in 1937 and named for then Governor General Baron Tweedsmuir of

Elsfield. Within the park is Lonesome Lake, made famous through the action of Ralph Edwards, a semi-hermit who chose in 1912 to homestead in the depths of the wilderness. With his family, he fed and probably saved the lives of trumpeter swans who wintered at the lake. Lonesome Lake is accessible either by a long hike or by a combination of air, foot and canoe travel.

From here, the highway crosses the height of land and descends along the Bella Coola Valley to the coast (see the Bella Coola Valley section in the next chapter, The Coast).

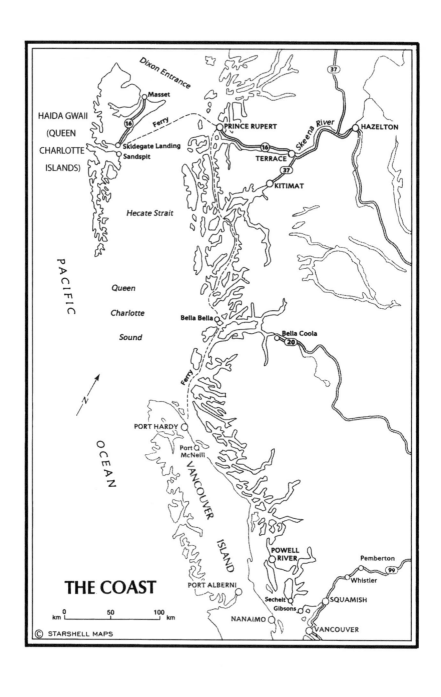

THE COAST

THE COAST

In the 21st century, almost every section of the coast of British Columbia is linked more strongly by road to inland regions than by sea to other parts of the coast. Few towns or cities break the coastal ranks of fjord, narrow channel and high mountain. Modern highways allow coastal dwellers to move freely by land and to work, play or shop in inland cities that provide the services they require.

Travellers will see, for example, that residents of the area immediately north of Howe Sound look south to Vancouver; many commute daily or weekly via ferry and highway to that metropolis. People who live in the Bella Coola Valley "go out" by highway to the Interior. Road and rail join Prince Rupert to Prince George.

Only the Queen Charlotte Islands and the long, scarcely populated stretches between the rare dots on the coastal map still turn, almost defiantly, to the sea. They are the inheritors of a historical tradition that in other centuries tied the coast together as a region. As few as 60 years ago, the links between the lower coast to Bella Bella and Bella Coola, between the Skeena Valley and the central coast, were still strong and self-evident. For British Columbians of that and previous eras, it would not have seemed odd to include the area around Sechelt, the central coast, the Skeena Valley and the Queen Charlotte Islands in a single region.

In the early days of human habitation on the coast, travel by land to coastal points was arduous or even impossible. A glance at the map shows why: deep inlets break the shoreline every few kilometres, and mountains rise sharply not far from the sea. Travel by water was the main and often the only way to reach coastal points.

You need only look at the magnificent Haida canoe *Loo Taas* at Skidegate on the Queen Charlotte Islands, a vessel designed to crest and conquer the waves of the open ocean, to realize the relationship of the earliest coastal residents to the sea. The Haida were the greatest of the early seafarers, respected and feared from Vancouver Island to the Nass River for their sea-going skills, but each coastal native culture built canoes to travel by sea—to trade, to fish, to hunt sea mammals and to conduct raids on their coastal neighbours. Though cedar trees provided material for canoes, housing, clothing and more, most food came from the sea: salmon—the greatest resource—as well as shellfish, whales, eulachon and other fish.

Eighteenth-century European explorers who arrived by ship saw the coast as neither friendly nor sustaining. As they sailed along this coast, they shuddered in their diaries at the forbidding forested shores that rose sharply from deep, dark inlets. Men in sailing ships often fear the land as much as they welcome it, for wind and tide can thrust them onto rocks or pin them to the shore. In those days, captains failed to note rivers and misinterpreted coastline that we take now for granted, because they could not risk their ships in foggy, windy inshore waters.

To them, the inlets seemed bereft of life; they saw few game animals on land. With no interest in permanent settlements, these 18th-century explorers were happy to return to known anchorages on the west coast of Vancouver Island and even happier to set sail for the South Pacific as winter approached.

Settlers who came to the Pacific Northwest in the wake of the mid-19th-century Cariboo gold rush took another look at the coast. Some sailed or rowed north of Howe Sound and pre-empted land in the most accessible areas. Some continued north by boat. The Queen Charlotte Islands, site of the first British Columbia gold rush in 1851, attracted would-be farmers, prospectors and loggers (though more failed and fled than stayed).

In 1866, men building the Russian-American telegraph line, an attempt to link North America to Europe via British Columbia, the Yukon, Alaska and Siberia, set the first sternwheel steamer onto the Skeena River. By 1871, gold-rushers headed for the Omineca had also made use of the Skeena. Between the 1870s and 1911, a series of steamers took prospectors, settlers and others upstream,

This petroglyph
is etched into
the rocks at
Thorsen Creek
near Bella Coola.
(Gary Green
Photography)

261

together with supplies and equipment. For almost 40 years, the route up the coast and along the Skeena to the head of navigation at Hazelton was the standard route for anyone coming into—or leaving—the northwestern Interior.

For some, the fact that the coast was accessible only by sea was a draw, not a drawback. In 1894, 84 Norwegians left their adopted home in Minnesota and came by ship to the Bella Coola Valley, where the land reminded them of Norway and where, they were assured, taverns and other unsavoury influences did not exist. The settlement prospered; the valley today contains many descendants of those Norwegian settlers.

The salmon runs that sustained native peoples all along the coast attracted the attention of others in the 19th century. By 1900, canneries operated from the Fraser River to the Skeena. By the 1930s, 80 canneries dotted inlets and bays, with clusters at Rivers Inlet and the Skeena mouth. During that

Depression decade, many a handliner made a bare living catching salmon in protected channels and delivering them to the canneries where workers gutted, cleaned and processed the silvery fish. By tradition, most of the fishermen were native or Japanese Canadian, while the cannery workers were usually Chinese immigrants and native women who worked under white overseers.

Incomers finally saw the value in the gloomy forests that had repelled early explorers but sustained the First Nations. Small floating logging camps known as *gyppos* were built in place or towed up the coast. In many places, the loggers stayed just long enough to fell the more accessible timber at water's edge, then moved on, and bright green splashes of alder showed where cedar and hemlock had been cut. In other places, more permanent camps and mills were established. The first pulp mill in western Canada started operations at Port Mellon in 1908 and sawmills operated at various coastal points.

Settlers, fishers, cannery workers, loggers, mill workers and miners moved back and forth by boat and similarly received their supplies, mail and visitors by sea. Settlers paddled canoes and small boats from their tiny pieces of turf to community wharves. Steam, then motor, ships were tied up at the wharves or stood off alongside the camps. Logs were boomed along ocean passages; canned fish departed aboard ship; freighters docked at mills to load lumber or pulp, near mines to load ore. The ships of the Union Steamship, Canadian Pacific, Canadian National and Northland Navigation fleets linked the coastal communities to each other and to the world.

Times change. In the 20th century, "rubber-tire traffic" and "economies of scale" became catchphrases that increasingly expressed a new way of life. Travel by land became more important, travel by sea less so. Larger companies prospered; smaller ones died. As land links were built from the interior of the province to the coast and as enterprises such as canning and milling were concentrated in single, rather than multiple locations, the coast began to lose its old identity.

In the north, the process began with the building of the Grand Trunk Pacific Railway. From the 1880s on, surveyors argued the merits of railway routes across British Columbia north of the Canadian Pacific Railway. Where would a new railway reach the coast—at Bute Inlet, Bella Coola, Douglas Channel or the

262

mouth of the Skeena? When the Grand Trunk chose the route via the Skeena, it assumed—and rightly so—that its new town of Prince Rupert would become the major city and deep-sea port on the north coast. The railway spelled the end of steamer traffic on the Skeena. When a road was built beside the railway in World War II, it strengthened Prince Rupert's ties to the Interior and loosened those along the coast.

Soon after World War II, car ferries began their first runs from the Vancouver area across Howe Sound and linked Sechelt and the Sunshine Coast more firmly to the Lower Mainland. As mentioned in the previous chapter, in 1953, Chilcotin and Bella Coola Valley residents succeeded—against the odds and with little government aid—in completing a road across the Chilcotin and the mountains to Bella Coola. An overland trip that had taken several days on horseback now became possible by car. Though a ferry continued to serve Bella Coola for some years, service eventually ceased, to return only in the 1990s as a seasonal service used mainly by tourists.

The fates of Ocean Falls and Powell River provide concrete examples of changes on the coast. The mill at isolated Ocean Falls closed down in 1981, judged "no longer viable," and the town was all but abandoned. By contrast, Powell River, not far from the Lower Mainland and linked to it by car ferry, survives, its pulp

This abandoned BC Packers cannery on Denny Island in the mid-coast area is one of many along the coast. (Gary Green Photography)

and paper mill still operating—though often threatened by closure as the forest industry in the province weakens. All along the coast, canneries closed as fish packers delivered fish to larger, more central canneries. When one by one Union Steamships, Canadian National and Canadian Pacific withdrew their coastal boats from service, it was only confirmation of the continued depopulation of the coast.

It was no accident that the coastal communities that survived without road links were those with the most vibrant First Nations cultures. Bella Bella, long home of the fiercely independent Heiltsuk, is the lone large community on the central coast that thrives with transport only by water or air. On the Queen Charlotte Islands, the Haida nation, much reduced from pre-contact numbers by smallpox epidemics in the 19th century, have reclaimed abandoned village sites and revived their traditions.

Travellers interested in history can see irony in the fact that the ocean route along the Inside Passage is often described as British Columbia's Highway on the Sea. They can also witness clearly here evidence of a worldwide trend that has seen smaller abandoned for larger, and tiny rural settlements deserted for the brighter lights, better services and greater promise of the cities.

———— • • ————

This chapter on the coast is divided into six sections: the Sunshine Coast from Langdale to Powell River; the southern Inside Passage from Desolation Sound to Bella Bella; the Bella Coola Valley; the Northern Inside Passage; the Queen Charlotte Islands; and the Skeena Valley.

The Sunshine Coast: Langdale to Powell River

Howe Sound is the first of the ocean inlets that slash into the mainland coast north of Vancouver. Ferries carry passenger and vehicle traffic across the sound from Horseshoe Bay to Langdale. Highway 101 leads from Langdale north to the Sechelt Peninsula and a second ferry links Earls Cove to Saltery Bay. The highway continues from the north side of Jervis Inlet through the Powell River area. This area is known as the Sunshine Coast.

 This section of the guide begins at the Langdale ferry terminal.

A road leads from the terminal to **PORT MELLON**, site of the oldest pulp and paper mill in British Columbia, built circa 1908 and upgraded in this century to state-of-the-technology status. Originally called Seaside, Port Mellon was renamed for a Royal Navy captain and early Vancouver resident, Henry Augustus Mellon, who was the mill company's first vice-president. Most place names in this area, however, derive from Shíshálh and Sliammon words or from the names of early settlers. Many have "Landing" tacked on to a settler's name, from the days when most traffic was by water. Settlers began pre-empting land here in the 1880s and building wharves. Small villages developed with each cluster of houses. **GRANTHAMS LANDING**, just south of the ferry terminal, is named for Frederick Charles Grantham, apparently a "Vancouver lime juice manufacturer," a description that asks more questions than it answers. He built a summer cottage, then subdivided his land and built a wharf and water system.

GIBSONS was originally Gibsons Landing, named for George Gibson, who went from Vancouver to Nanaimo in 1886, then set sail looking for a place to settle. A strong wind blew the boat, with Gibson and his two sons, off course to Howe Sound. The next day, they found the land they sought at the entrance to the sound. At the Gibsons infocentre (corner of Lower Marine Drive and Gower Point Road) is a burial plot for the Gibsons. A statue of Gibson stands nearby at Pioneer Park. At Stonehurst (1914)—the large white house by the park—

J. S. Woodsworth and Dr. Fred Inglis worked on a socialist philosophy that led to the founding of the CCF (Co-operative Commonwealth Federation), later to become the NDP. Near the junction of Gibsons Way, North Road and School Road are the Heritage Playhouse (formerly the Women's Institute Hall, built in 1929), St. Bartholomew's Church (1892) with a 1901 steamship bell in its belfry, and a 1911 school building.

Finnish immigrants, many of them disillusioned residents of Sointula, the Utopian settlement on Malcolm Island to the north, came here in about 1905 and began growing a variety of berries and fruits. They developed a co-operative cannery in the 1920s, producing jam that was sold around the province. New machinery bought in 1931 proved a disaster: no one knew exactly how to operate it and customers returned huge batches of undercooked jam. Business grew worse but the cannery survived until 1952.

The Sunshine Coast Museum at 716 Wynn Road in downtown Gibsons focuses on maritime history, with displays on the fishers, loggers and farmers who settled the area and on the First Nations. A cairn at Chaster Park, on the waterfront off Gower Point Road, marks the spot where George Vancouver is thought to have come ashore in 1792.

Sechelt Peninsula

A narrow neck of land joins the Sechelt Peninsula to the mainland. SECHELT, on that neck, has long been the home of the Shíshálh, though the smallpox epidemics of the 1860s reduced their numbers to as low as 200. The remaining Shíshálh moved to a new village around a mission site selected by Catholic priests. The long battle the group staged to regain control of their own lives and lands is celebrated at the House of Héwhíwus (House of Chiefs), a cultural centre at the entrance to Sechelt. The Shíshálh achieved self-government in 1986 and signed a draft treaty with the B.C. government in 1998, one of the first aboriginal groups in the province to do so. The House of Héwhíwus contains a theatre and the Tems Swiya Museum. Nearby, five totem poles represent the people and the present life of the Shíshálh. Also nearby is the shíshálh tl'e enak-awxw (Feast House), opened in 1996 on the Sechelt Indian Band's tenth anniversary of self-government.

Union Steamships occupy a chapter of their own in coast life. These red-and-black-funnelled ships served the coast from 1889 to 1959, calling at more than 200 settlements—industrial towns, logging gyppos, fish canneries and holiday resorts. The end of the line truly meant the end of the line for any number of coastal communities, whose isolation became almost complete when the Union whistle blew for the last time.

Rockwood Lodge, at the top of Cowrie Street on Sechelt, was built in 1936 as a resort for passengers arriving by steamship. Extensively renovated, it is now an arts centre and the location of an annual writers' festival and workshops for writers. Also in Sechelt are Sechelt Elementary School (1939) and St. Hilda's Anglican Church (1936).

Uncertainty surrounds the naming of Smugglers Cove north of Sechelt. Some suggest Chinese were picked up here to be smuggled into the United States after the building of the Canadian Pacific Railway. This seems an unlikely story, but something was undoubtedly smuggled in or out of here at some time. Since it's located next to Secret Cove, one can conjecture at some connection.

At Garden Bay Provincial Marine Park, farther north on the peninsula, Mount Daniel was a setting for Shíshálh puberty rites. There is an ancient cemetery on the waterfront.

Powell River Area

From Earl's Cove, named for another settler, a ferry takes travellers across Jervis Inlet to SALTERY BAY. Shell middens along the shore at Saltery Bay Provincial Park mark the location of old Shíshálh campsites. A fish saltery operated near here in the early 1900s.

With a population of over 13,000, POWELL RIVER, north of Saltery Bay, is by far the largest community between Langdale and Prince Rupert. Though it was named in 1885, for civil servant Israel Powell, Powell River was little more than a name until logging started in the area in 1908. In 1911, the first newsprint manufactured in western Canada rolled out of the new mill. For many years, the mill dominated the western Canadian market. Traces of old oxen roads, logging railways and abandoned logging camps remain in the forests around the town.

The Powell River Historical Museum, at 4798 Marine Avenue, contains many historic photographs and displays on area history. A walking-tour brochure for the Powell River townsite is available from the tourism infocentre.

The old townsite, designated a National Historic District, is the only original intact mill townsite left on the coast. It occupies an area of about 10 blocks near the mill. The tour begins not far from the mill site, near the ships' hulks sunk offshore to provide what is billed as the world's largest floating breakwater.

Scotsman John McIntyre was the townsite manager from 1919 to 1931 and designed almost all the townsite buildings constructed during this time. Among them was the Bank of Montreal, built in 1931 at the corner of Walnut and Ash. The Canadian Imperial Bank of Commerce had originally banked for the mill company until the CIBC turned down a loan request for a paper machine and a power dam; the company invited the Bank of Montreal to town and got its money that way.

Other interesting buildings in Powell River are St. Joseph's Roman Catholic Church (1916) and St. John's Protestant (1913), a union church for various Protestant denominations, both at the corner of Ash and Sycamore; and the first row of houses built on the townsite, on Sycamore one block east of Marine. Some early houses in Powell River have roofs that curve upwards at the edges. The Rodmay Hotel looks somewhat different from the 30-room Powell River Hotel built in 1911, but the basic structure is still there.

The Powell River Forestry Museum is at Willingdon Beach; the museum society maintains the 20-minute Willingdon Beach Trail, flanked by explanatory displays and equipment such as a steam donkey.

Ferries leave Powell River for Comox and for **TEXADA ISLAND**, the largest island in the Strait of Georgia. Texada attracted interest when gold, copper, iron and limestone were discovered in the late 1800s. The mining camp of Vananda at the north end of the island grew at the turn of the century when a copper smelter was blown in (started operations)—but Vananda's life was brief: the last mine of that time closed in 1919. An iron mine reopened near Gillies Bay in 1952 closed again in 1976, but the community continued, attracting those who wished a rural lifestyle. Texada also contains rich limestone deposits. In the 1930s and

1940s, much of the island was logged. Old mine shafts, the remains of the iron-mining operation, logged-over forests and the still-operating limestone quarries provide evidence of Texada's history.

Back on the mainland coast, **LUND** is the end of the road. Founded in 1889 by the Swedish Thulin brothers, Lund still contains the hotel that the Thulins built in 1905, renovated and restored in 2000 and run by the Sliammon First Nations and a Powell River partner. For many years a major stop on the Union Steamship runs, Lund is now a small fishing village and the jumping-off spot for tours into Desolation Sound.

INSIDE PASSAGE SOUTH
Desolation Sound to Bella Bella

North of Lund, the coastal road ends and travellers must take to sea or air. The growing number of visitors who sail their own boats along the Inside Passage between Desolation Sound and Prince Rupert can find much historical evidence of long-time native habitation, of abandoned logging camps, canneries and mines and of failed attempts at settlement. But most who travel these waters do so aboard the seasonal BC Ferries Discovery Coast run from Port Hardy on Vancouver Island to Bella Coola, on the ferry run from Port Hardy to Prince Rupert, or on a cruise ship. None of these has the time or capability of exploring the many inlets, coves and bays on this much-indented coast, though the Discovery Coast ship does visit a number of historic communities, and crew point out many of the less-known historic features.

Though this section of the guide includes mainly sites that can be seen from the deck of the ferry or by way of the one road that crosses to the coast, sites now seen only by a few adventuresome travellers but important to the history of the coast are also listed.

Pilings and wharves along the way mark where ships of the Union Steamship, Canadian Pacific or Canadian National lines used to dock at canneries, logging camps or tiny settlements where optimists fished and planted pocket-sized gardens. Forest and brush now mostly cover the remains of these hopeful attempts, noticeable only for the bright green of alder in spring and summer.

Bute Inlet cuts deep into the coast. The Homathko River empties into the inlet through a valley that extends almost to Tatlayoko Lake in the Chilcotin. Though little marine traffic uses the inlet, it once inspired great hopes and dreams. Alfred Waddington, a surveyor who came to Victoria in 1858, noted the short distance between the Interior plateau and the Homathko and decided that a wagon road from the head of Bute Inlet to the Cariboo would be considerably shorter and easier to build than any of the routes up the Fraser River. His attempts to survey that road precipitated the Chilcotin War (see Chilcotin section in Chapter Six, The Interior Plateau). His dreams died with the conflict. He sold his plans to the Canadian government in 1871, confident that the planned transcontinental railway binding B.C. to the rest of the country would come to tidewater at Bute Inlet. He was, of course, wrong, but his ambitions are remembered in Mount Waddington, Waddington Harbour and Waddington Inlet.

MAMALILACULLA, on Village Island near the mouth of Knight Inlet, was for years the home of the Mamalelaqala Kwakwaka'wakw band. In the 1960s, the Department of Indian Affairs encouraged them, along with others, to move to larger centres, closer to services such as education and health care. Many did so, and as a result, many lost the benefits available to natives living on reserves. An old longhouse, school and moss-covered poles still exist. Tours are by permission of the band.

As ships emerge into the open ocean north of Vancouver Island, they pass **PINE ISLAND,** a tiny islet between Vancouver Island and the mainland. The lighthouse here was built in 1907.

Queen Charlotte Sound borders the only area of the mainland coast that is open to the Pacific. It was named by an early British trader for the wife of King George III. The lighthouse on **EGG ISLAND,** established in 1898, warns of the approaches to Fitz Hugh Sound and Smith and Rivers inlets. In 1948, fierce storms swept away the light just after the lighthouse keeper and his wife had fled. The light now flashes from a steel mast on the island's highest point.

At the north end of Smith Sound, ferries and other water traffic enter the protected passages once more, sailing between small islands and the mainland coast. At the mouth of Rivers Inlet lies Walbran Island, named for Captain John

T. Walbran, whose book *British Columbia Coast Names* contains not just the derivation of names but also a wealth of information about the coast. Walbran worked the coast as master of the steamer *Quadra* from 1891 to 1903. He and his crews placed buoys and beacons, drew new charts and improved existing ones and patrolled the coast. As Walbran notes, Rivers Inlet owed its name not to rivers but to Rivers: George Pitt, first Baron Rivers, was thought "brutal and half-mad" but had a wife who was "all loveliness within and without."

The sockeye runs on the inlet were legendary. As recently as 1950, more than a dozen canneries operated on its shores. Now little but pilings, rotting wharves and decaying buildings mark the sites of most, though several have been transformed into sport-fishing camps.

To the north again, at **NAMU** near the mouth of Burke Channel, is evidence of the long history of First Nations history on the coast. Here, archaeologists have uncovered the layered story of the past 10,000 years. Namu is one of the longest continuously inhabited sites in Canada. Stone tools, bones and giant shell middens found here date well back in this history. Native sites at Namu are protected: disturb nothing, take nothing. In 1893, much later comers to the coast established a fish cannery at Namu. Up to 1,000 fishers and cannery workers lived here in houses along the boardwalks. Fire destroyed some major buildings in 1962. Though the cannery was completely rebuilt, it closed in 1969 and the village was gradually abandoned. In 1992, BC Packers sold the community to new owners to run as a resort. Since then, various owners have had big plans for Namu. Some of the houses and warehouses, plus some of the other buildings, were partly restored. Namu has recently operated as a base for a sport-fishing camp.

Through Lama Passage, named for the Hudson's Bay Company brig *Lama* (sometimes spelled *Llama*, though why a northern fur-trading company owned a ship named for a South American camel is anybody's guess), is **BELLA BELLA**, also known as Waglisla, a stop on both the Inside Passage and Discovery Coast BC Ferries runs. More precisely, since the beginning of the mid-coast ferry run, the ships stop at McLoughlin Bay, just south of Bella Bella. The Heiltsuk, or Bella Bella, people lived for many years on nearby Denny Island. After the HBC built Fort McLoughlin on Campbell Island in 1833, the Heiltsuk moved to

Waglisla Island near the fort, then established New Bella Bella at the present site. When the mid-coast ferry run was scheduled to start, the people in town took a second look at the wisdom of allowing so many tourists to come ashore at the village. They and BC Ferries agreed on a new wharf at **MCLOUGHLIN BAY** to the south; a short road joins the two communities. A native interpretive centre and Big House at McLoughlin Bay incorporate some of the history of the coastal First Nations; a trip from McLoughlin Bay to Shearwater, across the water, by native canoe or a tour of ancient village sites may be available.

SHEARWATER was a World War II Royal Canadian Air Force base for flying boats. It was and continues to be the site of a marine repair yard; it now also houses a fishing resort and marina, making the town a base for exploring the surrounding area.

The once-thriving town of **OCEAN FALLS**, on Cousins Inlet off the main waterway of Dean Channel, is a fascinating site, an almost modern ghost town. A lumber mill opened here in 1909; a paper mill powered by the falling water of the town's name followed in 1912. Several generations of mill workers' families went to the schools, relied on the hospital and used the excellent recreational facilities. But isolation and the need for expensive modernization closed the mill in 1981. The ferry ceased to call and few stayed behind. Some of the houses were bought up by absentee owners; the town was maintained by the few remaining residents. With the new mid-coast ferry, Ocean Falls has regained a little life but just 35 people live here full time, and the lack of employment and the deep isolation suggest that it will never regain its previous status.

Bella Coola Valley

It's not a great deal easier to get close to Alexander Mackenzie's rock today than it was when that explorer completed his cross-Canada trip over 200 years ago. The mid-coast ferry glides by, sometimes slowing so eager photographers with very long telephoto lenses can get a shot, but the rock in Elcho Harbour is really visitable only by private boat or float plane. Wrote Mackenzie on the rock, using vermilion: "Alexander Mackenzie, from Canada by land, the twenty-second of July, one thousand seven hundred and ninety-three." The message has been made permanent and a plaque erected by the Historic Sites and Monuments Board. Inquire locally about transport to Mackenzie's rock.

Farther inland near the head of the North Bentinck Arm of Burke Channel, where the only road across the Interior plateau meets the sea, is **BELLA COOLA**. Though residents now look more to Williams Lake and the B.C. interior for their supplies and for "escape," Bella Coola's history ties it firmly to the coast, a historical connection celebrated by the entire population of the town in 1996 when the mid-coast ferry arrived, the first scheduled passenger service to arrive by sea for 20 years.

The valley, which runs from the head of the arm to the mountains, has long been home to the Nuxalk nation, a group whose history is not fully known. Though they are surrounded by peoples who speak languages related to the Wakashan and Athapaskan language families, their own language is of the Coast Salish family.

Until the 20th century, they lived at villages in the valley and along inlet shores, but since the 1920s they have clustered at the town of Bella Coola. Archaeologists have found evidence of several Big Houses and many artifacts at the largest of the settlements, Nus'qalst. Nuxalk heritage is magnificently displayed at the Acwsalcta School east of Bella Coola (where a totem pole erected in 2002 was the first to be carved in 38 years), and in the Nuxalk village within Bella Coola. Nuxalk tours to the petroglyph sites in the valley are available.

The Nuxalk originally lived, as did white settlers, on the north shore of the Bella Coola River, which receives more sunlight than the south shore in the mountains' shadow. In the late 1850s and early 1860s, some newcomers looking for a different route to the Interior showed up in the Bella Coola Valley; a few stayed to homestead. The Hudson's Bay Company established a post at Bella Coola in 1867. HBC factor John Clayton resigned from the company and bought the post in 1886, establishing a farm there. The remains of a house built for Clayton's son are still visible at the north end of the village.

Floods in the 1920s persuaded white settlers to move to the south bank of the river where they established a new village. The Nuxalk held out until 1936, when another flood destroyed their water supply, and contaminated water

Emmanuel United Church at Bella Coola was floated across the river when floods chased residents from the north to the south shore. (Gary Green Photography)

274

resulted in cases of typhoid. Then they, too, moved. Their church, Emmanuel United, was floated across the river and hauled to its present site.

A boatyard now occupies the space where Bella Coola's first cannery was built at the inlet head. Remains of a number of other canneries can also be seen along the inlet west of town. A boat tour goes to the nearby Tallheo Cannery, where visitors can stay in a 1920 cannery bunkhouse, or explore the remaining cannery buildings; there is a restaurant on-site.

The Bella Coola Valley Museum is housed in a building that was once two: a small cabin built in 1892 for a surveyor and a larger building from 1898 that was the town's second schoolhouse. Both were constructed in traditional dovetail style—the walls contain no nails.

About 20 kilometres up the valley is the settlement of **HAGENSBORG**. In 1894, Norwegians who lived in Minnesota emigrated once more, drawn to the Bella Coola Valley by the resemblance to Norway and the valley's isolation. Fearing floods, they settled up the valley, founding the community of Hagensborg, which still retains some of its Norwegian heritage in the typical farm architecture of houses and barns. The main building of the Augsburg Church dates to 1904; the building finally got indoor plumbing on its 100th anniversary. **FIRVALE**, farther inland, was established by Seventh Day Adventists circa 1912. The Sons of Norway Heritage House dates from around 1900 and is furnished in the style of a typical Norwegian house of that era.

At the western entrance to Tweedsmuir Provincial Park, which is at the eastern end of the valley, is **BURNT BRIDGE**, near the traditional but now abandoned Nuxalk village of Nutl'lhiixw, called Friendly Village by Mackenzie when he arrived here exhausted and hungry after his trek across the mountains. The Nuxalk-Carrier Grease Trail, the traditional route that the Nuxalk used to trade eulachon grease inland, can be entered near Burnt Bridge. **STUIE**, 12 kilometres farther east, was the traditional meeting place of coast and interior First Nations. Tweedsmuir Park Lodge nearby, built in the 1930s and rebuilt after a fire in 1950, at first drew hunters and now draws nature-lovers, who use it as a base for exploring Tweedsmuir.

The Big Hill, the last remaining stretch of gravel road on Highway 20, in part because gravel provides better winter traction on the treacherous curves and inclines, is the pride of the Bella Coola Valley. Road builders from the valley and the Chilcotin, who defied government pessimism to build their own road, carved the last few kilometres of the road along this difficult hill. The ascent marks the end of the coastal region and, across the Coast Mountains, the beginning of the Interior plateau. For information on this area, see the Chilcotin Section of Chapter Six, The Interior Plateau.

The guide now returns to the roadless coast.

INSIDE PASSAGE NORTH
Bella Bella to Prince Rupert

Almost no sign of human habitation breaks the coastline between Bella Bella and Kitimat. Among the few that do are the lighthouses that warn ships of dangers in the narrow, deep channels. Dryad Point light (1899) is on Campbell Island; Ivory Island light (1898) is near Milbanke Sound; McInnis Island (1921) lies at the approaches to Milbanke Sound; and Boat Bluff (1907) is at the entrance to Tolmie Channel.

KLEMTU, on Swindle Island, was founded in the 1870s by a single native man who was lured by the abundance of traditional foods and was soon joined by others. The 500-strong village of Kitasoo/Xai'xais people is now the northernmost port on the mid-coast ferry route. Ferry visitors are shown island history by way of dance, food and a tour. Residents will tell you the island is so-named because it is where the whites swindled the natives, but it is undoubtedly named for a Mr. Swindle.

Most of the tiny dots on older maps indicate logging camps and canneries abandoned long ago. At SWANSON BAY, opposite Princess Royal Island, are the remains of a short-lived (1909–18) paper mill and planking and shingle mill. More substantial are the timbers and concrete of BUTEDALE, established

The Dryad Point Lighthouse (established in 1899, this tower built in 1919) warns of hazards near Shearwater. (Gary Green Photography)

in 1918 on Princess Royal Island. The lake behind Butedale was dammed to produce power. Relics of a fish-processing plant, wharves and a mine recall Butedale's past.

GRENVILLE CHANNEL, named by George Vancouver for British Baron Grenville, is deep, narrow and scenic. Walbran damns the baron with faint praise. In the House of Lords, "his weighty and sonorous speeches, though long and sometimes tedious, were listened to with great appreciation."

Grenville Island leads north towards Porcher Island and Prince Rupert.

Prince Rupert

PRINCE RUPERT looks both seaward and landward. In so doing, its residents follow a centuries-old tradition. Though the Tsimshian—"people going into the river of mists"—lived from the sea, they traded with other native groups along the Skeena River and farther inland. The history and traditions of the Tsimshian are most dramatically portrayed at the Museum of Northern British Columbia (at First Avenue and McBride) through the museum building itself, built to represent a longhouse, and also through displays, an ancient petroglyph, totem poles, a new longhouse and the nearby carving shed. Tours are offered in summer (reservations required) to some of the 150 archaeological sites in the area, including those on Laxspa'aws (Pike Island) across from Metlakatla. Tsimshian poles are located throughout the downtown area. Haida traditions from the neighbouring Queen Charlotte Islands are represented in a Ninstints housefront and totem poles near the city hall.

Explorers and fur traders came to the area in the late 18th century. The Russians arrived first, ranging south from their posts on the Alaska Panhandle. In the 1820s, the HBC agreed to supply the Russians with provisions from their southern posts; in return, they took over the area near Prince Rupert. The HBC founded Fort Simpson, at the mouth of the Nass River, in 1831. Three years later, the fort was moved to its present location north of Prince Rupert and renamed **PORT SIMPSON**. The site has been for years a Tsimshian town (**LAX KW'ALAAMS**), reachable—as are a number of other north coast villages—only by water or air.

Missionaries followed the traders. William Duncan arrived on the north coast in 1857. At METLAKATLA, 20 minutes by boat north of Prince Rupert, Duncan and a group of Tsimshian created a Utopian Christian settlement: an attempt at a model community where natives would absorb the best and be protected from the worst of European civilization. Metlakatla and its Tsimshian were successful on these terms for 25 years. Then Duncan quarrelled with his sponsoring society and his bishop and moved beyond their authority, to New Metlakatla, south of Ketchikan in Alaska. Though fire has destroyed most of the buildings, the original site of Metlakatla can be visited as part of various tours of the harbour or area. Ask at the museum or infocentre in Prince Rupert.

Prince Rupert is situated at the mouth of the Skeena on Kaien Island, all but uninhabited when Grand Trunk Pacific Railway president Charles Hays chose it as the western terminus of the second cross-Canada railway. In a matter of months in 1910–11, the forest became a townsite, the townsite became a tent town and the tent town acquired hotels, doss-houses, churches, homes and taverns. In preparation for the arrival of the rails and in an atmosphere of frenzied land speculation, prices increased ten- and twenty-fold in just a few weeks. But the grand plans that Hays devised for this city needed a "plan master" and Hays went down with the *Titanic*, on his way back to North America.

Eight hundred kilometres closer to Japan than is Vancouver, Prince Rupert was designed to dominate trans-Pacific trade. Wharves and docks were built for ships loading grain and timber, and Prince Rupert laid claim to the rarely contested title of Halibut Capital of the World. In the 1940s, when the Canadian and American governments feared that the Japanese would attack the railway line leading inland, they built a highway paralleling the railway.

The aforementioned Museum of Northern British Columbia also presents displays of railway, road and pioneer history. The museum and the infocentre have available a walking tour (on paper and on cassette) of historic Prince Rupert. Two railway stations are close, by the waterfront. The Kwinitsa CNR station (the GTP became part of the CNR) was moved to its present location from Kwinitsa, 70 kilometres east of Prince Rupert; it dates from 1911. The Prince Rupert GTP/VIA Rail station (1922), just above the Kwinitsa Station, was

Prince Rupert was still being built, roads above ravines and buildings supported by pilings, when this photo was taken in 1911. (J.D. Allen photo, courtesy of the Prince Rupert City & Regional Archives.)

destined for grander things: designed by Victoria architect Francis Mawson Rattenbury, it was to be part of an imposing complex centred on a magnificent railway hotel—but somehow the hotel never happened. The Kwinitsa Railway Museum presents railway and port history.

Many of the buildings along Third Avenue West in the city centre date from Prince Rupert's early and ambitious days. Among them are the restored art deco City Tel Building (1930); the Besner Building (1928), built in Spanish Renaissance style; the Capitol Theatre (1925), once home to vaudeville; the former Bank of Montreal building (1911), across from the theatre and now a café and bed and breakfast; and a variety of retail buildings.

The Pioneer Rooms at 167 Third Avenue East, built in 1913 as a boarding house for Japanese workers, is now a hostel. Also worth a look are a number of homes on Fourth Avenue East and West that date from circa 1910; the courthouse (1923) on Market Place; and the art deco City Hall (1938).

With its protected harbour and easy access to Queen Charlotte Strait, Kaien Island must have seemed an ideal location for the railway terminus. But the low land here is boggy, and early roads and buildings were built on pilings that rested on bedrock. Down in Cow Bay, named for the place where the city's first dairy cows swam ashore, Smiles Café still serves fish and chips in an old section of the city's docks. Built in 1922 as a prototype fast-food café, Smiles was open 24 hours a day during World War II, when up to 10,000 American servicemen were stationed in town.

The guide now leaves the mainland and moves to the Queen Charlotte Islands. The tour begins at Skidegate Landing.

QUEEN CHARLOTTE ISLANDS

The Queen Charlotte Islands—also known as Haida Gwaii—lie across Hecate Strait from Prince Rupert and the mainland. Long the home of the Haida nation, they were the first part of what would become British Columbia to be sighted by a European explorer. Juan Josef Perez Hernandez did not land, but his men traded with the Haida for dried fish. In 1851, gold was discovered on the Charlottes, and they were the site of the first northwest gold rush.

The Haida culture remained strong despite depopulation caused by smallpox. Though many of the Haida villages scattered through the forests and along the coast were abandoned during the epidemic and later, the Haida have now reclaimed much of their heritage on these old sites, including those in the Gwaii Haanas National Park Reserve and Haida Heritage Site. The Haida make up about half the population of the Charlottes.

History on the Charlottes centres on the Haida and on the logging, fishing and mining undertaken by them and by new settlers. Today, visitors to the islands travel by ferry from Prince Rupert, by private boat or by air. Those who choose the ferry route arrive at Skidegate Landing on Graham Island, the northerly of the two main islands that make up the Queen Charlottes. Those who fly in usually arrive at the Sandspit airport on Moresby Island. This guide begins at the ferry landing.

From Skidegate Landing, a side road leads west along Skidegate Inlet to **QUEEN CHARLOTTE CITY**, the administrative centre for the island. Logging roads from Queen Charlotte City rejoin Highway 16 near **JUSKATLA**.

On Highway 16 just east of the ferry landing is the Haida Gwaii Museum, opened in 1976 and enlarged in 1988. It is housed in a modern-day replica of a

Haida longhouse and is now part of the Haida Heritage Centre at Ḵaay Ll-nagaay in Skidegate. Officially opened in 2008, the centre contains five cedar longhouses, including the museum and a carving shed, and celebrates 12,000 years of Haida history and culture. Centre administrators stress the centre is an expression both of the Haida past and of a living culture. Here is the world's best collection of carvings in argillite, a black slate found only in the Queen Charlottes. The Haida keep its source secret. Also on display are tools and equipment used by early settlers.

Next door is the office of the Haida Gwaii Watchmen, guardians of the ancient villages of the Haida, with the 15-metre-long Haida canoe *Loo Taas* nearby. Shown at Expo 86 in Vancouver, *Loo Taas* was paddled to its permanent home here in 1987. It was the first Haida canoe carved since 1909. Check at the office for tours that explore the heritage of the island.

The merging of ancient traditions with present ways of life is evident at most Haida villages on the Charlottes. Information on visiting the ancient Haida villages throughout the islands is available at Ḵaay Llnagaay and at the Gwaii Haanas office in Queen Charlotte City.

Many of the settlers who arrived on the islands early in the 20th century settled along the east coast of Graham Island. Isolation and uncertain weather drove some of these settlers away; the weathered walls of abandoned houses and clearings where brush has overtaken farm fields are evidence of these failed attempts to make an inhospitable island home.

These rocky shores have been equally unwelcoming to ships. Though most wrecks occurred on the west coast of the islands, some took place along the east coast. A trail in Naikoon Provincial Park from the highway along the Tlell River leads to the wrecked bow of the *Pesuta*, a log barge flung ashore in 1928 when the tow line between tug and barge snapped. The trail starts at the parking lot on the north side of the river.

Masset Inlet cuts deeply into Graham Island from Dixon Entrance to the north. The highway swerves inland from the coast to Port Clements and roughly follows Mexican Tom's Trail. William Thomas Hodges was not, in fact, Mexican; stories suggest he got his name by killing Mexicans when he worked on cattle ranches in the American south. He spent some years knocking around in Port Simpson and on the Skeena, then arrived in the Charlottes to round up cattle left to run wild by a disillusioned rancher. He blazed a trail overland for a Cornishman who wanted to found a private empire on the islands. The Cornishman eventually retreated to calmer country on Moresby Island; even Mexican Tom, content on the beach, stayed away from the trail that bears his name. But the name remained.

PORT CLEMENTS is both inland and on the ocean. After settlers founded Port Clements in 1907, it became a logging, farming and mining centre. During World War I, aircraft manufacturers used the light but strong wood from island spruce trees for their craft. Information on this and other Port Clements lore is available at the Port Clements Museum, on the main road into town.

A side road from Port Clements south towards Juskatla leads to a spur road marked by a sign with a canoe silhouette. A boardwalk and trail take walkers to an unfinished dugout canoe begun more than a century ago. Haida canoes were some 23 metres long. This one, abandoned for some unknown reason, lies near the stump of the tree from which it was to be made.

Highway 16 continues from Port Clements along Masset Sound to the largest community on the islands, **MASSET**, which is primarily non-native. Old Masset is the largest Haida community. Masset centred on a Canadian Forces base until the mid-1990s, when the base closed; now, Haida and non-natives manage the base assets as new settlers move in to the CFB houses.

A Haida canoe and several carving sheds are in Old Masset, together with a number of totem poles. Permission to visit some of the old village sites on Graham Island may be available from the Old Masset Council offices; the village sites are within Duu Guusd Tribal Park.

The west coast of Graham Island, remote from roads, is open to the full Pacific. Remains of ships that foundered on this coast can be seen: the USATS *Clarkesdale Victory*, near Hippa Island (the ship sank in 1947, with 49 lives lost); the MC *Kennecott*, at Hunter Point (sunk 1923, with no lives lost); and two seiners near East Narrows.

The guide now returns to Skidegate Landing.

Travellers can cross Skidegate Inlet by ferry to Alliford Bay and thence to Sandspit on Moresby Island. Little of historic interest on Moresby and South Moresby is accessible by road, though travellers may chance upon abandoned logging camps such as the one at Aero on Cumshewa Inlet. Charter flights and guided boat tours leave from Sandspit for the magnificent Gwaii Haanas and the abandoned Haida villages of Cumshewa, Chaatl, Haina and Tanu. Travellers to Gwaii Haanas must have a reservation and take part in an orientation session before visiting.

It's not surprising that the village at Red Cod Island Village, or **NINSTINTS**, on Anthony Island (also known as Sgung Gwaii) at the southern tip of the Charlottes has been declared a UNESCO World Heritage Site. The Kunghit Haida lived here for unnumbered years. Many were killed in the 19th century by smallpox or by American traders. Today, no one of Kunghit ancestry remains. But they are not forgotten: the weathered totems, posts and beams from 20 Big Houses all half-hidden in the forest evoke a long-gone era. Other abandoned Haida villages throughout the Gwaii Haanas and other parts of the islands provide a sense of that era.

Weather, economic pressure and isolation ended many white attempts at farming, mining, whaling and fish canning. What remains of these endeavours is scattered along island inlets, most reachable now only by boat or float plane. **JEDWAY,** on Skincuttle Inlet near the south end of the islands, attracted prospectors in the early years of the 20th century. Revived as an iron-mining town in 1961, it was abandoned again in 1968. Though the buildings were destroyed, some remnants are still barely visible in the encroaching forest.

TASU, on the west coast in Tasu Sound, is a more recent ghost town. This company town was built in the mid-1960s. When the mine closed in 1983, the people left but the buildings were not razed. The scars left by the open-pit copper mine are clearly visible.

And **PACOFI BAY**, across Moresby Island from Tasu, hides a mysterious past. Alvo von Alvensleben built a cold storage and fish-processing plant here but left after just a year. Later excavations revealed concrete construction that some suggested might have been intended as a German submarine base. The cannery buildings were demolished more than 50 years ago.

The guide now returns to the mainland at Prince Rupert and continues east with the Skeena Valley.

SKEENA VALLEY

East of Prince Rupert, the division between "the coast" and "the north" is somewhat arbitrary. In this guide, the coastal region continues to Terrace and Kitimat. The region to the east, where the Coast Mountains give way to the Nass range and the Skeena Mountains, is assigned to the north.

The first cannery at the mouth of the Skeena opened in 1876. By 1900, more than a dozen canneries were clustered close by. The North Pacific Cannery at **PORT EDWARD**, about 10 kilometres east on Highway 16, then south on Skeena Drive, was built in 1899 and closed only in 1969. It is now a National Historic Site, encompassing a restored cannery village and museum, with period fishboats, canning lines, boardwalks, docks, mess hall, bunkhouses, store, offices, net loft and boat hoist. A bed and breakfast on-site lets visitors experience some of the feeling of living in a cannery village, and a café serves the type of food that would have been available in working cannery days. Since it is not surrounded—as are the Steveston canneries near Vancouver—with modern bustle, and the buildings have not been over-restored, it is highly successful at evoking the isolation and daily routine of the many canneries that used to line coastal shores.

Fifty years ago, Port Edward itself was bustling: American armed forces used it as a base for the many personnel who were posted here or who shipped out on navy ships during World War II.

Highway 16 meets the mile-wide Skeena across from **PORT ESSINGTON**. On the south bank of the river, Port Essington is accessible only by boat. A few of the original fishing port and trading centre buildings still stand. In 1870, trader

Robert Cunningham established a trading post and townsite at this location that had been a Tsimshian campsite for centuries. For more than 30 years, steamers and other boats left Port Essington for waypoints on the Skeena, carrying prospectors, traders, natives, settlers and other travellers. Then the building of the railway on the river's north bank doomed the town. And a 1961 fire destroyed many buildings. There are plans afoot to make the port into a tourist attraction.

From where it joins the Skeena, Highway 16 runs beside river and rail in a narrow valley that crowds the transportation systems of three eras together: the earliest, of canoes then steamboats; the middle, after 1912, of trains; the latest, of automobiles, buses and trucks. Those who travel this section can easily imagine the difficulties road and rail builders experienced and see why railway workers needed 4.5 million kilograms of explosives to break through rock between Prince Rupert and Terrace. A no-longer-used 300-metre tunnel 69 kilometres east of Prince Rupert shows some of the problems, as do other tunnels and blasted rock faces.

Red Sand Lake Demonstration Forest, off a side road west of Terrace, contains evidence of historic native use of trees: strips of bark have been peeled away for use in making clothing, baskets and rope. Signs of abandoned farmsteads established early in the 20th century are visible in the undergrowth.

Several kilometres west of Terrace, the Nisga'a Highway (also known as Kalum Lake Road) heads north towards ancient Nisga'a communities along the Nass River. The lava that flowed from a volcanic cone around 1775 destroyed several Nisga'a villages, killed perhaps 2,000 people and changed the course of the Nass River. The twisted and hardened lava flow is visible along this route, at Nisga'a Memorial Lava Bed Provincial Park.

GITLAKDAMIX (or New Aiyansh) is the headquarters of the Nisga'a nation, who signed a treaty with the provincial and federal governments in 1998 after 111 years of negotiations. The original village is across the river; flooding at the older site led the residents to move to the present location. Look for the administrative centre built in longhouse style, with a totem pole at the entrance and the inner part of the building shaped like a lava cone.

A gravel road follows west along the Nass River, the historic Nisga'a trade and transportation route. **GITWINKSIHLKW** (or Canyon City) is some nine kilometres along this road. A pedestrian-only bridge that crossed the Nass here has been replaced by a road bridge, where carved poles representing the four Nisga'a clans of wolf, eagle, killer whale and raven stand. The original, daunting suspension bridge still sways above the river.

At the mouth of the Nass is LAXQALTS'AP (or "Greenville"), a traditional site for the various First Nations of the region to gather to harvest eulachon, a small and oily fish prized both for food and lamp oil. Accessible now by road, GINGOLX (or "Kincolith"), at the edge of Portland Inlet, contains four traditional tribal smokehouses, as well as a longhouse and carving shed. Visitors can see the preparation of traditional foods; a July Crabfest is a multicultural celebration of dancers, music and food. A waterfront boardwalk offers the opportunity to see the river that has sustained the village for centuries.

A secondary road branches from Nass Road north of Nass Camp to ALICE ARM, named for the wife of missionary Robert Tomlinson. Alice and Robert travelled for 24 days in a massive Haida canoe to reach their mission station at Kincolith. Later explorers in this area were prospectors who found and mined silver deposits.

Terrace

On the eastern edge of the Coast Mountains, TERRACE, like many other towns in the Skeena and Bulkley valleys, was created by the railways. Before 1910, a few settlers had taken up land where the Kitsumkalum River meets the Skeena. One such was George Little, who snowshoed up the Kitimat Trail from Douglas Inlet in 1905. Others arrived aboard the paddlewheelers that strove upstream from the 1860s on. Some thought that the new town the railway builders planned to establish would centre around Eby's Landing at the mouth of the Kitsumkalum, but canny Little offered free land for a station on his farm. He then laid out a townsite around the station.

The George Little House (1914), after two moves at the base of Kalum Street, houses the VIA Rail station and a carving shed, as well as various events, including flea markets, teas and meetings. Here you can get walking- and driving-tour information for Terrace.

A 1908 square-timbered house built by early resident Henry Frank still stands south of the railway, next to the river, together with buildings from the dairy farm Frank and his sons operated until 1956. Not far away, along the route of an old trail, off Highway 16 beside Kalum Lake Road, is Kitsumkalum's pioneer graveyard. A view from the graveyard shows remnants of orchards that were planted in the 1920s and 1930s.

Canadian National Railway tracks are on Skeena's north bank. The highway crosses to the south bank in Terrace. You can still see the original road bridge north of the present bridge. Built in 1925 to replace a ferry service, it was damaged by a 1936 flood that converted large areas of low-lying farmland into swamp. At the bottom of Eby Street is the restored Kwinitsa railway foreman's house, now housing an ice cream parlour.

Reminders of pioneer history are preserved at Heritage Park on Kerby Road off Kalum Hill Road from the town centre. The park contains log buildings transplanted from the surrounding area, among them the 1920 Kalum Lake Hotel, a mid-1920s dance hall, a 1912 barn containing early farm equipment, a miner's cabin, a homestead building, a 1919 linesman's cabin from the Dominion Telegraph Line and a trappers' cabin with windows small enough to exclude the hungry bears for which the area is famous. A heritage garden is also at the site.

Also worth a look in Terrace are a B.C. Provincial Police Station from 1912 on the corner of Kalum Street and Lakelse Avenue; the Kalum School (1914) on Lakelse at Kenny; and army buildings left over from World War II, when Terrace was base a camp for 3,500 soldiers.

Highway 37 South/Kitimat

Across the Skeena, Highway 37 turns south towards Lakelse and Kitimat, following the route of an old trail between the native communities of Kitamaat and Kitselas. A spur line was built from the CNR to the instant town of Kitimat in 1953. The road followed in 1957—though it was described then as "a sort of a road."

The highway passes Lakelse Hot Springs, now known as **MOUNT LAYTON HOT SPRINGS**, long a rest stop for people travelling the Kitamaat trail. In 1910, a would-be resort operator pre-empted land here, hoping the railway would run to the Douglas Channel, not to Skeena's mouth. Though disappointed, he persevered, building a hotel in 1910 and seeing it burn, then building a second hotel in 1929 and seeing it burn down too. A resort still operates here.

Everybody likes to call places by names that relate to their own experience. There's no better example than **KITAMAAT**: the Haisla residents on the east shore of Douglas Channel called their village Dsemosa, "the place of logs," because tides and storms dumped huge quantities of uprooted trees near their village. But the coastal Tsimshian, visiting for winter ceremonies, were awed by the immense depth of the snow that fell here—an average of 450 centimetres a year and sometimes three times that much. They dubbed their neighbours the *Kitamaat*, "people of the falling snow." That name stuck, and that's what the Haisla village is called. Though many Haisla work across the inlet at the Alcan smelter or elsewhere, many still follow traditional ways, fishing and drying or smoking salmon along the inlet shore.

Kitamaat village, now the headquarters of both the Haisla and the Henaalsiala people from farther south, is the departure point for five-day or longer tours to the Kitlope Heritage Conservancy, a park that contains the watersheds of the Kitimat and Kitlope rivers. The park contains trees used for traditional purposes; the river mouths are the site of eulachon fisheries. Visitors are expected to follow Haisla tradition by washing their faces as they enter the region, to signify to the spirits that they mean no harm to the watershed.

Missionaries came to the Kitamaat Valley in the 1880s and 1890s, and some settlers cleared farms and built houses at the channel head after 1900, hoping that the railway would come to the sea here. But they had departed by 1943, leaving the valley once more to the Haisla. Then, in the early 1950s, the Aluminum Company of Canada (Alcan) built an aluminum smelter here. To power it, they diverted water from the Fraser River system south of Burns Lake across the mountains to the ocean, channelling it through a powerhouse at Kemano to the south of Kitimat.

The company built the modern town of **KITIMAT** for its employees and other town residents. The Haisla village curves naturally along the east shore; the new town across the inlet is less organic. In a sense, the town is one historical document, a blueprint of social ideas prevalent in the early 1950s. Residential areas are set back from the water, carefully separated from commercial and industrial areas. The beer parlour, for example, is well distant from the houses, lest a child see a drunk. Streets are named in alphabetical clusters, and walkways cut through the green spaces that the houses face. Interestingly, in deciding to reverse the traditional location of front and back yards, the planners neglected to think about where the clothesline would go: in the front, facing green space, or in the back beside the road. In the 1950s, workers and their families came from across Canada and Europe, recruited from Scandinavia, Portugal (mainly the Azores) and other southern European areas. Today, close to a third of Kitimat is of Portuguese descent.

Of specific historic interest is the railway station, shuttered and declining, in the industrial area, and the smelter itself. The Kitimat Centennial Museum, in the commercial area at the city centre, displays native, pioneer and more recent history, including information on the destruction of eulachon fishing in the inlet because of pollution from the mill.

The guide returns to Highway 16 at Terrace. For information on the area to the east, see the next chapter, The North.

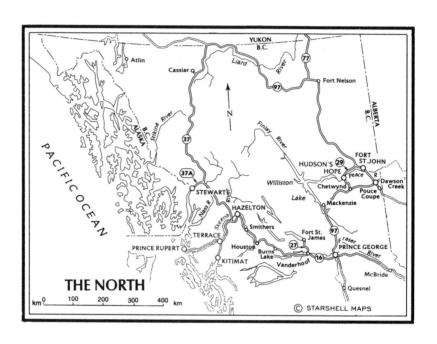

PACIFIC OCEAN

YUKON
B.C.

Atlin

Cassiar

Liard

River

77

97

Fort Nelson

ALBERTA
B.C.

Stikine River

B.C.
ALASKA

37

N

Finlay River

HUDSON'S
HOPE

29

FORT
ST. JOHN

37A

Williston

peace

R.

Dawson
Creek

Chetwynd

Pouce
Coupe

STEWART

Lake

Mackenzie

Nass R.

HAZELTON

Skeena

River

Smithers

Fort St.
James

97

Fraser

PRINCE GEORGE

TERRACE

Houston

27

River

PRINCE RUPERT

Burns
Lake

Vanderhoof

16

KITIMAT

McBride

Quesnel

THE NORTH

km 0   100   200   300   400   km

© STARSHELL MAPS

THE NORTH

The history of the northern half of British Columbia is indeed diverse, a diversity mandated by the geography of this huge region and first established in a historical sense by the area's native inhabitants. Widely populated by First Nations for thousands of years, the north encompasses groups with coastal, interior and plains affiliations. Nations with river links to the coastal way of life lived—and live—very differently than those whose territories are on the eastern side of the Rockies.

The north was one of the first areas to feel some effects from newcomers who came west across the prairies and through the mountains to explore, trade and establish posts. Yet after those contacts, little changed in the region between the 1860s and early 1910s, while the south changed greatly. In the north, major change came only after the building of railways in the years following 1912 and during and after World War II. Even today, cities are rare in the great expanse of the north and roads and railways absent from much of its map.

The north contains vast differences of terrain. One part of the area, that east of the Rockies and south of the borders with the Yukon and Northwest Territories, is relatively flat. Elsewhere, range after range of mountains angles northwest, with only small plateaus, river valleys and narrow lakes in between. The climate can be harsh and, in winter, unforgiving.

The region farthest west was the most hospitable for the native people. The Tlingit, the Tagish and the Tahltan lived relatively settled lives in villages along the rivers where each year salmon came to spawn. They traded with the native peoples of the Interior along trails used to transport valuable eulachon oil eastwards. (The grease from these oily smelts was a prized trade good for coastal peoples, and the trails eulachon traders followed were known as grease trails.) Though diseases brought by white intruders wiped out many of these villages, all these groups still live in the northwest and their cultures and traditions are being revived.

The Gitxsan and Wet'suwet'en people who lived along the Skeena and the Bulkley river valleys profited from the salmon runs that fed them and that allowed them to develop a settled culture. Farther east, the Dakelh people found life a little more difficult. Living between the Skeena and Omineca mountains and on the plateau, they followed a more nomadic lifestyle. Across the Rockies, the Dunne-za, Sekani, Dene-thah, Saulteaux and Cree centred their existence on hunting and gathering.

In 1793, Alexander Mackenzie, travelling for the North West fur-trading company and accompanied by native guides and voyageurs from Quebec, explored the Peace and Fraser rivers, then became the first outsider to cross overland to the Pacific. His trip had little impact on the residents of the north until a decade later when other "Nor'Westers" established the first trading posts in the region they called New Caledonia. Between 1805 and 1808, Simon Fraser and his men built posts at present-day Hudson's Hope (Rocky Mountain Portage Fort), at McLeod Lake, at Stuart Lake (Fort St. James), at Fraser Lake and at the junction of the Nechako and Fraser rivers near the present site of Prince George. These posts were the first year-round, continuing sites of non-native habitation in what would become British Columbia.

The posts continued to operate after the North West Company merged with the Hudson's Bay Company in 1821. Despite the presence of HBC, the region was little troubled by newcomers for many decades thereafter.

The few who did slog the trails of the north in search of gold in 1861 were inadvertently responsible for the location of B.C.'s eastern border. The maps of 1858, drawn when B.C. became an official colony of Britain, show a border line that follows the Rocky Mountains north. In 1861, two successful prospectors set off a minor gold rush along the Parsnip and Peace rivers. The British government wanted this area to be under British control, so colonial officials redrew the boundary north of the 54th parallel of latitude along the 120th meridian of longitude, including the region east of the Rockies in the only organized territory that existed in the area at that time. Nine years later, Canada acquired the northwest from the Hudson's Bay Company and Britain and created the Northwest Territories, a region that would evolve into the Prairie provinces. Had the border between B.C. and what would become Alberta been drawn after that acquisition, it would logically have followed the Rocky Mountains, and the Peace River district might well have been part of Alberta.

In the 1860s, surveyors for the Russian-American telegraph line (see page 305) sought a route along the valleys and between the mountains of northern B.C. They followed Takla Lake north, then went overland to the Stikine before deciding an easier route would go by way of Fraser Lake and the Bulkley and Kispiox rivers. The line was some kilometres into the Kispiox when a telegraph cable beneath the Atlantic was declared a success; the overland project was cancelled and the line through the north abandoned.

Other attempts to open the northwest met with similar fates. In the 1870s, prospectors were lured north by a gold rush in the Cassiar and Omineca, and the usual hotels and boarding houses were opened on Dease Creek. By 1876, the excitement had abated and the country had returned to normal. Atlin was founded at the turn of the century in the excitement of another gold rush, one that lasted a little longer and was linked to the Klondike rush. Gold, silver and copper mining began at Stewart around 1910.

Before the turn of the century, promoters promised would-be settlers that a railway would soon run along the Bulkley Valley. Homesteaders struggled overland from Bella Coola to take up land in the Lakes Country and along the river. But no railway came until 1914, when the Grand Trunk Pacific laid tracks from the east through B.C. to the town they created at Prince Rupert. Their timing was bad: even before the last spike was driven on the GTP, the economic boom that had begun around 1900 had collapsed. Yet the building of the railway was sufficient to make Prince George, at the crossing of north-south and east-west corridors, the central supply and service town for the north.

World War I drew all attention away from the hinterland. Though prosperity made a brief appearance in the 1920s, it was followed by the Depression in the 1930s. Perhaps the greatest change in the north during these years came when bush pilots began flying chartered and scheduled service in the 1930s, making northern isolation a relative condition.

On the other side of the Rockies, writers were praising the Peace River country as "the last best west," needing only labour and capital to be transformed into waving wheat fields and bustling cities. The provincial government had withheld this land from homestead claims so that the federal government could have first choice of land in the Peace River Block. This was in return for help Canada had given B.C. with its railways. In 1907, Ottawa selected its land; in 1912, some was opened for settlement.

Between 1872 and 1914, all manner of suggestions were made and two dozen charters granted for railways that would run through the Peace River region, connecting it to the east and the coast. A number of syndicates surveyed in the Peace in the 1920s, seeking minerals and rail routes. But not a kilometre of track was laid on any of them until the Northern Alberta Railway extended a line to Dawson Creek in 1931.

The federal government returned control of the Peace River Block to B.C. in 1930. Throughout the '30s, Prairie farmers left the dustbowl lands of southern Alberta and Saskatchewan for Peace River country, but distance to market and transportation difficulties made farming an iffy business.

World War II began a new era in northern history. In 1942–43, the United States greatly feared that the Japanese would invade Alaska. American military engineers, with Canadian civilian help, built a highway north to Alaska. They looked at routes along the Finlay River and Stuart and Takla lakes and through the coastal valleys. But they chose instead to go northwest from Dawson Creek, along the eastern flank of the Rockies. Ironically, Peace River country had a road link to Alaska 10 years before it got one to Prince George.

After the war, new settlers moved to the Peace and shipped more and more grain east through Alberta from Dawson Creek. Ninety years after it became part of B.C., the region still had no direct road or rail connection to the rest of the province. Some residents began to campaign to join Alberta. Finally, in 1952,

British Columbia completed the John Hart Highway from Prince George to Dawson Creek. In 1958, the Pacific Great Eastern Railway crossed the Rockies; the "Prince George Eventually" had become the "Fort St. John at Last." With the expansion of the lumbering and pulp industries, the population of Prince George more than tripled between 1961 and 1971.

Expansion continued in the 1960s and beyond. In 1968, the building of B.C.'s largest hydroelectric dam changed the course of the Parsnip and Peace rivers, first described by Alexander Mackenzie almost 200 years earlier. Oil derricks were raised in wheat fields, and both oil and gas were piped from the Peace region and the Fort Nelson area.

Between the Rockies and the coast, along the railway line from Prince George to Prince Rupert, towns grew up as loggers, lumber workers and miners plied their trade in forest and mountain. In 1942, driven by the same fear of Japanese attack that underlay the building of the Alaska Highway, the Canadian government, with American help, built a highway west beside the railway. More than the steamers that first plied the rivers, more than the railway, the road opened the region, even though Smithers, Houston, Burns Lake and Vanderhoof had a total population of just 15,000 by the 1980s—a number good or bad, depending on your opinion of urbanization and development.

The north still remains a land apart—in fact, two lands apart, one on either side of the Rockies. Much of it is still characterized by its relative isolation. The patterns of history repeat themselves: in the 1970s, BC Rail, the successor to the PGE, announced with much fanfare that it would extend its tracks to Dease Lake. Abandonment of the project some years later was much quieter; for years, the railway, like the old PGE, ran from nowhere to nowhere. Only in the 1990s was part of the line opened, to carry logs out of the north. And closing of mines at Cassiar and Stewart reminded both northerners and travellers how precarious the northern economy still is.

——— · ◆ · ———

This guide divides the north into three sections. North Central includes the region from the Mountain Spine west to Prince George, north to the Rockies and on through Lakes Country to Burns Lake. The Northwest includes the area between the Coast Mountains and the Lakes Country north to the Yukon border. The Northeast includes the Peace River country and the area north to the Yukon and Northwest Territories border.

NORTH CENTRAL

The guide begins at Prince George, the largest city of the north, at the junction of Highways 16 and 97 just 90 kilometres from the geographic centre of the province.

Prince George

As much as any place, **PRINCE GEORGE** embodies the contradictions of early and late development in the north. For centuries, the land at the junction of the Fraser and Nechako rivers was a meeting and gathering place for the Dakelh. In 1807, Simon Fraser founded the fur-trading post of Fort George here, making this one of the earlier posts south and west of the Rockies. But the following century saw very few attractions for outsiders in this area. Indeed, so well-loved was the HBC posting at Fort George that the settlement was known as Little Siberia.

Not much changed until 1907, when the Grand Trunk Pacific Railway announced plans for a northern transcontinental railway that everyone was convinced must logically follow the Fraser west from the Rockies. For once, everyone was right. Land speculators immediately moved in and established two separate and competing townsites, Fort George and South Fort George. Always loath to see anyone else profit from the railway, the GTP then surveyed their own townsite. Not surprisingly, the GTP site won out; in 1915 residents voted 153 to 13 to improve their image by adopting the name of Prince George, applied by the GTP to their townsite, presumably because it sounded more impressive than Fort George.

It mattered little to the GTP or to BC Express Company owner Charles Millar that the area at the confluence of the rivers was part of the Fort George Indian reserve. They battled in court over who should have the right to the land; the GTP won but turned over land at Shelley, located on the Fraser to the northeast, to the native people. Millar got 80 hectares, which was later developed as the Millar Addition.

The excitement of these railway days soon subsided, and Prince George reverted to quieter ways. In 1952, the Pacific Great Eastern Railway finally reached Prince George (thus its sobriquet "Prince George Eventually"), and that same year, the John Hart Highway linked Prince George to Dawson Creek and the Alaska Highway. Over the next decade, many of the tiny sawmills in the forests surrounding the city were closed, and lumber and pulp production centralized in town. With the opening of three major mills in the 1960s, Prince George became a major northern city.

A number of reminders of Prince George's early days remain. A Dakelh burial ground is preserved at Fort George Park, which is also the location of Simon Fraser's original fur post. Also at the park, where 17th and 20th avenues meet the cliffs that rise from the Fraser, is The Exploration Place at the Fraser-Fort George Regional Museum. Although the museum now stresses natural history, particularly that of dinosaurs, its displays and archives—especially its historic photographs—also present a good picture of city and area history. Look for the history and traditions of the Dakelh and the history of transportation—from canoes to steamboats that plied upriver to support the railway building to the railway itself. A tiny narrow-gauge steam train runs on tracks in the park in summer months. The museum may be the only one in British Columbia where visitors can play in a re-created historic billiard hall or sit in a tiny jail cell.

The museum or infocentres can supply information on heritage walking tours in the city, including a pamphlet on the Millar Addition (south of Connaught Drive), its streets named alphabetically for trees and bushes from Ash to Quince. The area contains a number of dignified residences built between 1914 and the 1940s. The houses at 1420, 1466 and 1480 Gorse Street are the earliest remaining: they were built for GTP workers who decided to stay in Prince George.

Connaught Hill, between Connaught Drive and Patricia Boulevard, was in Dakelh legend a huge beaver lodge. When the Fraser River flooded in 1898, Fort George natives fled to the top of the hill for safety. In the park at the top of the hill is the flywheel from an early sawmill.

The Heritage River Trails that follow the Fraser and Nechako rivers pass by a number of historic sites, including the Cameron Street and the GTP bridges. Infocentres can give details of the trails that run between the Cameron Street overpass and Carrie Jane Gray Park.

The Prince George Railway and Forestry Museum, on a three-hectare site beside Cottonwood Island Nature Park at 850 River Road, includes the 1914 GTP station from Penney (upstream on the Fraser), a bunkhouse, a heritage fire hall and more than 70 pieces of rolling stock such as a 1913 steam crane and a 1903 snowplough, as well as more usual railway and forestry vehicles. Upstream from the 1978 bridge that carries Highway 16 across the Fraser is the dual-purpose steel bridge that incorporates a drawbridge. It was built in 1914 and shared thereafter by vehicles and trains; trains had the right-of-way.

Prince George heritage suffered in the 1960s when growth and massive redevelopment saw a variety of historic buildings torn down. The city designated its first two heritage buildings in the 1990s: the former downtown liquor store at Sixth Avenue and Dominion, built in art deco style in 1949 with glass blocks and ceramic design, a standard liquor-store style in the 1940s and 1950s; and the federal post office, built in 1939, at 1288–1294 Third Avenue.

East of Prince George

East of Prince George, Highway 16 leads through logging cuts and pine forest towards the Rocky Mountains. Almost no buildings break the roadside between here and McBride, not particularly surprising since this section of road opened only in 1972. Settlement that preceded the road developed along the rail line and around small lumber mills that processed the timber cut in the region. Follow Highway 16 east, then turn north about 10 kilometres out of town for Shelley, Willow River and Giscome. When Northwood Pulp bought out the independent mills in the 1960s and 1970s, centralizing milling in Prince George, these towns lost much of their reason for existence. **WILLOW RIVER** still survives, however, and is a pleasantly historic community near the mouth of the Willow. **UPPER FRASER**, a tiny community at the end of pavement on a scenic back road, was reduced to ghost-town status when its last remaining operating mill closed in 2003. Farther east off Highway 16, residents of **PENNY** on the river's north bank must leave town by crossing by boat or ice bridge in winter or by whistling down the train in the middle of the night since there is no road access to their hamlet.

To continue east on this route, see the Valemount and Robson valley sections of Chapter Five, The Mountain Spine.

North of Prince George

The John Hart Highway (Highway 97), connecting Prince George to the province's northeast, was opened only in 1952, but trails through the area have existed for centuries. About 37 kilometres north of Prince George, turn east on Mitchell Road to Giscome Portage Regional Park and the Huble Homestead. In 1905, Al Huble built a trading post here at the south end of the Giscome Portage that connects Pacific and Arctic watersheds. He transported goods across the portage for fur traders and would-be settlers. At one point, interest groups in Prince George wanted to move Huble's house to a heritage park at Prince George, but the Giscome Portage Historical Society dug in its collective heels and preserved the squared-log house, barns and warehouse on-site. You can hike the Giscome Portage route, about eight kilometres back to Highway 97. The trail is named, a little unfairly since the native people knew it well, for a black prospector from Jamaica who arrived in the area in 1862, looking for gold. Delayed at Fort George by the winter, he was told of this shorter route north by a native guide. John Robert Giscome wrote about his trip for a Victoria newspaper. In 1871, the government widened the trail into a wagon road to serve the Omineca goldrushers.

Near where the portage route returns to the highway, Summit Lake marks the divide between creeks that run down to the Fraser and, eventually, the Pacific Ocean, and those that run north to the Peace River, the Mackenzie and the Arctic Ocean.

West of Prince George

The central region west of Prince George is a fairly flat forested area cut through by rivers and long narrow lakes. The guide traverses this region along Highway 16 west of Prince George.

About 61 kilometres west of Prince George, the Cluculz Creek rest area presents signs detailing the history and culture of area Dakelh communities.

VANDERHOOF, a further 26 kilometres west, lies very close to the geographic centre of the province. It is named for Herbert Vanderhoof, an American who was working as a publicist for Canadian railways circa 1910. A sometime writer himself, he envisioned a writers' retreat here, with a luxury hotel beside the Nechako River—but the retreat stayed on paper and was never built. Ranchers and loggers came in with the railway instead. The Vanderhoof Heritage Village Museum is located on a 12-hectare site beside the highway, developed as a reconstructed 1920s farming community, with 11 relocated buildings. These include the Board of Trade Building, which houses charts and natural science displays; the O.K. Café, with summer service and reconstructed rooms displaying 1920s artifacts; and the Reimer/Redmond House, a two-storey frame building from 1918. On occasion, a Waterloo steam engine pulses into town; wagon rides may be offered.

South of Vanderhoof on Kenny Dam Road lies Sai-Kuz Park in the First Nation village Sai-Kuz (Stoney Creek). In the park are two totem poles and a rock war-memorial to soldiers from the village who died in the two world wars; nearby in the village is a large log potlatch building. Also south of town is a hike-able section of the old Dominion Telegraph Line trail; ask locally for directions. Kenny Dam Road eventually leads to the Kenny Dam (1952) some 87 kilometres south of Vanderhoof. The dam significantly changed the landscape: visitors can see the canyon of the Nechako River, once home to a raging river dried up by the dam that turned the river around and sent it westward. See page 304 for more information.

A pleasant road wanders from the centre of Vanderhoof through farm fields to join up with Highway 27 north to Fort St. James and gravel roads to the Omineca. At Dog Creek on this road, the old HBC trail leads west towards Fort Fraser.

FORT ST. JAMES was one of the first fur-trading posts in British Columbia, founded by Simon Fraser in 1806 as the headquarters of New Caledonia. Fraser spent an unhappy winter here, relieving his loneliness by entering "upon the matrimonial state" with a local woman. The fort continued as a trading post through the 19th century into the 20th, rebuilt four times. A National Historic Site, the fort has been restored to the 1890s period and is one of the most interesting and attractive historic sites in the north, providing a window to early fur-trading days. On-site are the general warehouse and fur store and the men's residence. Artifacts, trade goods, photographs and diaries give a good reconstruction of the conditions of the fur trade in the 19th century.

A variety of historical evidence exists in or near Fort St. James. The Hudson's Bay Company cemetery is located on Stuart Drive beside the Anglican Church. The grave site of Dakelh Chief Kwah is located near the river; follow the first right after the Necoslie River bridge on the way out of town. Twenty-one pictograph sites have been identified on the cliffs along the shores of Stuart Lake; guides take visitors to the sites by boat.

On Lakeshore Drive in the town of Fort St. James are the Lady of Good Hope Church, third-oldest standing church in B.C. (built in 1873). Father Adrien Gabriel Morice, who wrote the first history of the northern Interior of the province, was a priest here for 19 years. The cabin where he printed Dakelh-language prayer books and newspapers is behind the church and a nearby plaque commemorates his work. In the church graveyard are gravestones inscribed in Dakelh syllabics.

Not far from the church in Cottonwood Park is the Junkers Memorial, for bush flyers such as Russ Baker, founder of Central BC Airlines, which became Pacific Western Airlines, then evolved into Canadian Airlines and now is taken over by Air Canada. The memorial is a one-third scale model of a Junkers aircraft, one of the aerial workhorses of the north in the 1930s and 1940s. It's a fitting place for a bush pilot memorial: Fort St. James is the centre of bush flying in the north-central region. Every year, Fort St. James hosts a Junkers festival, to commemorate the pioneer bush pilots, and Vanderhoof is the location of an international air show.

The Tom Creek steam shovel, also at Cottonwood Park, arrived in the area in the 1930s.

The Cunningham Forestry Road, off Sowchea Bay Road, leads west from Fort St. James to the 15-kilometre portage between Stuart and Babine lakes used by the Hudson's Bay Company on its supply and fur-transport route between Fort St. James and Port Simpson. Supplies and furs travelled up the Skeena by sternwheeler, overland by track train to Babine Lake, along the lake by boat, then over Babine Portage and once more by water along Stuart Lake. Ask locally for directions to the portage route.

North of Fort St. James on Stuart Lake is Douglas Lodge, built in 1924 as a fishing and hunting resort. One of its claims to fame was the visit of then U.S. president Herbert Hoover. The lodge welcomed travellers until the 1960s, when it closed; it functioned as a logging camp in the 1970s and is now once more a resort.

Also north of town is Mount Pope Provincial Park. Mount Pope stands above the village and is named for Franklin Pope, who explored the region while seeking a route for the doomed overland telegraph line that was to lead from the United States to Europe via Canada and Siberia.

Follow the unpaved Mackenzie Highway north of Fort St. James into the OMINECA. The Omineca gold rush in 1869–71 resulted in the founding of towns such as Manson Creek and Germansen Landing. For a brief time, the *Fort St. James Journal* and newspapers in the outside world recorded the comings and goings of such people as Dancing Bill, Black Jack, Dutch Henry, Red Alick and French Frank, who travelled by canoe, or on the steamship *Enterprise,* which was brought into the country in 1871 and on a trail cut through that same year. It's not unusual still to see prospectors in downtown Fort St. James who fit the old mould, though you'll also see helicopter-borne surveying teams who seek minerals from the air.

MANSON CREEK is 180 kilometres north of Fort St. James, GERMANSEN LANDING 207 kilometres. Both are fascinating, rarely visited gold-rush sites. It would be interesting to invent a story about the origin of the name of the Toodoggone River, farther north on this road. But, in fact, the name comes from a Sekani word meaning "water's arms." A First Nations graveyard on the east side of the Omineca River, several historic trails and mining sites are part of Omineca Provincial Park. A few broken remnants of the Germansen flumes, built in the 1930s for use in hydraulic mining, can be seen at Germansen East along the road to Germansen Lake.

The guide returns to Highway 16 west of Vanderhoof.

Fort Fraser to Burns Lake

Thirty-seven kilometres west of Vanderhoof, a kilometre east of Fort Fraser, a roadside plaque identifies the location of the last spike driven on the Grand Trunk Pacific Railway on April 7, 1914. **FORT FRASER** dates from 1806, when Simon Fraser established a fur-trading post at the east end of Fraser Lake. A cairn in Beaumont Provincial Park marks the approximate site of the fort.

FRASER LAKE and **ENDAKO** were railway towns. Fraser Lake stayed small, supported by sawmilling, until Endako Mines chose it as a townsite. The village was incorporated in 1966. Three sets of pictographs are on the north side of Fraser Lake on Indian reserve No. 2. Endako had a brick roundhouse for locomotive repair and the tallest water tower on the GTP line. The roundhouse and water tower are now gone.

The GTP helped found **BURNS LAKE**, 128 kilometres west of Vanderhoof. The town became the entry point into the rolling hills to the south for those who homesteaded and farmed in the area after 1912. A historic walking-tour guide is available online, or from the Burns Lake and District Chamber of Commerce, part of a heritage centre in a 1920s forestry building at 540 Highway 16 West. A museum in this centre houses a 1920s operating room and features logging displays. Among the stops on the walking tour are a hospital (on Government Street) built in the 1930s, now an office building; and a square-cut log building known as the Bucket of Blood (on Fifth Avenue), once a fur-trading office, then a gambling den where a poker game shooting resulted in the building's name. Look here for memorabilia of town founder Barney Mulvaney.

Highway 35 leads south from Burns Lake to Francois Lake (a free ferry crosses the lake) and Ootsa Lake. Near the shore of Ootsa Lake (follow the road to Ootsa Lake and turn right along the shore), a cairn at the Wistaria Community Hall stands in memory of the pioneers of Ootsa. The community of Wistaria exists more in memory than in reality. The massive Alcan project to provide power for the aluminum smelter at Kitimat dammed the Nechako River, turned the waters of the lake to drain westward to the Pacific rather than eastward to the Fraser and flooded both farmland and the villages and traditional territories of the Cheslatta Dakelh (Carrier) people who had fished, hunted and lived here for centuries.

The Nechako River curled north from Cheslatta Lake through Fort Fraser then east through Vanderhoof and on to the Fraser. It is now a small replica of its historic self. The Kenny Dam, built in the 1950s for the Alcan powerhouse in Kemano on the coast, reduced water flow by more than half. The river is larger than it might have been: a coalition of area people successfully fought further diversion in the 1990s. Though the 1950s diversion went all but unnoticed in the southern part of the province, the *Nechako Chronicle* printed an obituary in 1952 for "the ageless and mighty Nechako River . . . [The dam] has destroyed forever a thing of beauty and of divine creation."

When built, Kenny was the largest rock-filled dam in the world. Roads lead to the dam from both Lejac (located six kilometres east of Fraser Lake; take Holy Cross No. 1 Road) and Vanderhoof.

Highway 16 now leaves the watershed of the Fraser River, draining southwest to saltwater near Vancouver (except where diverted), and enters the watershed of the Skeena, flowing westwards to Prince Rupert. The guide continues in the northwest section of this chapter.

THE NORTHWEST
West of Burns Lake

West of Burns Lake, Highway 16 follows the widening Bulkley River Valley out of the sub-boreal forests of the province's interior into the northwest.

A paved road from Topley, about 50 kilometres west of Burns Lake, leads to 170-kilometre-long Babine Lake, billed as the longest natural lake in the province and one of the many long narrow lakes in the area that were used as transportation routes by both native peoples and fur traders. In **TOPLEY** is the restored Our Lady of Fatima Church, built in 1948.

HOUSTON began as a tie-cutting centre for the railway and continues today as a major logging and milling centre.

A rest stop overlooking the Bulkley 43 kilometres west of Houston gives a capsule resumé of the Russian-American telegraph line that was to unite North America and Europe. Colonel Charles Bulkley, late of the U.S. Army, was chief engineer on the project during construction between 1864 and 1866. He was proud of what his men accomplished: he summed up their endeavours in Siberia by saying, "against all obstacles they have struggled faithfully and bravely, and accomplished more than the most sanguine could have expected." But all the faith and bravery in the world could not compete against the successful Atlantic cable, and the overland telegraph project was abandoned. After the project, Bulkley left his wife and two sons behind in California while he went to work in Guatemala, where he died in 1894.

TELKWA, another seven kilometres west, was the main community in the valley for a brief period, until it lost out to Smithers when the railway came through, a result made worse when fire destroyed many businesses in 1914. Telkwa survived and a variety of houses, stores and businesses still stand. A self-guided

Ice blocks the river and overflows into the streets of Telkwa in 1919. (BCA B1753)

walking tour is available from the museum in the 1920 schoolhouse on Highway 16. Three houses on Fifth Street between Hope and Hill were built between 1908 and 1912. St. Stephen's Anglican (1910) is at Highway 16 and Hill. Regrettably, the revised brochure no longer notes that Jack McNeill, whose house on Fifth Street was built in the 1920s, was "one of the more colourful figures of his era because of his penchant for fast horses, cars and women," simply saying that McNeill liked to invite travelling salesmen in for a drink. Also check out Hong Chong's laundry and bathhouse (circa 1920) on Riverside near Hankin.

Telkwa's claim to fame in Ripley's Believe It or Not was the three bridges across two rivers all anchored on one rock at the junction of the Bulkley and Telkwa rivers. Pilings are still visible where the rails, Riverside Street and the rivers meet. Coalmine Road, an extension of Riverside Street, leads to the site of an old coal mine, one of many worked in the area in the 1920s and 1930s.

The old trail to the site of Aldermere (see the Smithers section below) and the Telkwa wagon trail can both be walked; each is about half a kilometre long. Locations are on the walking-tour brochure.

Smithers and Area

SMITHERS is in the ancestral hunting grounds of the Wet'suwet'en Dakelh people, the westernmost extension of Athapaskan-speaking native peoples. Before the building of the Grand Trunk Pacific Railway, non-natives who ventured into the area were mainly just passing through, either working on the telegraph lines or using the telegraph trail to get to the Klondike gold rush. Some promoters speculated and schemed—this was, after all, part of British Columbia, and the Bulkley Valley had been adjudged fertile farmland by government surveyors—and at one point, the B.C. government tried to settle 8,000 Boer War veterans here. Only 100 veterans applied for the free 160 acres (65 hectares) each was entitled to, and half of those sold their scrip to speculators. Even the GTP didn't want to go through the present site of Smithers: the surveyors preferred a slightly shorter route. But the government insisted that the rails serve the Bulkley Valley and, by 1913, the head of steel was at Hazelton farther west.

In what must be the only case of its kind amid the rampant land speculation that always accompanied railroad building in B.C., residents at **ALDERMERE**, one of the sites being considered as a divisional point, objected strongly. "Resolved," they declared, "that the Board of Trade of Aldermere pledges itself to resist to the utmost the attempts on the part of the Grand Trunk Pacific to thrust a station down our throats with its accompanying hordes of shacks and cons."

The Aldermerians got their way. In supposed secrecy, the GTP hired a surveyor to survey a different townsite—but the surveyor managed to buy up all the area farms on the cheap. Smithers, named as was often the case for a GTP official rather than for any local hero, was born. The usual early development so feared by Aldermere explains why Smithers was nicknamed "Squatterville," but by late in 1914, Main Street was lined with relatively solid buildings, and residents sported lapel pins crowing "5,000 population by 1915." Aldermere, its board of trade wishes granted, had all but disappeared by 1920. The townsite is east of Highway 16, just south of Telkwa.

As elsewhere, World War I put an end to optimism and growth, and Smithers struggled along, briefly buoyed by a burst of enthusiasm in the 1920s when mines on Hudson Bay Mountain and elsewhere sustained the village's economy, and then sinking again through the Depression. Even the building of the Yellowhead Highway during World War II did little for permanent growth. Only after the war did Smithers begin to expand once more.

Fire, the constant enemy of those who built towns of wood, levelled many of the early buildings in the 1930s. Still standing, however, are the GTP station (built 1919, located at the foot of Main Street south of the highway) and the Central Park building (at the top of Main beside the highway), built in 1924–25 for the provincial government. The latter houses the Bulkley Valley Museum, with First Nations, railway and mining displays. The infocentre is next to the museum in a buffet car from the CN line between Montreal and Toronto. The 1913 St. James Anglican Church, abandoned for many years, now serves as a performing arts centre.

The Wet'suwet'en have lived for perhaps 5,000 years at **MORICETOWN**, also known as Kyah Wiget, where the Bulkley squeezes through a short narrow canyon. Five clans make up the Wet'suwet'en: the Gitamdan, symbolized by the black bear, wolf and grizzly; the Laksamshu, symbolized by the whale, grouse and moon; the Laksilyou, symbolized by the caribou, frog and goose; the Gilser-hyou, symbolized by the wolverine and nighthawk; and the Tsayou, symbolized by the goat and beaver. The transition here from the coast to the Interior is evidenced in these symbols.

In pre-contact days, the Kyah Wiget fishermen built a weir across the river and used nets and baskets to catch fish. In the late 1800s, pressure by commercial fishers resulted in the banning of these methods and the introduction of gaffing at Moricetown. The Wet'suwet'en continue to fish from the rocks beside Moricetown Falls. Part of the canyon was blasted out in 1928 to make it easier for salmon to move upstream, and two fish ladders aid the fish in low water.

Moricetown is named for Father Adrien Gabriel Morice, a Catholic missionary and explorer of northern B.C. who worked in the northwest 1883–1904. His book *The History of the Northern Interior of British Columbia: Formerly New Caledonia, 1660-1880* is a classic of its time. An account of the native people and early settlement days of the northern Interior, it was written partly because of his annoyance at the "unaccountable ignorance of the area," something that many northerners feel has changed little today.

A trail in the area leads from Moricetown and eventually to the Cronin Mine and back to Smithers; it was a horse and mule-packing trail for the mine.

West of Moricetown begins the traditional territory of the coastal native nations. Not far west is Hazelton, the head of navigation on the Skeena and the point where settlers coming up the Skeena transferred to land transport.

Three Hazeltons are clustered near the junction of the Bulkley and Skeena rivers. Both New Hazelton and South Hazelton, south of the Bulkley, were built when the rails of the GTP were being laid after 1911. **NEW HAZELTON** was the winner in the station sweepstakes and is the larger of the two villages now. An infocentre at the western end of New Hazelton contains displays about the history of the area. The statue outside the centre is of Cataline—Jean Jacques Caux, a packer who came, probably, from the Basque region of Spain and who was legendary from the Cariboo to the Stikine for his ability to carry huge loads, and for the fact that he was said to change his clothes just once a year. Cataline was buried in the Hazelton cemetery (see below) when he died at the age of 92.

A Wild West sidelight on history was the gunfight that occurred near here in 1914, when seven Russian anarchists—history does not reveal what they were doing here—stole the railway payroll. Inspired by their success, they tried to repeat it. But this time, townsfolk were quickly alerted and bullets were fired. Three of the robbers were killed, three were wounded and one—the one with the money—escaped.

A number of years ago, locals laid out a Tour of the Totems, with Hands of History signs that designate interesting historic sites in the area. Though some of the signs have disappeared, others still pinpoint sites along the back roads. You can buy an inexpensive copy of the tour description at the Hazelton village office (see below); the route information and historic background provide an excellent primer for this fascinating region of British Columbia.

The road to the oldest of the Hazeltons leaves Highway 16 beside the info-centre and crosses the Bulkley River at Hagwilget. In about 1820, a rock fell into the river here, preventing large numbers of salmon from travelling upstream to the traditional Wet'suwet'en fishing spots at Moricetown. After suitable discussions—though some say it was after some battles—the Wet'suwet'en came to this place, traditionally Gitanmaax territory, to resume fishing here. The rock was blasted out of the river in 1958.

The bridge across the river here is, with its predecessors, one of the most famous and picturesque in the province. The original bridges were woven by the Gitxsan of poles and cedar rope, flimsy but serviceable ways for the native people to cross the river. When the overland-telegraph builders abandoned their line, the native people incorporated the wire into the 44-metre-long bridge. A third bridge was built with the arrival of the railway; the fourth and most recent 75-metre steel suspension span was built in 1931.

Four Mile, on the road into Hazelton, was traditionally the place where pack trains were loaded by those heading out overland from Hazelton. Two Mile was less salubrious: it was home to those not welcome in town.

The town at the junction of the Bulkley and Skeena rivers was for many years a Gitxsan trading centre called Gitanmaax. In 1868, the Hudson's Bay Company opened a short-lived trading post here. In 1871, the same trader, now operating independently, returned to start a general store. Prospectors seeking the gold of Omineca that year came upriver by paddlewheel steamer to Hazelton, bought last-minute supplies at the store and followed a Gitxsan trade trail—improved by the B.C. government as the rush grew—overland to Babine Lake. In 1880, the HBC returned to open a store of its own in Hazelton that operated until after World War II.

Today's town of **HAZELTON** is a pleasant village, an amalgam of white and native heritage. A walking guide is available at the Hazelton village office, and riverboat excursions detail the past and present of the river and the communities along its banks. Among the historic highlights in Hazelton are a steam donkey engine, a paddlewheel shaft (circa 1910), a sternwheel replica and St. Peter's Anglican Church (circa 1890s). The Hazelton Pioneer Museum and Archives is in the same location as the public library.

But the real highlight of Hazelton is 'Ksan, the Gitxsan village that re-creates the life of the native people of the area and brings it into the modern era. Seven communal houses have been built here; in each, aspects of traditional life are explored through artifacts, artistry and guided tours. The treasure room and exhibition centre, the carving shed, the studio, the 'Ksan shop, the Fireweed House, the Wolf or Feast House and the Frog House of the Stone Age contribute to an understanding of what life was and is like for the Gitxsan. 'Ksan is open daily mid-May to mid-October with winter hours as posted. Walk through the village and stand by the river, looking up at the mountain—"Rocher de Boule" to Europeans, "Stii Kyo Din" to the native peoples—to gain symbolic entry to one of the most magical places in the province.

To further involve yourself in this magic, return back up the hill from the town and turn left on the Kispiox road, then make a left onto the gravel road to reach the cemetery where native and white graves along the bluff overlook the town and the river. Many of the magnificent grave houses that used to mark the graves are gone, but a number of small totems and interesting gravesites remain.

The Kispiox road leads on along the Skeena, then branches with the Kispiox River up the Kispiox Valley. Five kilometres along the road, a Hands of History sign outlines the story of Simon Gunanoot, accused of murder in 1906, who spent 13 years in the forests and mountains of the region as a fugitive, evading capture with the help of those who either believed him innocent or wanted to help him regardless. He surrendered in 1919 and was acquitted of the charges against him.

GLEN VOWELL, off the main road to the right, is the result of a split among the Gitxsan people a century ago. During the split, dissidents had appealed to a native agent for help; he sent surveyor Arthur Vowell to create a new village site north of Kispiox. A Salvation Army missionary arrived, and Glen Vowell became one of the few army missions in the north.

At the meeting of the Kispiox and Skeena, a cairn commemorates Fort Stager, the last post on the Russian-American overland telegraph line. On October 26, 1866, when the work parties stopped for the winter, they had strung more than 800 kilometres of line in British Columbia from New Westminster to a point 40 kilometres farther up the Kispiox. A stretch of the surveyed route, later used by the Dominion Telegraph Line that was strung to the Yukon in 1900–01, has been identified north of Kispiox village along Cullon Creek to Deep Canoe Creek. Ask locally if you are interested in hiking this trail.

KISPIOX itself is an ancient Gitxsan village. The Department of Indian Affairs, however, named the village: the word means "loud talkers," a tribute or a judgment, depending on your point of view, on the people who lived here and insisted on defending their land. The two dozen totem poles here, set back from their original sites along the river, are one of the most impressive displays of poles in the northwest. Check at Kispiox Cultural Centre for more information, including info on three-to-four-hour walking tours of the village.

Back roads continue up the Kispiox Valley, crossing and recrossing the river. Sometimes rough and sometimes good gravel, these roads continue on to intersect with Highway 37 north near Cranberry Junction. You can also take the Kitwanga back road, which branches from the road to Kispiox about 20 kilometres from Hazelton. Tam Lax Aamid (Temlahan), noted on a plaque about 13 kilometres along this road, is the Gitxsan Garden of Eden, their ancient land of plenty, the place that they believe they came from.

This guide now returns to Highway 16 west of New Hazelton.

About 25 kilometres west of New Hazelton is **KITSEGUECLA**, with carved poles and painted carvings on the elementary school. Poles are often erected to commemorate events, as when a new chief takes over from one who has died. The poles here, as elsewhere, are on native property; ask before exploring.

Some 16 kilometres farther west, Highway 37 heads north into the deep northwest. To follow this route through native and mining history, see the "Highway 37 North" section later in this chapter.

About 33 kilometres west past this Highway 37 north junction, a viewpoint looks out over Skeena River Boat Passage, a reference to the steamboats that battled the heavy river current upstream before the age of rail. The Skeena is not a gentle river. When spring meltwaters cascaded down its many tributaries, the fast-flowing swollen stream flooded farm fields and riverside communities and undercut bridges. The problems the Skeena sternwheelers encountered are commemorated in various place names, among them Hardscrabble Rapids, the Devil's Elbow and the Hornet's Nest.

Many small communities were founded along the GTP railway north of the river after 1912. When the road was built south of the river during World War II, it killed most railway towns on the north bank. **USK**, about 70 kilometres from the Highway 37 junction, is one that survived. Linked to the south bank by one of the few remaining reaction ferries in the province (the tiny ferries, tethered by cables, are powered by the river current), Usk was, but is no longer, a railway station village.

About four kilometres past the Usk ferry road is Kleanza Creek Provincial Park, the nearest landmark to **KITSELAS CANYON**, a National Historic Site that embodies both native and steamboat history. Several modern longhouses and an interpretive trail at the canyon give life to the traditions of the Kitselas people and evoke steamboat days.

Centuries ago, the Kitselas people found a flat place suitable as a landing place and fishing stage near the bottom of this canyon and established villages on the terraces above, thus becoming the guardians and gatekeepers for traffic on this part of the Skeena. The largest of these villages contained 17 longhouses and many totem poles. When overland-telegraph parties tried to go up the Skeena through the canyon in 1866, they were considerably frightened by the Kitselas massed on the cliff above them—but the native peoples seized their tow lines and hauled them upriver.

When a steamboat was introduced onto the river to carry telegraph supplies, crews soon discovered how strong the current through the canyon was and hired Kitselas canoes instead. Sternwheelers that ran the river between 1890 and 1914 often had to wait at the western end of the canyon for lower water. A white settlement grew up here. Ringbolts used to line steamboats through the canyon are still cemented to the rocks of Ring Bolt Island, an island accessible at low water in late summer.

The Kitselas abandoned the villages in the 1860s and 1870s when smallpox killed many of the villagers. Recent archaeological investigations have provided much information about the Kitselas villages and discovered a number of petroglyphs in the canyon. For tours, consult the Kitselas band administration office at 4562 Queensway in Terrace.

Highway 16 continues west, into the coastal region. To continue with it, refer to Highway 16: Prince Rupert to Terrace in Chapter Seven, The Coast.

Highway 37 North (the Stewart-Cassiar)

The guide now follows the Stewart-Cassiar, or Highway 37 north from Highway 16 west of Hazelton. This is still the most rugged route to the far north, completed only in 1972, and cutting through scenery far more splendid than that along the Alaska Highway. Much of the route was gravel until recent years. Each year more kilometres are paved, but some sections are still rough and require extra care.

Across the Skeena, a road leads left along the river's north bank to the hamlet of **CEDARVALE**. For several decades from 1888, this was the Holy City of Minskinish, founded by missionary Robert Tomlinson on the precepts of

William Duncan at Metlakatla. Tomlinson gathered together a band of Gitxsan from Kitwanga to the north and built a non-sectarian, self-sufficient community with church, school, houses, sawmill, brickyard and gardens. No one might land or leave the village on a Sunday and no work was performed on the Lord's Day. Tomlinson left for New Metlakatla in 1908, and Minskinish declined under the tutelage of Tomlinson's less effective son. Little remains of the original community, though the son's house still stands beside the railway tracks, abandoned and ever deteriorating.

Back on Highway 37, a second side road leads east (right), then circles back to the highway through the village of **GITWANGAK**, the first of a number of native villages and other historic sites in the area. Gitwangak is home to a cluster of totem poles, at least one of which dates back to 1875. Opposite the totems is St. Paul's Anglican Church, an 1893 building with 400-year-old stained glass windows brought here from England.

The Kitwanga Back Road heads east off Highway 37. About 1.5 kilometres along, a sign marks Tam Lax Aamid, the ancestral Gitxsan land of plenty.

North again (follow signs from Highway 37) is **KITWANGA** and the Battle Hill National Historic Site. The Gitxsan built a 13-metre hill here and a fort atop it, so that they could roll logs down the slope onto their enemies. Though the cedar palisades and plank buildings are gone, the hill remains. A series of interpretive panels placed on the trail to Ta'awdzep, "the battle hill," explains the story of Nekt, the last defender of the fortress, a warrior who was feared from Kitamaat to the Nass.

The Nass is one of the best eulachon-fishing rivers in the world, and several "grease trails" branch from the river (see pages 291–292). In this area, Highway 37 follows the route of one of these trails.

North again, just to the west of the highway (follow the signposts), is the site of **GITANYOW** (also known as Kitwancool), which has a fine display of totem poles. The oldest of the 18 major poles—about 140 years old—is "Hole in the Ice" or "Hole in the Sky." Painter Emily Carr did some of her finest work based on these Gitanyow poles.

At **CRANBERRY JUNCTION**, a road with restricted access (check locally for logging traffic and hours of public use) branches west towards the mouth of the Nass River. This road joins up with the Kitsumkalum Road that spears north from Terrace, an easier route to the tiny communities on the Nass. For information on this area, see Chapter Seven, The Coast.

Highway 37A branches west at Meziadin Junction to the northernmost coastal community in British Columbia. **STEWART**, at the head of Portland Inlet, was founded circa 1903. The town limps along, closer and closer to ghost-town status now that the mine that sustained it has closed, though mining promoters continue to tout the region and 500 residents still live here. Back in 1903, prospectors lured north by the promise of Klondike gold were exploring this region for equal riches. Robert, John and James Stewart looked at this location and imagined a thriving mining town. For a few years, it looked like their dreams were based on reality: by 1910, 10,000 people were sustained here by gold, silver and copper mining, and ore went by rail to ships waiting at dockside in Portland Canal. And the town, if not the boom, prospered until the 1990s, when the last of the big mines closed. It's still a marvellous place to visit, its past very visible in its present and its low housing prices and scenery seductive.

The town museum is housed in the old fire hall at Sixth and Columbia streets. A telegraph room documents the history of both Russian-American and Dominion telegraph lines; a mining room takes visitors through the hardrock era. Pilings that supported the original buildings are still visible, along with two mine sites with buildings and workings on the road to Salmon Creek. Check at the museum, the Chamber of Commerce or local stores for driving/walking tours that pinpoint the historic buildings, such as the hotel, the Masonic building and the 1905 home of the town founder. And have a look at what must be the only Toaster Museum in the world, a museum featuring a century's worth of this kitchen appliance.

The border with Alaska, just southwest of town, is marked by an 1896 stone storehouse. Hyder, in Alaska, markets itself as the friendliest ghost town in that state—though more people come now to see the grizzly bears that fish the river just outside town, seemingly unconcerned by the presence of massive telephoto lenses bearing down on them.

Bush flying transformed the north, making accessible vast regions of lake and forest. This 1925 mining party used a Vickers flying boat at Dease Lake, in the first aerial exploring party in B.C.'s north. (BCA H6353)

North of Meziadin Junction, Highway 37 snakes through the Iskut River Valley past a series of lakes and across the Stikine River. The Grand Canyon of the Stikine begins just downstream. Early travellers in the region were overwhelmed by the wildness and beauty of this canyon; those coming upstream were equally overwhelmed by its impassibility.

At **DEASE LAKE**, centre of a 1970s mining boom and projected terminus of the ill-fated BC Rail extension, an unpaved road heads west towards the Stikine River, Tahltan and Telegraph Creek. This is a fabled part of B.C. that has lured adventurers and writers from the 1860s to the present. As far back as the 1860s, prospectors were struggling up the Stikine from the coast, attracted by the idea and sometimes the reality of gold. Nellie Cashman, prospector and traveller supreme who worked almost all the mineral rushes in western North America from the 1870s to the 1920s, travelled the Stikine between Wrangell and Dease Creek a number of times, once in winter when all feared for her safety. The Americans sent out the military to rescue her; when found, she was sitting happily beside a fire cooking supper. The soldiers took tea with her and returned, while she went on to the Cassiar.

TELEGRAPH CREEK, on the Stikine, was named when telegraph workmen brought supplies upriver here. Some 10,000 optimists followed the Stikine upriver in their attempt to reach the Klondike circa 1898. They included 200 men of the Yukon Field Force, four nurses and reporter Faith Fenton, who slogged through mud and muskeg on the barely broken trail to Teslin, in the Yukon.

The church and cabins of the native community of **TAHLTAN**, a name also given to a now-extinct breed of dogs, still stand on the riverbank above the river. Tradition and development have been clashing here for almost a decade, as two factions within the Tahltan nation argue for and against coal-bed methane mining in a valley some elders consider sacred. At Telegraph Creek, the 1898 Hudson's Bay Company post has been converted into a café, general store and lodge. It is the atmosphere and rushing river more than the old buildings that recall an era when steamboats fought the current as they pushed upstream and gold seekers panned the sandbars and drank in the town bars.

The road ends at **GLENORA**, originally a Tahltan and Tlingit fishing camp, then an HBC trading post, then a tent city for Klondike miners and the planned beginning of a new railway to the Klondike. It is now once more a Tahltan fishing camp.

CASSIAR, built in the 1950s to sustain an asbestos mine, became a 1990s ghost town when it became clear that developing new asbestos mines and carrying the asbestos the long distances to market was not an economic endeavour. The site is closed. The irony is that the communities the highway was named for and built to serve—Stewart and Cassiar—have both dropped out of the mining mainstream. But the highway itself still has an important function, carrying travellers who seek the beauty of such areas as Mount Edziza Provincial Park and the tumultuous waters of the Stikine.

Atlin

Highway 37 leaves British Columbia, then soon joins the Alaska Highway near Upper Liard in the Yukon. At Jakes Corner, farther west, Highway 7 heads south back to B.C. again, to Atlin Lake and the town of Atlin. This is one of those corners of the province that bring people back again and again with their beauty and mystery. At the turn of the century, this area lured with its gold: thousands of prospectors, entrepreneurs and hangers-on streamed into

Discovery City, on Pine Creek where gold was first panned, and Atlin City sprang up with all the speed and fervour of gold-rush towns everywhere. The year 1899 was Atlin's grandest: hotels (19 in total), banks, pleasure palaces, boarding houses, restaurants and government offices served the incomers. Discovery and Atlin underwent a slow decline after that. Discovery became a ghost town, while Atlin learned to live at a slower pace. Lillian Alling, a 1920s adventurer who was determined to walk home to Russia from New York City—and who may have made it—showed up here in the summer of 1928, having walked in via the old telegraph trail. She bought a pair of shoes and carried on.

Atlin is now an alluring community beside the lake, home to some 500 people year-round and a goodly number more in summer. The Atlin Courthouse (circa 1900) has been restored and is used by a school and by the Northern Lights College. Fittingly, it is also where circuit court sits quarterly. The Atlin Pioneer Cemetery east of town has been restored; graves date from the period 1898–1948. The first grave in the cemetery was that of a man, possibly named Sinclair, who drowned while skating. A second cemetery, first used in 1948, is at the end of the airport runway. A story persists that an Atlinite who had suffered from chronic rheumatism wanted to escape his affliction after death. Not wanting to be buried in the pioneer cemetery with its high water table, he surveyed the new site instead.

On the shore of Atlin Lake is the MV *Tarahne*, a ship that sailed the lake from 1917 to 1936 for the White Pass and Yukon Railway. In 1927, the ship was hauled ashore, cut in two and a nine-metre section built in the middle. A smaller ship took her place in 1937. Somewhat more decrepit, the 1911 vessel *Atlinto* lies beside the *Tarahne*.

The Atlin Museum, in a 1902 schoolhouse at Third and Trainor, has Tlingit, gold-rush and pioneer exhibits. Other turn-of-the-century buildings give Atlin a look that combines Victorian ornamentation with Wild West false fronts. A walking tour of the historic town is available from the museum or online.

Mining-rush towns had their share of entertainment and sporting events. Here, men compete in the 200-yard race in Dominion Day festivities at Discovery, near Atlin, in 1899. (BCA D9418)

The Northwest Corner

In the far northwest corner of British Columbia, at the apex of a triangle caught between the Yukon and Alaska, Highway 2 cuts across from Carcross in the Yukon to Skagway in Alaska. Where it crosses the Alaska border, the highway parallels, at a distance, the famous Chilkoot Trail used by thousands during the Klondike gold rush in 1898 and years following. So arduous were the conditions on the trail and in the Klondike, and so unprepared the prospectors, that the North West Mounted Police sent to monitor the pass turned back anyone who did not carry a year's supplies. Photographs show, nonetheless, a long file of gold seekers, plodding up the mountain slope on their way to boats that would take them along Bennett Lake to the Yukon River.

The White Pass and Yukon Railway, which was completed in 1900, runs a historic train in summer from Skagway up through the White Pass on the Canadian border to Bennett Lake.

The meeting of the Yukon and Alaska borders marks the end of British Columbia's northwest region.

The Northeast

Despite its relatively recent land links with the rest of British Columbia, the province's northeast remains to a great degree separate from the rest of the province, connected by ties of history and geography more to the Alberta plains than to the British Columbia mountains and coast. The native peoples who live in this region are part of the great family of Athapaskan-speaking peoples. They are here as the result of migrations from the east, and their way of life is more related to the hunting societies of the plains than to the more settled fishing societies of the west. Both fur traders and the farmers who followed a century later moved in from the plains, not from the coast. Oil and gas exploration is linked more closely to Alberta as well.

This section of the guide begins at Summit Lake on Highway 97 north of Prince George, heading north and east into the Arctic watershed.

Though the highway is new (historically speaking), trails in this area date back centuries to the movements of the native peoples, and were among the first followed by non-natives into present-day B.C. A cairn at **MCLEOD LAKE**, about 140 kilometres from Prince George, commemorates the building in 1805 of Fort McLeod, the first fur-trading post west of the Rockies. The first store operated by the North West Company was located here, as was an HBC store that continued on into the 1950s. Buildings at this site date to the 1920s and 1940s.

North again, the highway crosses the Parsnip River, which was followed by both Alexander Mackenzie and Simon Fraser as they sought a route to the great river that flowed to the sea. The Parsnip has its source to the southeast in Arctic Lake, 817 of Mackenzie's paces away from Portage Lake, the source of James Creek, which runs into McGregor River and thence to the Fraser.

Just beyond the Parsnip, Highway 39 leads to **MACKENZIE**, an instant town created in 1965 to support pulp and lumber mills. At Mackenzie is the world's largest tree-crusher, used to clear "non-merchantable" timber from land that was to be flooded by Williston Lake when the W. A. C. Bennett Dam was built in 1968. The town is named for Alexander Mackenzie, who camped near here on his cross-country trip in 1793. The town museum at 86 Centennial Drive has footage of the Finlay River before the dam.

Peace River Country

Some 53 kilometres north of McLeod Lake, the highway crosses the summit of Pine Pass, 869 metres above sea level. As early as the 1870s, the pass was suggested as the best route for the Canadian Pacific Railway. Joseph Hunter, surveying the area in 1877, considered giving up his attempt to find the pass until he heard "the repeated distant call of a loon, coming faintly from a point ahead in the direction of our line of travel." The presence of a loon suggested a lake and perhaps a pass. Hunter and his men continued on, finding the lake, the loons and, the next day at noon, the pass. A stop-of-interest sign marks the pass and a viewpoint overlooks Azouzetta Lake.

Towns are few and far between in this northern country. Another 105 kilometres to the east is **CHETWYND**, known as Little Prairie when the first white settlers arrived in 1912. The Little Prairie Heritage Museum is on the hill two kilometres west of town in a 1949 store/post office building, together with an old trapper's cabin.

From Chetwynd, the guide follows Highway 29 north. The road passes **MOBERLEY LAKE**. Beside the lake is a cairn to Henry John Moberley, fur trader and explorer who "discovered" the lake in 1865 and remained in the area until 1868. Farther north, the highway crosses the Peace River and follows the north bank to **HUDSON'S HOPE**. Simon Fraser paused here at the foot of the Peace River Canyon, warned by Mackenzie's diary that the trip through the canyon should not be attempted by canoe. Fraser built Rocky Mountain Portage House here in 1805.

It's difficult for the visitor to envision much of what was, since dams have changed the Peace and its tributaries almost past imagining. The Peace Canyon Dam is just above Highway 29 where it crosses the river. The road to the W. A. C. Bennett Dam and the Gordon Shrum Generating Station leads west from Hudson's Hope. Williston Lake, named for yet another politician, is the dam reservoir, which stretches back 362 kilometres through Peace Reach (once the

Peace River), Parsnip Reach (once the Parsnip River) and Finlay Reach (once the Finlay River). The largest reservoir in B.C., it took five years to fill. Tours are available.

A heritage park in Hudson's Hope, opposite the infocentre on 105th Avenue, incorporates a number of historic buildings. Fossil collections and trapping and coal-mining artifacts are on display in the Hudson's Hope Museum, in the old HBC store here. St. Peter's Church, a log church built in 1938, is beside the museum.

Travellers can follow Highway 29 to Fort St. John or return to Highway 97 at Chetwynd.

This guide returns to Chetwynd and proceeds east towards Dawson Creek.

Just east of Chetwynd, Highway 29 south leads to **TUMBLER RIDGE**, an instant town built in the 1980s to serve the Quintette coal development close by. Though Tumbler Ridge is fairly new, travel by visitors to the area is not. Early in the 1900s, fur trader and farmer Alex Monkman decided a route through the pass that now bears his name would be perfect for a road or railway from the Peace River country to the coast. He convinced very few, but those few carried on the fight: Monkman Pass Highway Association volunteers built a trail from Rio Grande, Alberta, through Monkman Pass in 1937, and continued on towards Hansard, near Prince George, until they were interrupted by the outbreak of World War II. Monkman Provincial Park can be reached by rough road from Tumbler Ridge. Check in Tumbler Ridge for information on the 63-kilometre Monkman Pass Memorial Trail, a very tough trail through the pass re-opened in 2008.

Highway 97 continues east from Highway 29 across the Pine River into a region closely linked with Alberta's Peace River country, both in appearance and in history. Side roads are straight now, in square sectional prairie fashion, and wheat fields and oil derricks become more common than vegetable gardens or dairy farms. To get to Dawson Creek you will pass through a hamlet called **PROGRESS**: even the name sounds like that of a Prairie settlement.

Dawson Creek

DAWSON CREEK is at the junction of Highways 97, 2 and 49 (the latter two run west from Alberta) and the end of a BC Rail line and the Northern Alberta Railway line. Named for surveyor George Mercer Dawson, who was particularly positive about the potential of the Peace River region, the town saw its first permanent non-native settler in 1907. The townsite was established in its present location in 1931 with the arrival of the Northern Alberta Railway. Twelve years later, when American engineers and soldiers trucked into the north to build the Alaska Highway, Dawson Creek boomed as a supply town. It's now the centre of Peace River farming; it has been supplanted by Fort St. John as the largest city in the region.

The Walter Wright Pioneer Village sits in the V created when Highway 97 makes a sharp left turn to head north from Dawson Creek at the west side of town. A well-set-out historic site, it contains local pioneer buildings, including two churches, a furnished log house, a general store, a blacksmith's shop, a trapper's cabin, two schools, farm machinery and homesteader's tools.

The official Mile Zero of the Alaska Highway has moved around some. The original Mile Zero marker was on a street corner until a car hit it. The Dawson Creek Jaycees created a new, three-metre-high painted wooden post which stands at the centre of 102nd Avenue and Tenth Street, with the showy old Alaska Hotel making a photogenic background. A stone cairn and metal sign were set up in NAR Park on Alaska Avenue (Highway 97) near the traffic circle. You can have your picture taken with either marker.

A museum, opened in 2007 across from the 102nd Avenue Mile Zero marker, commemorates the building of the highway with maps, archival photographs, and memories from those who helped build the road, as well as a 1942 Willy's military jeep.

Centrepiece of NAR Park is the original NAR Dawson Creek Station, built in 1931, added to in 1942 and 1947 and restored to a circa-1930s/1940s appearance. It houses the Station Museum, with exhibits showing Peace pioneer history, construction of the Alaska Highway and geological and archaeological displays (including a mastodon tusk found nearby). The restored Alberta Pool grain elevator next door dates from 1949. Also here is a restored circa-1900 railcar.

Highway 2 cuts southeast from Dawson Creek to **POUCE COUPE**, named for someone's cut thumb and pronounced *poose coopy*. First settled in 1898, Pouce Coupe was the first seat of government for the Peace River Block and the original end of steel for the Northern Alberta Railway. For many years, it was also the only place where you could buy liquor in the region. All those distinctions were eventually lost, and it is now a village of some 800, overshadowed by Dawson Creek and Fort St. John. The Pouce Coupe Museum is in the old railway station building at 50th Street and 49th Avenue, with a heritage house, trapper's cabin and caboose nearby. The original government building (1920–21) is privately owned. The United Church built in 1929 is now a senior citizens' hall. Christ Church Anglican (1932) still serves as a church. Check with the museum or infocentre for the route to the last wooden railway trestle remaining from the original NAR line from 1931.

Between Pouce Coupe and the Alberta border are the two tiny settlements of Tomslake and Tupper, both founded in the late 1930s by refugees from the Sudetenland, a region claimed by Hitler from Czechoslovakia for Germany. Sudeten Provincial Park is between the two villages, the land donated by a settler from the Sudeten.

The guide now returns to Highway 97 north of Dawson Creek.

From Dawson Creek, Highway 97 angles back northwest. Along the road are various signs erected in 1992 (the 50th anniversary of the building of the Alaska Highway), signs marking important points on the highway. One such is off Highway 97, on the original highway route. Turn right 30 kilometres north of Dawson Creek on Road 64 towards Kiskatinaw Park to reach a curved, banked bridge across the Kiskatinaw River. Since load limits were in force on the bridge, heavy trucks had to ford the river until the road was rerouted in 1978. This was the first curved wooden bridge built in Canada, and is now the only curved, banked trestle remaining in western Canada.

Highway 97 crosses the Peace River just south of the town of **TAYLOR**. Herbie Taylor and his family were the first family to settle on "the flats." Taylor and pioneer Bob Barker battled over the town name. When Taylor left to work his trapline, Barker put up a sign reading "Barker Flats"; when Taylor came home, he put up his own sign. Taylor won out when a post office opened on his farm. Though these early settlers were farmers and trappers, Taylor celebrates mining, not farming. The World Invitational Gold Panning Championships are held at Peace Island Park each August.

The first bridge across the Peace River was built here in 1942, a suspension bridge rumoured (as are other bridges on the Alaska Highway) to contain materials from Galloping Gertie, a bridge that collapsed in Tacoma, Washington. The Taylor bridge also collapsed in 1957, and was replaced by a new bridge in 1960.

The Church of the Good Shepherd at the north end of town on Spruce Street below the highway was built by volunteers in memory of four daughters of Otto Hoffstrom. The girls drowned in the Peace River when Hoffstrom's car plunged off the ferry that used to be the only way across the river.

Fort St. John

Fort St. John may rightfully claim to be the oldest non-native settlement in British Columbia—and also one of the oldest *native* settlements. At Charlie Lake, just northwest of Fort St. John, archaeologists have found evidence of the Paleo Indians who lived here more than 10,000 years ago. The Charlie Lake cave and bead display, in the North Peace Museum in Fort St. John (behind the oil derrick visible from Highway 97), includes artifacts such as a fluted spear point, stone tools, bones and the replica of a stone bead dated to 10,500 years ago, the earliest evidence of human adornment in Canada. The artifacts were discovered in a cave near the east shore of Charlie Lake.

The museum also contains a reconstructed schoolhouse, a trapper's cabin and information on earlier Forts St. John. In 1794, the North West Company founded Rocky Mountain Fort upstream on the Peace where the Moberley River flows in. It was followed by four other forts built between 1806 and 1925 at various other locations on the Peace and nearby rivers. Fort d'Epinette, another

North West Company post, was at the confluence of the Peace and Beatton rivers, a location worth visiting now as much for the magnificent cutbanks of the rivers as for the historical importance. The HBC founded a fort nearby in 1820, then merged the two when the companies joined. They decided to move their operation west in 1822; the Dunne-za were dismayed, regarding the decision as a betrayal. Five company employees were killed, and the HBC subsequently closed all its posts in the Peace River region, opening a new post only in the 1860s, on the south bank of the Peace River opposite present-day Fort St. John. From the 1870s until 1925, the fort was on the north bank. Today's Fort St. John is in its sixth location. A monument to first fort founder Alexander Mackenzie is in Centennial Park beside the museum. Also near the museum is the Anglican Chapel of the Holy Cross, built by Monica Storrs, a church worker who came here from Britain in 1929 and stayed until 1950.

The oil derrick beside the museum is testament to the changes that have driven the Fort St. John and North Peace economy since the 1950s. Gas and oil were discovered in the area in 1952, and an oil refinery and gas plant were built in nearby Taylor in 1957. Fort St. John now rightfully claims a place as the energy capital of B.C.

The Treaty 8 Tribal Council has its headquarters in Fort St. John. Between 1899 and 1914, seven First Nations communities in B.C. signed Treaty 8 with the federal government, the only native groups in the province to sign treaties up to the present day. B.C. Treaty 8 people—including the Sekani, Dunne-za, Denethah, Saulteaux and Cree who live between McLeod Lake and the Yukon border—hoped that the treaty would guarantee their ancestral way of life, the way they lived and hunted throughout the region. They did not anticipate the wave of settlers, farmers and gas and oil seekers who have overwhelmed the area.

The farmlands east and north of Fort St. John are laid out in Prairie fashion, although the twists and turns of deep-cut rivers interrupt the fields of wheat and canola. Ask at the infocentre for a hard-to-find farming map of the area, or beg for a local back-roads map: either will help you find your way home after backroading through a maze of roads that are simple to decipher for locals, a little more difficult for visitors. Along these back roads, you'll discover tiny farming communities with perhaps a general store and a cemetery set on a hill, reminders of the decades since 1912, when farmers began to enter the region. Check out Rose Prairie, Montney, North Pine and Cecil Lake, the last of these on a pleasant back road that leads towards the Alberta border.

The Alaska Highway

From Fort St. John, the Alaska Highway heads north into land that remains something of a wilderness despite the many inroads of loggers and oil and gas companies. In 1942, after the United States entered World War II, American military analysts feared a Japanese attack on Alaska, isolated at the edge of the continent. In eight months, with the help of 16,000 Canadian and American civilians, the U.S. Army Engineers built more than 2,300 kilometres of rough road from Dawson Creek to Alaska. In 1943, road builders improved the highway to an all-weather gravel surface. In 1946, Canada took over the route between Dawson Creek and the Alaska border.

Though the highway cut into the isolation of B.C.'s far northeast corner, it brought few settlers into the area between the Rockies and the Alberta border. For the most part even now, the land on either side of the Alaska Highway north of the fertile Peace River plains is still a region of boreal forest, lakes and rivers. However, trappers, loggers, mill workers, oil and gas workers and the occasional rancher have joined the Treaty 8 people who make their homes in this area. Those who cater to tourists and truck drivers have set up shop at various motels, cafés and gas stations along the way. The native people in the area work in the oil and gas industry—but they also continue traditional ways that include hunting moose and drying the meat. Historical evidence is rare along the highway because development is still relatively new.

Along the way from Dawson Creek to the Yukon border, however, are a number of places of historical interest. Markers erected during the celebrations of the highway's 50th anniversary in 1992 mark some of these spots. Those markers use imperial measures: you will see mileposts, not kilometre posts, on the Alaska Highway. Those who try to convert historic miles to kilometres are, however, doomed to frustration: the route of the highway has been straightened and shortened, so historic miles and actual miles/kilometres no longer correspond. But don't worry: you may get slightly confused, but you can't get lost in this one-highway region.

CHARLIE LAKE, home of the fascinating archaeological discoveries that date human occupancy here back millennia, was Mile Zero of the original U.S. Army Tote Road, a road that was the real beginning of the Alaska Highway. The general store here provides a glimpse into northern life—though microwave popcorn and videos aren't exactly of historical interest, survival kits and fishing and hunting gear set up a balance between old and new lifestyles.

At kilometre 162—or historic Mile 101—is WONOWON, once known as Blueberry. The buildings just south of the village (you'll see a plaque about the buildings on the right of the road) date from wartime, when this was a military checkpoint. Historic Mile 148 marks Suicide Hill, a steep decline that earned its nickname. Beyond historic Mile 173, the road takes a new route around Trutch Mountain; army engineers chose to scale the heights rather than fight the muskeg, but later road engineers have used the lower route. At Kilometre 366 (Mile 233), the native settlement of PROPHET RIVER features a church built in 1942. Around historic Mile 234, the road stretches straight—but until 10 years ago, it curved and twisted to follow natural features north; rerouting eliminated many of these curves.

FORT NELSON, at Kilometre 470 (Mile 300), was established in 1805 as a fur-trading post. It is the only incorporated municipality in the Fort Nelson Liard Regional District, which encompasses 10 percent of British Columbia's land area. The first post here was destroyed by natives; four other posts were built between 1813 and 1890. An economy once dependent on the fur trade turned to logging and lumbering in the 1920s, then to natural gas after the 1950s. The Fort Nelson Heritage Museum, just west of the Mile 300 milepost, has pioneer artifacts, a highway construction display, a spruce-bark canoe, exhibits of fur-bearing animals and area information. On the museum grounds are a log cabin, a telephone operators' building, a factor's house and diesel generators that powered the first electrical service in the town.

The museum also offers the story of Harry Rusk, the first North American native to perform at the *Grand Ole Opry*. Rusk's only brother, mother and father all died of tuberculosis while he was still young, and Rusk himself spent four years in a TB sanatorium. Country singer Hank Snow visited the san in 1952, and Rusk decided to emulate Snow. Over the next four decades, Rusk cut records and appeared on television shows. He also appeared in a television movie about his life.

The Fort Nelson-Liard Native Friendship Centre, across from the post office, offers a window to traditional lifestyles in the northeast. A "Welcome Visitors" program on summer evenings presents area information; history is sometimes a part of these presentations. The Trappers' Rendezvous each March brings together trappers working today and others whose lifestyle is part modern, part traditional.

Kwadacha Wilderness Provincial Park, accessible by air or trail from the Fort Nelson area, takes its name from the Athapaskan word for "white water." Less aptly named is the park's icefield, Lloyd George, so-called by American Paul Haworth who explored the area in 1916 and who greatly admired the British prime minister. Canadian authorities followed his lead, naming other area ranges Churchill, Roosevelt and Stalin.

At **TOAD RIVER**, at historic Mile 422 (Kilometre 672), a sign tells the story of Dennis and John Callison, who led surveyors through here in 1941, then stayed behind.

MUNCHO LAKE, at Kilometre 700, takes its name from the Kaskan word for "big lake." At Kilometre 800, the bridge crossing the Liard River is said to contain materials from the collapsed Tacoma bridge, Galloping Gertie (much like the first bridge across Peace River). *This* bridge, however, remains intact. At Kilometre 765 are **LIARD RIVER HOT SPRINGS**, used for centuries by native people and an inviting oasis for the builders of the Alaska Highway and for modern travellers. First mentioned by outside travellers in 1835, the hot springs became part of legend: in the 1920s, many thought there was a tropical paradise here, complete with parrots and banana plants.

At Kilometre 839 is **FIRESIDE**, named for disaster: British Columbia's second-largest forest fire burned an enormous area in 1982.

Crews working on the highway from north and south met at **CONTACT CREEK** (historic Mile 588, Kilometre 909) on September 24, 1942.

LOWER POST, at historic Mile 620 (Kilometre 958), was once a Hudson's Bay Company trading post; Upper Post was to the north, on a tributary of the Dease River.

And finally, the Yukon border is at Kilometre 1,009/historic Mile 627.

INDEX

Numbers in italics refer to photographs in the text. *CS* refers to the colour section between pages 172 and 173.

335

338

About the Author

ROSEMARY NEERING has been writing about the byways of British Columbia for more than 30 years. A sucker for a good story, she finds the history of the province endlessly interesting, and can always be tempted into following the road less travelled, whether it be into the backwoods or down a dusty archival alley. She is the author of a number of books that seek out the quirky side of British Columbia, or that invite travellers to come along on journeys in search of unusual and interesting people and places. Among her books are *Wild West Women: Travellers, Adventurers and Rebels* and *Down the Road: Journeys Through Small-Town British Columbia*. She lives in Victoria with her husband, Joe Thompson, and when she isn't travelling she gardens, creates hand-built pottery and plays tennis and squash.